"Jesus taught plainly and often al
meaning of his words has occupied theologians for centuries. This volume
captures the biblical perspective—not just Jesus' words but the full scope of
Scriptural insight—in a comprehensive, readable, and thorough fashion. God
will use it to reveal insight about his kingdom and change your perspective
on kingdom living."

Jeff Iorg, President, Golden Gate Seminary

"Morgan and Peterson have put together a collection that brings clarity and precision to an often blurry discussion. Like the other volumes in
the Theology in Community series, it is biblically informed, theologically
incisive, and pastorally sensitive. Those looking for a guide to understanding
the significance of the kingdom—past, present, and future—will do well to
consult *The Kingdom of God*."

Stephen T. Um, Senior Minister, Citylife Presbyterian Church, Boston,
Massachusetts; Adjunct Faculty, Gordon-Conwell Theological Seminary

"A timely and refreshing look at an oft neglected, misunderstood, but central doctrine of the Bible—*The Kingdom of God* will inspire, inform, and
edify pastors, students, laymen, and scholars alike. This work charts a course
between the Scylla of an overspiritualized conception of the kingdom and
the Charybdis of an overrealized understanding of the kingdom of God. It
does so by following the contours of the Bible in its arrival at a relevant biblical understanding of the kingdom consistent with the best of the evangelical
tradition. A must-have in the library of every serious student of the Bible!"

John David Massey, Associate Professor of Missions, Southwestern
Baptist Theological Seminary

"The essays within provide a fresh and helpful assessment of the multifaceted
meaning of the kingdom of God—from the Old Testament and the ancient
covenants, to the New Testament and today's Christians, and on to the consummation. For those in my generation captured by George Ladd's 'already/
not yet' understanding of God's kingdom, this work is a noteworthy twenty-
first-century expansion of how complex and important the kingdom theme is
both for orthodoxy and for orthopraxy."

Kendell Easley, Professor of Biblical Studies, Union University; author,
The Illustrated Guide to Biblical History

"In this elegant volume, seven distinguished theologians wrestle with the big questions surrounding the biblical notion of kingdom—ultimately forging a path for the church where there is no inherent conflict between kingdom preaching and kingdom living, between orthodoxy and orthopraxy. As ambassadors of the king, God's people proclaim the kingdom and embody God's rule in every dimension of society and culture, and across the fabric of human life."

> **Bruce Riley Ashford,** Dean and Associate Professor of Theology and Culture, Southeastern Baptist Theological Seminary; editor, *Theology and Practice of Mission*

"At a time when scholars continue to wrangle over various interpretations of the kingdom and pastors seek to find clear, concrete ways to express kingdom living to their congregations, we have in this volume a foundational work that will assist scholars and pastors alike for years to come. It's all here—the history of the debate, biblical theology, systematic theology, and very practical application. As I finished reading this book, I knew that my understanding of the kingdom was forever enlarged; perhaps more significantly, I knew that my heart would never again be satisfied with anything less than kingdom life."

> **Michael Honeycutt,** Associate Professor of Historical and Practical Theology, Covenant Seminary

"Chris Morgan and Robert Peterson have done a masterful job of searching out a comprehensive construct of the concept of the kingdom of God. Through world-class scholars, they have presented, as promised, "the historical, biblical, theological, and ethical" precepts of the kingdom. What a gift of understanding they have given to the body of Christ."

> **Jim Parker,** Associate Professor of Biblical Interpretation, New Orleans Baptist Theological Seminary

THE KINGDOM OF GOD

Other Books in the Theology in Community series:

The Deity of Christ (2011)

The Glory of God (2010)

Suffering and the Goodness of God (2008)

THE KINGDOM OF GOD

edited by CHRISTOPHER W. MORGAN
and ROBERT A. PETERSON

WHEATON, ILLINOIS

Trade paperback ISBN: 978-1-4335-0918-6
PDF ISBN: 978-1-4335-0919-3
Mobipocket ISBN: 978-1-4335-0920-9
ePub ISBN: 978-1-4335-2358-8

Library of Congress Cataloging-in-Publication Data

The kingdom of God / Christopher W. Morgan and Robert A. Peterson, editors.
      p. cm. — (Theology in community)
    Includes bibliographical references (p.   ) and indexes.
    ISBN 978-1-4335-0918-6 (tpb)
    1. Kingdom of God. 2. Kingdom of God—Biblical teaching. I. Morgan, Christopher W., 1971–   II. Peterson, Robert A., 1948–
BT94.K49   2012
231.7'2—dc23   2012010785

Crossway is a publishing ministry of Good News Publishers.

VP		21	20	19	18	17	16	15	14	13	12
15	14	13	12	11	10	9	8	7	6	5	4	3	2	1

To our team at Crossway
with whom it is a joy to serve the Lord:

Al Fisher, Justin Taylor, Jill Carter,
Lydia Brownback, and many others

CONTENTS

LIST OF ABBREVIATIONS

BBR	*Bulletin for Biblical Research*
BDAG	*Greek-English Lexicon of the New Testament and Other Early Christian Literature*
BECNT	Baker Exegetical Commentary on the New Testament
Bib	*Biblica*
DCG	*Dictionary of Christ and the Gospels*
DLNTD	*Dictionary of the Later New Testament and Its Developments*
DNTB	*Dictionary of New Testament Background*
DTIB	*Dictionary for Theological Interpretation of the Bible*
HALOT	*The Hebrew and Aramaic Lexicon of the Old Testament*
HvTSt	*Hervormde teologiese studies*
Int	*Interpretation*
JETS	*Journal of the Evangelical Theological Society*
JPT	*Journal of Pentecostal Theology*
JPTSS	Journal of Pentecostal Theology Supplement Series
NAC	New American Commentary
NIDB	*New Interpreter's Dictionary of the Bible*
NIDNTT	*New International Dictionary of New Testament Theology*
NIGTC	New International Greek Testament Commentary
NovT	*Novum Testamentum*
PNTC	Pelican New Testament Commentaries
SBLDS	Society of Biblical Literature Dissertation Series
SBT	Studies in Biblical Theology
SR	*Studies in Religion*
TB	Theologische Bücherei
TBei	*Theologishe Beiträge*
TJ	*Trinity Journal*
TZ	*Theologische Zeitschrift*
WBC	Word Biblical Commentary
WTJ	*Westminster Theological Journal*
WUNT	Wissenschaftliche Untersuchungen zum Neuen Testament
ZEC	Zondervan Exegetical Commentary

SERIES PREFACE

As the series name, *Theology in Community*, indicates, *theology* in community aims to promote clear thinking on and godly responses to historic and contemporary theological issues. The series examines issues central to the Christian faith, including traditional topics such as sin, the atonement, the church, and heaven, but also some which are more focused or contemporary, such as suffering and the goodness of God, the glory of God, the deity of Christ, and the kingdom of God. The series strives not only to follow a sound theological method but also to display it.

Chapters addressing the Old and New Testaments on the book's subject form the heart of each volume. Subsequent chapters synthesize the biblical teaching and link it to historical, philosophical, systematic, and pastoral concerns. Far from being mere collections of essays, the volumes are carefully crafted so that the voices of the various experts combine to proclaim a unified message.

Again, as the name suggests, theology *in community* also seeks to demonstrate that theology should be done in teams. The teachings of the Bible were forged in real-life situations by leaders in God's covenant communities. The biblical teachings addressed concerns of real people who needed the truth to guide their lives. Theology was formulated by the church and for the church. This series seeks to recapture that biblical reality. The volumes are written by scholars, from a variety of denominational backgrounds and life experiences with academic credentials and significant expertise across the spectrum of theological disciplines, who collaborate with each other. They write from a high view of Scripture with robust evangelical conviction and in a gracious manner. They are not detached academics but are personally involved in ministry, serving as teachers, pastors, and missionaries. The contributors to these volumes stand in continuity with the historic church, care about the global church, share life together with other believers in local churches, and aim to write for the good of the church to strengthen its leaders, particularly pastors, teachers, missionaries, lay leaders, students, and professors.

For the glory of God and the good of the church,
Christopher W. Morgan and Robert A. Peterson

ACKNOWLEDGMENTS

We are grateful to the Lord for giving us this opportunity to serve him. Among his faithful servants, we thank:

Beth Ann Brown, Lydia Brownback, Allan Sholes, and Rick Matt, for expert editing. Special thanks are due Elliott Pinegar, Robert's teaching assistant, for editing the entire manuscript and compiling the bibliography.

Tony Chute, Jeff Mooney, and Mike Honeycutt, for reading and making suggestions.

Our librarians, James Pakala and Steve Jamieson at Covenant Theological Seminary, and Barry Parker at California Baptist University, for professional, timely, and courteous assistance.

CONTRIBUTORS

Gregg R. Allison (PhD, Trinity Evangelical Divinity School), Professor of Christian Theology, The Southern Baptist Theological Seminary

Clinton E. Arnold (PhD, University of Aberdeen), Professor of New Testament Language and Literature, Talbot School of Theology

Anthony B. Bradley (PhD, Westminster Theological Seminary), Associate Professor of Theology and Ethics, The King's College (New York)

Gerald Bray (DLitt, University of Paris-Sorbonne), Research Professor of Divinity, Beeson Divinity School

Christopher W. Morgan (PhD, Mid-America Baptist Theological Seminary), Professor of Theology and Dean, School of Christian Ministries, California Baptist University

Stephen J. Nichols (PhD, Westminster Theological Seminary), Research Professor of Christianity and Culture, Lancaster Bible College and Graduate School

Robert A. Peterson (PhD, Drew University), Professor of Systematic Theology, Covenant Theological Seminary

Bruce K. Waltke (PhD, Harvard University), Distinguished Professor of Old Testament, Knox Theological Seminary

Robert W. Yarbrough (PhD, University of Aberdeen), Professor of New Testament, Covenant Theological Seminary

INTRODUCTION

> It is clear that no view of <u>Christ's person and work</u> which
> is separated from the context of the Kingdom [of God]
> can claim to reflect a biblical mode of thought.[1]

David Wells is right. A good grasp of the kingdom of God is indispensable for a proper understanding of Christ and the redemption that he accomplished. The kingdom of God is a very large biblical category indeed. Accordingly, a comprehensive understanding of the kingdom would illuminate many aspects of theology. But to obtain such an understanding is not so easy! In fact, to attempt to gain a comprehensive understanding of the kingdom of God is to invite many problems. We begin by considering one of those problems.

Jesus' Statements about the Kingdom Appear to Be Contradictory

At first glance Christ's statements concerning the kingdom appear contradictory.

Is the kingdom present or future?
But if it is by the Spirit of God that I cast out demons, then the kingdom of God has come upon you. (Matt. 12:28)

I tell you I will not drink again of this fruit of the vine until that day when I drink it new with you in my Father's kingdom. (Matt. 26:29)

Does the kingdom concern salvation or judgment?
Then the King will say to those on his right, "Come, you who are blessed by my Father, inherit the kingdom prepared for you from the foundation of the world." (Matt. 25:34)

Again, the kingdom of heaven is like a net that was thrown into the sea and gathered fish of every kind. When it was full, men drew it ashore and sat down and sorted the good into containers but threw away the

---

[1]David F. Wells, *The Person of Christ: A Biblical and Historical Analysis of the Incarnation* (Westchester, IL: Crossway, 1984), 23.

bad. So it will be at the end of the age. The angels will come out and separate the evil from the righteous and throw them into the fiery furnace. In that place there will be weeping and gnashing of teeth. (Matt. 13:47–50)

Does the kingdom mean that God rules, or is it the place where he rules? And behold, you will conceive in your womb and bear a son, and you shall call his name Jesus. He will be great and will be called the Son of the Most High. And the Lord God will give to him the throne of his father David, and he will reign over the house of Jacob forever, and of his kingdom there will be no end. (Luke 1:31–33)

You are those who have stayed with me in my trials, and I assign to you, as my Father assigned to me, a kingdom, that you may eat and drink at my table in my kingdom and sit on thrones judging the twelve tribes of Israel. (Luke 22:28–30)

Of course, these questions provide false choices, and a deeper look at Jesus' words reveals that he views the kingdom as multifaceted. He speaks of the kingdom as both present and future, as including both salvation and judgment, as encompassing both rule and locus. In addition, the kingdom pertains to human beings, angels, and the heavens and earth.

Jesus Emphasizes the Kingdom

From first to last, Jesus' message underscores the kingdom of God. Matthew summarizes Jesus' early Galilean ministry: "And he went throughout all Galilee, teaching in their synagogues and proclaiming the gospel of the kingdom and healing every disease and every affliction among the people" (Matt. 4:23). Toward the middle of his ministry, Jesus defends himself against the wicked accusation that he casts out demons by Satan: "But if it is by the finger of God that I cast out demons, then the kingdom of God has come upon you" (Luke 11:20). And in the presence of Pilate before Jesus' crucifixion, he declares, "My kingdom is not of this world. If my kingdom were of this world, my servants would have been fighting, that I might not be delivered over to the Jews. But my kingdom is not from the world" (John 18:36).

Widely Divergent Views of the Kingdom

When Jesus speaks of the kingdom, he emphasizes God's action. R. S. Barbour correctly states, "Because this theme of God's action was so central to Jesus, the Kingdom of God has tended to become a cover-phrase for varied understandings of that action in the world."[2] This is an understatement, as quotations from representatives of five kingdom perspectives show: classic liberalism, the "social gospel," liberation theology, Christian reconstructionism, and postmodern evangelicalism.

First, the classic liberal theologian, Adolf von Harnack:

> The kingdom of God comes by coming to the individual, by entering into his soul and laying hold of it. True, the kingdom of God is the rule of God; but it is the rule of the holy God in the hearts of individuals; *it is God himself in his power.* From this point of view everything that is dramatic in the external and historical sense has vanished; and gone, too, are all the external hopes for the future. Take whatever parable you will, the parable of the sower, the pearl of great price, of the treasure buried in the field—the word of God, God himself, is the kingdom. It is not a question of angels and devils, thrones and principalities, but of God and the soul, the soul and its God.[3]

Second, the "father of the social gospel," Walter Rauschenbusch:

> The social gospel . . . plainly concentrates religious interest on the great ethical problems of social life. It scorns the tithing of mint, anise, and cummin, at which the Pharisees are still busy, and insists on getting down to the weightier matters of God's law, to justice and mercy. . . . The non-ethical practices and beliefs in historical Christianity nearly all centre on the winning of heaven and immortality. On the other hand, the Kingdom of God can be established by nothing except righteous life and action. There is nothing in social Christianity which is likely to breed or reinforce superstition. The more the social gospel engages and inspires theological thought, the more will religion be concentrated on ethical righteousness.[4]

Third, the most famous liberation theologian, Gustavo Gutiérrez:

> If we believe that the Kingdom of God is a gift which is received in history, and if we believe, as the eschatological promises—so charged with human and historical content—indicate to us, that the Kingdom of God necessarily implies the reestablishment of justice in this world, then we must believe that Christ says the poor are blessed *because* the Kingdom of God has begun: "The time has come; the Kingdom of

---

[2]*The Oxford Companion to Christian Thought,* ed. Adrian Hastings et al. (Oxford: Oxford University Press, 2000), 370.
[3]Adolf von Harnack, *What Is Christianity?* (New York: Harper, 1956), 56, italics original.
[4]Walter Rauschenbusch, *A Theology for the Social Gospel* (New York: Macmillan, 1917), 15.

God is upon you" (Mark 1:15). In other words, the elimination of the exploitation and poverty that prevent the poor from being fully human has begun; a Kingdom of justice which goes even beyond what they could have hoped for has begun. They are blessed because the coming of the Kingdom will put an end to their poverty by creating a world of fellowship.[5]

Fourth, the original Christian reconstructionist, R. J. Rushdoony:

> To ensure the continuity of Christ's kingdom on earth, the church was established to extend over all the earth the crown rights of the Lord of Glory, and to make disciples of all nations (Matt. 28:18–20). So great is the supernatural power of Christ's true and faithful church that the very gates of hell cannot prevail or hold out against it (Matt. 16:18). . . . The New Testament tells us that Jesus Christ is this Lord of Glory. It is thus the duty of the modern state to let Him in and to submit to Him, not to control Him. . . . In Scripture, the state has a specific ministry, the ministry of justice (Rom. 13:1). Its place in the plan of God is a real if limited one. The state must be the servant of the Messiah.[6]

Fifth, an influential evangelical postmodernist, Brian McLaren:

> According to him, the good news of the kingdom is a story of heaven invading earth and transforming it, saving it, healing it. . . . An ecclesia [a church] is a gathering of people who identify themselves as citizens of the kingdom of God, living by a higher calling—the way of Jesus and his message of the kingdom. . . . The kingdom of God, Jesus said, was "good news for the poor." There is a personal dimension to the kingdom of God, to be sure, in which we have a personal relationship with the King. But there is also a social dimension to the kingdom of God, a dimension that challenges normal human (and religious) assumptions about peace, war, prosperity, poverty, privilege, responsibility, religion, and God.[7]

Our Goal

Here are five very different conceptions of the kingdom of God—each containing at least elements of truth. But each also fails to capture the full biblical message of the kingdom. It seems that doing so is a difficult task, as Howard Marshall explains:

[5]Gustavo Gutiérrez, *A Theology of Liberation* (Maryknoll, NY: Orbis, 1988), 170–71, italics original.
[6]R. J. Rushdoony, *Christianity and the State* (Vallecito, CA: Ross House, 1986), 33, 72, 74.
[7]Brian McLaren, http://pomomusings.com/2008/01/14/brian-mclaren-on-the-kingdom-of-god/.

> Although the phrase [the Kingdom of God] has been the subject of much biblical research in recent years, and although it is banded about with great frequency in discussions of Christian social action, it is unfortunately often the case that it is used in a very vague manner and that there is a lack of clear biblical exposition in the churches on the meaning of the term.[8]

The purpose of this book is to remedy this situation. It seeks to capture a fuller understanding of the kingdom of God than any one of the five conceptions above. How? By adopting historical, biblical, theological, and ethical perspectives, it attempts to move closer to a comprehensive exposition of the kingdom.

A Road Map

A road map will guide readers. Stephen J. Nichols leads off with "The Kingdoms of God: The Kingdom in Historical and Contemporary Perspectives," in which he demonstrates the differences and similarities of varying ideas of the kingdom throughout history and their implications for theology and life today. Four chapters on the kingdom in Scripture anchor this volume. Bruce K. Waltke lays underpinnings by treating "The Kingdom of God in the Old Testament: Definitions and Story" and "The Kingdom of God in the Old Testament: The Covenants." Robert W. Yarbrough builds upon them in chapters that continue the biblical story in "The Kingdom of God in the New Testament: Matthew and Revelation" and "The Kingdom of God in the New Testament: Mark through the Epistles."

A biblical foundation is essential, but to construct a theological building we need a superstructure. The next four chapters are just that. Clinton E. Arnold deals with "The Kingdom, Miracles, Satan, and Demons" in the "already" and the "not yet." Gregg R. Allison explores the complex relationship of "The Kingdom and the Church" and its ramifications for the church's mission. Gerald Bray considers the present and the future, and time and eternity, in "The Kingdom and Eschatology." And Anthony B. Bradley concludes by applying the theology of the kingdom to eight principles of orthopraxis and justice in "The Kingdom Today."

Christopher W. Morgan and Robert A. Peterson

---

[8]I. Howard Marshall, *Jesus the Saviour: Studies in New Testament Theology* (Downers Grove, IL: InterVarsity, 1990), 213.

1

THE KINGDOMS OF GOD

The Kingdom in Historical and Contemporary Perspectives

STEPHEN J. NICHOLS

And this gospel of the kingdom will be proclaimed throughout the whole world as a testimony to all nations,
and then the end will come.—Matthew 24:14

For what other end do we propose to ourselves than to attain the
kingdom of which there is no end?—Augustine, *The City of God*

Leo Tolstoy, author of such classic novels as *War and Peace* and *Anna Karenina*, also tried his hand at nonfiction. In 1894 he penned one such piece, entitled *The Kingdom of God Is Within You*. The novelist went looking for a solution to the socio-political challenges his native Russia faced as the new century loomed. In most parts of the globe, optimism reigned as the new millennium approached. Such optimism especially ran high throughout most of Europe and in North America. But Tolstoy saw the roadblocks and hurdles in the path when it came to his homeland. He saw the hindrances that lay between his fellow countrymen and the safe and sound arrival of what many were hailing as "The Christian Century." Tolstoy went looking for a way into the utopian "Christian Century." He found what he believed to be the answer in Christ's words from Luke 17:21 (KJV), the words that he used to title his book. Tolstoy found the kingdom of God. Or, more accurately, he found what he thought was the kingdom of God.

The phrase, "the kingdom of God," not only captivated this Russian novelist; it has also captivated theologians, biblical scholars, churchmen, and laity through the centuries. Some have claimed the kingdom to be the central message of Jesus' teachings. In fact many have. And there are about as many interpretations of the kingdom as there are theologians addressing it. This essay lays out the history, the long and curious history, of interpreting the phrase the "kingdom of God," and its variants such as the "kingdom of heaven," throughout the Christian tradition. Looking deeply at this phrase reveals a number of things, chiefly the differences within the Christian tradition regarding understanding the kingdom and, more importantly, the far-reaching implications of understanding the kingdom for the rest of one's theology. Like the tentacles of an octopus, how one understands the kingdom of God reaches and stretches out to all other areas of doctrine.

The church can little afford to neglect theological consideration of the kingdom of God. As perplexing as it might be, and as much of a source of disagreement the kingdom and eschatology might be, the church must grapple with it. Such an understanding of the kingdom is first and foremost informed by the pages of Scripture. But we will also be aided by the work of those who have gone on before. In the pages of church history we will see wisdom, perhaps also a share of folly. Even such folly, however, can be good for us for it can alert us to our own folly—or at the very least our own limitation—in interpretation. To set the stage for this journey into the Christian tradition, consider the decades around the turn of the twentieth century, from the 1880s through the 1920s, the time period in which Tolstoy wrote his book, a time period in which the kingdom received a great deal of attention.

The Coming of the Twentieth Century and the Coming of the Kingdom of God: Setting the Stage for a History of the Kingdom

Returning to Tolstoy, what the Russian novelist found in this deceptively simple little phrase—"The kingdom of God is within you"—set him off articulating a strange, but not so foreign, concept in the modern age, that of pitting the Jesus of history against the Jesus of faith or the Jesus of Christianity. The Jesus of some parts of the four Gospels, the "historical Jesus," was a far cry, Tolstoy and a long train of others argued, from the Jesus of Christianity, the Jesus of the creeds. In his book, Tolstoy seems to have particularly the Nicene Creed in his sights. And, to Tolstoy, understanding what Jesus meant by the seven words of this Luke 17:21 phrase held the key to opening the door to understanding Jesus properly. In Tolstoy's hands, capable writer that he was, the phrase "The kingdom of God is within you" meant that Jesus was all about human life, human flourishing, in the here and now. He was not some God-man who died on the cross as a substitute, rose again bodily from the grave, and will come again visibly to bring swift justice and sweep all of humanity and creation into the long-awaited eschaton—all the dogma of the creeds. No, Tolstoy thunders on in his prose. Such theological platitudes had precious little to do with improving the plight of the peasant. The kingdom that Jesus spoke of, as Tolstoy understood it, is here and now:

> The Sermon on the Mount, or the Creed. One cannot believe in both. And Churchmen have chosen the latter.... People who believe in a wicked and senseless God—who has cursed the human race and devoted his own Son to sacrifice, and a part of mankind to eternal torment—cannot believe in the God of love. The man who believes in a God, in a Christ coming again in glory to judge and to punish the quick and the dead, cannot believe in the Christ who bade us turn the left cheek, judge not, forgive these that wrong us, and love our enemies.... The man who believes in the Church's doctrine of the compatibility of warfare and capital punishment with Christianity cannot believe in the brotherhood of all men.
>
> And what is most important of all—the man who believes in salvation through faith in the redemption or the sacraments, cannot devote all his powers to realizing Christ's moral teaching in his life.[1]

Tolstoy ironically becomes like one of the false prophets Jesus warned about. Jesus told his disciples that there would be those to come who would point and say, "There's the kingdom." Jesus told his disciples not to believe in such a message and not to follow such a messenger. When Tolstoy says, in effect, "Look here, at this ethical system, this is the kingdom of God," he could not be more off target.

At about the same time Tolstoy was writing in Russia, theologians and biblical scholars in Germany were striking similar keys on their typewriters, promulgating what has come to be called "realized

---

[1]Leo Tolstoy, *The Kingdom of God Is Within You* (Seaside, OR: Watchmaker, 2010), 43. One critic has hailed this work as the best of Tolstoy's many forays into nonfiction. Perhaps Tolstoy should have stayed with fiction.

eschatology." Tolstoy was not alone. In 1892 Johannes Weiss published
Jesus' Proclamation of the Kingdom of God. This book marks a watershed
in the so-called "quest for the historical Jesus" movement that occupied so
much of German theologizing in the nineteenth century (and would continue into the twentieth century as well). As Benedict Viviano explains,
"[Weiss's] book was so offensive because liberal theology had a bad conscience about its suppression of Jesus' eschatology. It was not ignorant
of it. It simply hoped to keep it a dirty little secret. Thanks to Weiss, the
liberal emperor was seen to have no clothes."[2] Weiss put eschatology and
Jesus' message of the kingdom at the center of the quest. The twentieth
century would be the century of the kingdom, as far as theological discussions were concerned.

Though Weiss himself held to a future realization of Jesus' kingdom
message and eschatology, other theologians followed the trajectory he set
out and left the future behind. In the hands of such English theologians
in the Anglican tradition as Charles Dodd, J. A. T. Robertson, and G. B.
Caird, the kingdom of God was understood to be entirely for the present
and not for the future. There would be no physical, visible second coming. There would be no apocalyptic kingdom. Eschatology consequently
became not a matter of the sweet by and by, but entirely a matter of the
gritty here and now. Just as some of Jesus' early disciples missed the point,
thinking he was speaking of a kingdom to come, so also centuries' worth
of theologians had done the same as they speculated and theorized about
some cataclysmic future event that would set in motion the end times.
When Jesus spoke of the kingdom of God as being in the midst of his contemporary audiences, Dodd and his fellow adherents of realized eschatology argued, Jesus meant it.[3]

In this teaching of "realized eschatology," the kingdom is entirely here
and now. Eschatology—and all that this subject of theology concerns,
including the meaning of the kingdom, the second coming, the events of
the end times, the future judgments, even heaven and hell—is fully *realized* now. All that is bound up in eschatology is made real and experienced
in this life, in this world.

---

[2]Benedict T. Viviano, "Eschatology and the Quest for the Historical Jesus," in *The Oxford Handbook of Eschatology*, ed. Jerry L. Walls (Oxford: Oxford University Press, 2008), 79. See also Wendell Willis, "The Discovery
of the Eschatological Kingdom: Johannes Weiss and Albert Schweitzer," in *The Kingdom of God in Twentieth
Century Interpretation*, ed. Wendell Willis (Peabody, MA: Hendrickson, 1987), 1–14.
[3]Viviano, "Eschatology and the Quest for the Historical Jesus," 81. While Dodd initially held to both a present
and future kingdom, he moved to see the "futuristic passages" as fully understandable within a framework of
realized eschatology. See C. H. Dodd, *The Parables of the Kingdom* (London: Nisbet, 1935).

And concurrent with Tolstoy and Weiss and the Germans, American theologians were also getting in on the act. Among the more liberal strands of American theology, realized eschatology appeared to win the day. In the hands of Baptist German-American Walter Rauschenbusch, realized eschatology would result in the Social Gospel movement. The gospel, Rauschenbusch argued in the early years of the 1900s, has nothing to do with sinners in need of salvation, but instead has everything to do with the socially oppressed and marginalized realizing justice.[4] Realized eschatology became the central driving force in his theology. For Rauschenbusch, the idea that the kingdom is now means that salvation is now, that judgment is now, that heaven and hell are now. Of course, for such things to be now requires that one take the New Testament teaching on these subjects as mere poetry, myth, and metaphor. And, from its proponents Tolstoy, Weiss, and Dodd, this realized eschatology also requires an uneasiness—if not flat-out rejection—of the Jesus of the creeds. There is an unbroken, almost necessary, linkage between how one defines the kingdom message of Jesus, how one understands the overall thrust of the ministry and message of Jesus, and what one believes about his person. If the definition of the kingdom is off, so is the rest. Once that false move is made, all the central and defining tenets of Christianity fall like dominoes.

But the social gospel liberals were not the only American theologians transfixed with deciphering the meaning of the kingdom of God. The dispensationalists, also getting started in this same time frame of the 1880s to the early 1900s, stand at the opposite end from the realized eschatology movement. This movement began with the writings of the churchman John Nelson Darby. Born in London, Darby went on to study at Trinity College, Dublin. Upon completing his degree, he became ordained in the Anglican Church of Ireland. Darby soon found his own thinking at odds with Anglicanism, from which he departed and began, along with others, the Plymouth Brethren movement. Through his writings, and his focus on biblical prophecy, Darby gave expression to dispensationalism, a view that holds a deep and wide distinction between Israel and the church and emphasizes a literal interpretation of biblical prophecy. Dispensationalism was nurtured in North American soil at prophecy conferences in such places as Niagara Falls; Winona Lake, Indiana; and

---

[4]Walter Rauschenbusch, *Christianity and the Social Crisis* (New York: MacMillan, 1907), and *A Theology for the Social Gospel* (New York: MacMillan, 1927).

Philadelphia. And it was brought to fruition with the 1917 publication of *The Scofield Reference Bible* (named after C. I. Scofield).

Dispensationalism stresses the *future* and apocalyptic piece to eschatology. Christ will come again. Actually, his second coming will have two parts. The first part will be the rapture, a secret coming in which Christ takes the church to heaven to be with him. Christ will then come again physically at the conclusion of the literal, seven-year tribulation. This will be followed by the thousand-year reign of Christ on the earth (the millennium), which will be followed by the final judgment, the damned to an eternity in hell, and the righteous to an eternity in the new heavens and the new earth. In the meantime, the kingdom of God has been put on hold. Instead of seeing the kingdom (or even seeing any part of the kingdom) as present, these early dispensationalists saw the church as a "parenthesis" in God's program, interrupting God's direct dealing with Israel. Someday in the future, God would return to deal with Israel, and the kingdom in all of its literal manifestation would come. For now, however, God is working through and in the church, and the kingdom is postponed. Contrary to the "realized eschatology" of the liberal theologians, dispensationalists proclaimed a wholly future eschatology.[5]

And so from Russian novelists to German theologians to American prophecy conference speakers, the kingdom of God received a boatload of attention. Four things can be gleaned from this brief foray into the eschatological conversation of the 1880s through the 1920s. First, consider the overwhelming emphasis on eschatology in the theologizing of this time period. The sheer volume of books published on the subject nearly outweighs books on eschatology from all previous centuries of the church's life combined. Further, this was not just an emphasis among academic theologians. Such masses of conference goers flocked to Winona Lake in the summertime that the Chicago Railroad built a designated line running from the city to the middle of the farm plains of Indiana. Prophecy and the kingdom of God were topics that had captivated the hearts and minds of the public as well.

The rest of the twentieth century evidences similar fascination. Hal Lindsey's *Late Great Planet Earth* dominated the *New York Times* bestseller lists in the 1970s. And its sales but shadow the *Left Behind* novels from the pens of Tim LaHaye and Jerry Jenkins. In 1996, while at the

---

[5]This scheme follows the pattern of Revelation, as dispensationalists interpret the book, seeing chapters 6–18 as referring to the seven-year tribulation, chapter 19 referring to the second coming, chapter 20 referring to the literal millennial reign of Christ, and chapters 21–22 referring to the final judgments and eternity future.

Christian Booksellers' Convention in Anaheim, California, I could not even make my way through the lines to get into the auditorium for that evening's main event, a prophecy conference. In the end I gave my prized ticket to a most grateful student of prophecy—the telltale sign being the particular study Bible firmly clutched in his hands—waiting with all the fervor of eschatological hope in the standby line. The meaning of the kingdom was crucial in this 1880s–1920s time period, and it remains crucial, if not central, to many to the present day.

The second thing to be learned from this eschatological discussion concerns how eschatology touches other areas of theology. One's view of eschatology has implications for how one views the person of Christ, the gospel, and the nature and mission of the church. One's view of eschatology informs and is also informed by—this is a theological version of the chicken and the egg conundrum—one's hermeneutics, one's understanding of the Old Testament, the Gospels, prophetic books, apocalyptic literature, and the relationship between the Testaments. Simply consider understanding the Gospel of Matthew. How you define the kingdom will govern how you read and interpret the first Gospel. In other words, how we view the kingdom of God is not an isolated piece of theology. The same is true of the rest of the biblical teaching on the kingdom. Our view of the kingdom of God stretches out to nearly every part of our hermeneutic, biblical understanding, and theology.

Third, we learn from this eschatological discussion of the 1880s–1920s of the broad and vast differences within the Christian tradition. This period reveals what will become the wide terrain of the Christian tradition on eschatology. There are myriad interpretations of the kingdom of God. Tony Campolo, in his inimitable way, once even defined the kingdom of God as, yes, a party.[6] It is far more accurate to speak of kingdoms (plural) of God. To put the matter another way: of the making of eschatologies there seems to be no end. What are we to make of all of these differences? This is a significant piece of the discussion, to which we will return in the conclusion of this essay.

Fourth and finally, this eschatological conversation of the 1880s–1920s reveals a center point to the discussion. Eschatology is vast, touching on all matters of biblical interpretation and views of the end times. When facing such broad horizons a center point can help bring focus, which in

---

[6]Tony Campolo, *The Kingdom of God Is a Party: God's Radical Plan for His Family* (Nashville: Thomas Nelson, 1992).

turn can promote understanding. To switch metaphors, we need a handle on the far-reaching subject of eschatology. And we find that handle in the center point of the discussion—the phrase "the kingdom of God."

In the pages to follow of this essay, we will explore the route this phrase has taken through the history of the Christian tradition in order to shed some light on what the phrase and its implications mean for the church today. We will look at the historical perspectives on this phrase in these successive eras: the early church, the medieval age, the Reformation and Puritan eras, and the modern age. To get a handle on the contemporary perspectives on this phrase we will look at both the twentieth century and the early years of the twenty-first. As with all surveys, what follows is more a summary of the high points than a comprehensive treatment. Nevertheless, we stand to be informed significantly by the distant and immediate past as we seek our own understanding of the kingdom of God.

"The Days Shall Come in Which Vines Shall Grow": The Kingdom of God in the Early Church

Papias, as tradition has it, was taught by the very elders who themselves had been taught by the apostle John. Sadly, though, our connection to Papias is mostly indirect, coming to us through the writings of Irenaeus— himself, as tradition holds, taught by the aged apostle John as well. Papias envisioned a future time of blessing, a future entrance into the fullness of God's promise. He writes with a fervor not unlike John the apostle:

> The days will come, in which vines shall grow, each having ten thousand branches, and in each branch ten thousand twigs, and in each true twig ten thousand shoots, and each one of the shoots ten thousand clusters, and on every one of the clusters ten thousand grapes, and every grape when pressed will give five and twenty metretes of wine.[7]

If you do the math—Papias's calculations have each grape yielding about 260 gallons—that's a lot of wine. He follows with a discussion of an equally impressive amount of grain. Though Papias uses earthly language to describe the bounties of this future, he, like his fellow church fathers, stressed that this was a future kingdom not contiguous with the present world. The present world, overrun by wickedness and under the spell of

---

[7]Papias, *Fragments*, IV, Michael W. Holmes, ed., *The Apostolic Fathers in English*, 3rd ed. (Grand Rapids, MI: Baker, 2006), 314–15; see also Irenaeus, *Against Heresies*, bk. 5, chap. 33; A. Cleveland Coxe, ed., *The Ante-Nicene Fathers, Vol. 1: The Apostolic Fathers, Justin Martyr–Irenaeus* (Grand Rapids, MI: Eerdmans, 1953), 562–63.

Rome, will come to an end. The present world will literally crash and burn. And then God's kingdom, not of this world and filled to the brim and beyond with wine, shall come.

Justin Martyr argued from this very position in his apologetics. As Charles Hill explains, "[Justin Martyr] castigates the Romans for assuming, when they hear that the Christians look for a kingdom, that this kingdom is a human one."[8] On the contrary, Justin argued that the kingdom of God was a kingdom not of this world. But Papias, Irenaeus, and Justin Martyr all saw this future kingdom of God as a physical kingdom, with material blessings. When they spoke of grapes and wine and grain and bread, they were talking about grapes and wine and grain and bread.

Tertullian follows suit, even adding a sharpness to an idea present in his fellow pre-Nicene church fathers, that of chiliasm or millennialism. This view, which later theologians would call "historic premillennialism," holds to a two-stage future, consisting first of a literal thousand-year reign of God on earth and then, second, of the eternal state. Here we begin to see the linking of the kingdom of God with a future cataclysmic event and the end times, opening the door to the millennium (viewed as a literal thousand-year time period; see Rev. 20:1–6), which then leads to the eternal state. The connection of the kingdom of God to millennial or chiliastic thinking was a crucial step in the historical development of the theology of the kingdom. Equally important to the discussion of the kingdom in the early church were the resurrection of the dead and the intermediate state. To pursue this, however, lies beyond the scope of this essay.[9]

The idea of chiliasm or millennialism merits attention. Previous studies have argued for a consensus view of these pre-Nicene early church fathers, claiming they were nearly all of the historic premillennial persuasion and singling out Origen as the proverbial exception proving the rule. Charles Hill has documented, however, that this was not the only view of the early church fathers up until 325 and that Origen did not stand alone. Against Papias, Irenaeus, Justin Martyr, Tertullian, and a cast of others, Charles Hill lines up Clement, Polycarp, Hippolytus, and another cast of others, not to mention Origen, who do not share this premillennialism. Some figures on this other side of the millennial fence even explicitly reject it.[10]

---

[8]Charles E. Hill, *Regnum Caelorum: Patterns of Millennial Thought in Early Christianity*, 2nd ed. (Grand Rapids, MI: Eerdmans, 2001), 23.
[9]See ibid. for a full discussion of early church views on the relationship between the intermediate state and the kingdom of God.
[10]Ibid., 1–20, 75–76.

The standout figure here is Origen with his spiritual view of the kingdom. No doubt (overly) influenced by Neoplatonic thought, Origen was
quite troubled by the physicality—like that of Papias's wildly fruitful grape
clusters—and literalness—like that of Tertullian's hermeneutic—afoot. In
his *Hexapla*, he lays forth the threefold sense of his hermeneutic, comprised of the literal, the moral, and the allegorical. He was captivated by
the latter, applying his allegorical method with abandon to the biblical
teaching of the kingdom, especially to the earthy descriptions of the kingdom in the scrolls of the Old Testament Prophets. When these prophets talk about grapes and wine and grain and bread, Origen argued, they
were *certainly not* talking about grapes and wine and grain and bread.
They were using the physical to point to the true, deeper, spiritual meaning. The kingdom of God is, according to Origen, spiritual. All of those
prophesied blessings speak of the glories of the soul's union with God.[11]
Benedict Viviano speaks of Origen's "interiorization" of the kingdom, citing as evidence his repeated reference to the kingdom of God "in us."[12]

Hill sets forth a nuanced view of the kingdom of God in the first few
centuries of the church's life, seeing both millennialist views (historic
premillennialism) and non-millennialist views. The upshot of this means
that, when it comes to thinking on the kingdom of God from 100 through
the 300s, there is one line of interpretation that stresses the future, literal,
and physical kingdom of God to come and another line of interpretation
that sees the kingdom of God as spiritual, realized in the soul's union with
God now, and to be consummated in the future.

* * * * * * *

As we move out of the 300s and into the 400s we encounter one of the
most significant stages of the historical development of the theology of
the kingdom of God—that of Augustine and his work. He seems to follow
in the train of Origen, and there are indeed similarities. But Augustine's
view, in the end, is all his own. His view is worth understanding because
it almost exclusively dominated the field for centuries and continues to be
deeply felt.

Though Augustine discusses quite a few subjects in his monumental
City of God (written on and off from 413–427), the kingdom of God takes
center stage. Augustine prefers the term *city*, from Psalm 87:3, though

---

[11]Origen, again following his philosophical commitments, puts exclusive stress on the soul.
[12]Benedict T. Viviano, *The Kingdom of God in History* (Wilmington, DE: Michael Glazier, 1988), 42.

he does not mean a geographical place. He writes, "These we also mystically call the two cities, or the two communities of men, of which one is predestined to reign eternally with God, and the other to suffer eternal punishment with the devil."[13]

Though Augustine was an ardent opponent of Neoplatonism, platonic ideas nevertheless do influence his thoughts on the kingdom. The physical descriptions of blessings, which Papias took literally, point Augustine past the shadow, the real, and on to the substance, the ideal. The abundance of physical blessings, in other words, served as the vehicle the biblical authors used to deliver their message of the real essence of the kingdom of God, which is the unadulterated union with the Triune God and the future absolute reign of God over all things. Augustine declares, "How great shall be that felicity, which shall be tainted with no evil, which shall lack no good, and which shall afford leisure for the praises of God, who shall be all in all."[14] Augustine's view of the kingdom, as that of Papias and Tertullian and the other literalists, involves a future kingdom, one that came once this life passed. So he writes with a faraway look in his eye of the kingdom to come, "whilst on our pilgrimage we sigh for its beauty."[15]

Augustine then stresses a figurative kingdom, derived from an allegorical or figurative hermeneutic, which will be consummated in the future. And in Augustine's philosophy of history, the kingdom is not only the end chronologically; it is also the end teleologically. So he writes, "For what other end do we propose to ourselves than to attain the kingdom of which there is no end?"[16] The *civitas terrena* (City of Man) will pass away and only the *civitas Dei* (City of God) will remain.

Two things emerge from this brief look into the early church's perspective on the kingdom of God. One concerns the variegated nature of the perspectives. It is an oversimplification to speak of the early church's understanding of the kingdom as monolithic. We should recognize that there are differences.

The second thing that emerges concerns the influence of the sociological or cultural situation on theologizing. That is to say, the various views of the kingdom of God put forth by the church fathers were influenced by their respective contexts. Martyrs and those facing persecution (including mostly, but not exclusively, figures from the pre-Nicene era)

---

[13]Augustine, *The City of God*, trans. Marcus Dods (New York: Modern Library, 1993), 473 (bk. 15, chap. 1).
[14]Ibid., 864 (bk. 22, chap. 30).
[15]Ibid., 166 (bk. 5, chap. 16).
[16]Ibid., 867 (bk. 22, chap. 30).

looked for a time when the tables would be reversed. The kingdom was to be a time of rich blessing for the poor, the outcast, those we would call today the socially marginalized. In another vein, Augustine developed a hermeneutic and a theology, specifically a theology of the kingdom, both impacted by his platonic tendencies and by the immediate circumstances of the fall of Rome. The earthly cities, no matter how glorious, have their limits and their final ends. What may be said of this dynamic of the cultural influence on theologizing about the kingdom of God applies equally to theologians and biblical scholars working in the centuries since and right up to the twenty-first century.

The End of the World: The Kingdom of God in the Medieval Church

As mentioned, Augustine's understanding of the kingdom of God and, consequently, his eschatology, dominated the medieval period. One notable exception, however, was the thinking of Joachim of Fiore (c. 1135– 1202). Joachim's work sparked an apocalyptic frenzy among followers on the one hand and received an anathema from the Fourth Lateran Council in 1213 on the other hand.

Joachim, taking his cue from certain verses of the book of Revelation and texts elsewhere in Scripture, uncovered a secret code outlining the three successive *status*, or states, of God's dealings with humanity. The third *status* was the time in which he lived and, as he saw things, which would come to an end at 1260, at which time the Antichrist would be revealed in a time of conflict, ushering in the end times.[17] Joachim reintroduced millennial thinking and linked such thinking to the political moves of the day, mixing temporal causes with the eternal cause of the reign of righteousness. This was the era of the Crusades. His followers, the Joachimites, ranged the spectrum from the tame to the fanatic. And his views, once they trickled down, were quite popular among the masses, and even among kings, like the famed Richard the Lionhearted. Joachim placed a focus on Revelation, a book sometimes obscured due to its complexity. The careful study of the last book of the New Testament, he argued, revealed hidden clues to understanding the climax of God's dealing with humanity. The pages of Revelation held the key to understanding all things.

---

[17]See Bernard McGinn, *Visions of the End: Apocalyptic Tradition in the Middle Ages* (New York: Columbia University Press, 1979), 126–41; Viviano, *The Kingdom of God in History*, 57–76. For the interested, see the technical discussion of Joachim's manuscripts by Stephen Wessley, "A New Writing of Joachim of Fiore: Preliminary Observations," in *Prophecy and Eschatology*, ed. Michael Wilks (Oxford: Blackwell, 1994), 15–27.

Joachimism was met theologically by Thomas Aquinas, who preferred more of an Augustinian hermeneutic and, consequently, understanding of the kingdom of God. Aquinas lacked any such millennialist approach in his understanding of the kingdom, seeing it instead as meaning both "Christ himself dwelling in us through grace" and the future realization of the kingdom in heaven.[18]

The vision-filled Joachiamite tradition, though, proved to be a formidable match for the theological sophistication of the Thomist tradition. This can be seen in no less a person than Christopher Columbus and in no less an event than the fabled "discovery of the New World" in 1492. In addition to making four voyages across the untamed Atlantic, Columbus also wrote a book, *The Book of Prophecies*, offered to his beloved patrons, Ferdinand and Isabella, king and queen of Spain. It is a book of quotations that Columbus garnered from the pages of Scripture, the patristic period, and the medieval era, including, of course, Joachim himself. This work, as well as his "The Account of the Fourth Voyage," leads Bernard McGinn to hang Columbus out on the same line as apocalyptic-obsessed medieval theologians. McGinn admits, "To those accustomed to see the discovery of America as the work of a hard-headed practical seaman flouting the traditions of the past, the picture of Columbus as a religious visionary strongly influenced by centuries of apocalyptic hopes may seem strange." Then McGinn adds, "But the existence of this element in the great explorer's complex personality is undeniable, and its force became stronger as he neared the end of his adventurous life."[19] A few lines from Columbus's "The Account of the Fourth Voyage" show McGinn's estimation not to be wide of the mark:

> Jerusalem and Mount Sion are to be rebuilt by the hands of Christians, as God has declared by the mouths of his prophet in the fourteenth Psalm (vv. 7Ex.8). The Abbott Joachim said that he who should do this was to come from Spain. . . . Who will offer himself for this work? Should anyone do so, I pledge myself, in the name of God, to convey him safely hither, provided the Lord permits me.[20]

Leaving the medieval era, we see two main strands of thinking on the kingdom of God. The first, following Augustine, stresses the allegori-

---

[18] As cited in Viviano, *The Kingdom of God in History*, 62.
[19] McGinn, *Visions of the End*, 284.
[20] Cited in ibid., 285. For the original text, see C. de Lollis, ed., *Scritti di Cristoforo Colombo: Raccolta di Documenti e Studi*, part 1, vol. 2 (Rome: Forzani, 1984), 202.

cal understanding of the kingdom, closely identifying the kingdom with the soul's union with God individually and collectively. The elect being in union with the triune God is the end, both teleologically and chronologically. The kingdom, in Aquinas's thought for example, is the beatification of the saints with God in heaven. Here he echoes the work of Augustine. The other strand of thinking on the kingdom of God in the medieval era is in the apocalyptic tradition. This view links global evangelism (understood in terms of baptism and membership in the Roman Catholic Church) of the heathen with the coming kingdom, stresses cataclysmic events as inaugurating the kingdom, and reads current events through the lens of biblical prophecies. This strand is marked by visionaries, chief among them Joachim of Fiore, who both interpret the times and lend their own predictions concerning the times.

"Christ Is the King": The Kingdom of God in the Reformation

Martin Luther's thoughts on the kingdom of God look, like the rest of his theology, quite different from that of the medieval churchmen and theologians. Bernard Lohse argues that Luther links his understanding of the kingdom of God—the two kingdoms, actually, that of God and that of the world—to his understanding of the difference between law and gospel, which amounts to, in Lohse's estimation, "help[ing] secure gospel purity and faith."[21] Simplifying these connections would not suffice because, for Luther, the stakes could not be higher when it came to rightly understanding the kingdom of God. Luther preferred to speak of two *kingdoms* rather than Augustine's two *cities*, seeing all of humanity as citizens of either the kingdom of God or the kingdom of the world. As for the former, Luther declares, "Those who belong to the kingdom of God are all the true believers who are in Christ and under Christ, for Christ is King and Lord in the kingdom of God, as Psalm 2 and all of Scripture says."[22] But then Luther, striking a different chord on the kingdom from Augustine's, adds, "For this reason [Christ] came into this world, that he might begin God's kingdom and establish it in this world."[23]

Lohse sees significant differences in Luther's thinking from that of Augustine.[24] Whereas Augustine preferred more of a dialectical relation-

---

[21]Bernard Lohse, *Martin Luther's Theology: Its Historical and Systematic Development* (Minneapolis: Fortress, 1999), 315.
[22]Martin Luther, "Temporal Authority: To What Extent Should It Be Obeyed?" (1523), *Martin Luther's Basic Theological Writings* (Minneapolis: Fortress, 1989), 662.
[23]Ibid.
[24]Lohse, *Martin Luther's Theology*, 314–24.

ship between this world and the next, between the spiritual (the *civitas Dei*, City of God) and the temporal (the *civitas terrena*, City of Man), Luther had a larger place for God to be at work in the world and, consequently, for the church to be at work in the world. This dynamic drives Luther's ethics, not to mention his politics.[25] Lohse further notes how Luther's and Augustine's differences stop when it comes to the eschatological perspective on the kingdom. Concerning the future consummation of the kingdom of God, the two were agreed. According to both, the ultimate realization of the kingdom would not be of this world.

Luther's more radical colleagues, who would soon break off from him altogether, dissented from his perspective on the kingdom of God. Chief among them is Thomas Muntzer, the Reformation's own version of Joachim of Fiore. By 1520, Muntzer had become rather fanatical. By the mid-1520s he took to interpreting dreams. For him, the kingdom of God would come to earth, rather violently, as God's people took to the battlefield in the name of righteousness. Muntzer attached apocalyptic significance to the Peasants' War, assuring the peasants that God was on their side against the godless nobles. It all ended rather badly for the peasants. Muntzer fared no better, eventually being captured and beheaded.[26]

Muntzer was associated with the Anabaptist movement, the majority of which renounced such violence. In fact, the Anabaptists came to be marked by a significant disinterest in the political affairs of the *civitas terrena*. The perspective of the Anabaptists may be summarized in the letter that Michael Saddler, an early Anabaptist leader and primary author of the Schleitheim Confession, wrote just before his martyrdom. "Flee the shadow of this world," he exhorted his congregation.[27] Far from taking up arms, the Anabaptist view of the kingdom that emerged consisted of championing the cause of the oppressed. John Howard Yoder's *The Politics of Jesus* (1972) and Donald B. Kraybill's *The Upside-Down Kingdom* (1978) reflect this Anabaptist understanding of the meaning of the kingdom of God to the present day.

Returning to the magisterial Reformers, John Calvin argued that the kingdom of God, as Christ proclaimed it, is the gospel and all that it conveys to believers. Calvin writes, "By the kingdom of God, which [Christ] taught was at hand, he meant the forgiveness of sins, salvation, life, and

---

[25]See Stephen J. Nichols, *Martin Luther: A Guided Tour of His Life and Thought* (Phillipsburg, NJ: P&R, 2002), 131–46.
[26]See Michael J. St. Clair, *Millenarian Movements in Historical Context* (New York: Garland, 1992), 153–90.
[27]Cited in Thieleman J. van Braght, *Martyrs Mirror* (Scottdale, PA: Herald Press, n.d.), 420.

utterly everything that we obtain in Christ."[28] Elsewhere, Calvin says, "God reigns where men, both by denial of themselves and by contempt of the world and of earthly life, pledge themselves to his righteousness in order to aspire to a heavenly life."[29]

It is notable that neither Luther nor Calvin made interpreting the book of Revelation a priority. As Benedict Viviano points out, Calvin did not "worry much about apocalyptic eschatology."[30] The same may be said of Luther. Both Reformers were far more interested in connecting their understanding of the kingdom to the gospel, both to proclaiming and living it. They had a future eschatology, but certainly not a detailed one.

Interlude

"Look! Here's the Kingdom":
The Kingdom of God in the Modern Age

It might be helpful to set the stage for the twentieth century by looking outside of theology and for a brief moment looking at the work of Georg Wilhelm Friedrich Hegel. Hegel's ideas significantly shaped the modern world, introducing his idea of progress. Progress comes through the dialectic, which Hegel used to explain the history of ideas. The dialectic starts with the thesis (the accepted idea), which is then met by the antithesis (an opposing idea), which then eventually emerges into a synthesis (a composite idea), which then becomes the new thesis. And so ideas march on, and humanity and history always progress to the newer, the better, and the higher. What is noteworthy here is how Hegel baptized this idea in an attempt to give it religious significance. God himself, the *Zeitgeist* (Time Spirit), is that which progresses, that which is newer, better, higher. The trickle-down effect of Hegel's thinking is enormous, especially on more liberal theologies. This philosophical perspective underlies realized eschatology, which comes to dominate liberal theology from the end of the nineteenth through the twentieth century. This philosophical perspective also underlies the politicization of the kingdom that also marks the modern age. The kingdom of God becomes politicized when it gets identified with or attached to an ideological agenda.

---

[28]John Calvin, *Institutes of the Christian Religion*, ed. John T. McNeill (Philadelphia: Westminster, 1960), 1:613 (1.3.19).
[29]Ibid., 2:905 (3.20.42).
[30]Viviano, *The Kingdom of God in History*, 97.

Lesslie Newbigin offers a healthy corrective to this modernist tendency to politicize the kingdom and co-opt God's agenda for one's own.
He writes of the necessity

> to insist that the fulfillment of Christ's commission must include the call
> to a total allegiance to Jesus, and to commitment to the company of His
> people, the company that bears his name, the church. Without this, talk
> about the Kingdom is too easily co-opted into a utopianism which owes
> more to the nineteenth-century doctrine of progress than to the essen-
> tially apocalyptic teaching of the New Testament about the kingdom.[31]

And so we are back to trying to understand both proclamations of
Christ, that the kingdom of God is at hand, that it is near, and that the
kingdom of God is not of this world. Very few theological discussions in
the contemporary age will play as prominent a role as that of the kingdom
of God. And it is to those discussions that we now turn.

"What Shall Be the Sign of Thy Coming?":
The Kingdom of God in the Twentieth and Twenty-First Centuries

As mentioned in the earlier look at the period from the 1880s through
the 1920s, the kingdom of God was a widely discussed and hotly debated
topic. The newer views of realized eschatology and dispensational premillennialism joined alongside historic premillennialism, amillennialism,
and postmillennialism to offer a virtual smorgasbord of eschatological
choices. For most of the twentieth century, adherents of these various
views drew sharp boundary lines. The views were not so much points
along a continuum as distinct camps with deeply and passionately held
differences. And, as to be expected, these different views resulted in a
variety of perspectives on the kingdom of God. In the twentieth century
especially, it is best to speak of the various and many kingdoms of God.

Consider dispensational premillennialism. This view, as discussed
earlier, sees a sharp distinction between Israel and the church, seeing
the promised kingdom only for Israel and as having a distinct and separate future from that of the church. In dispensationalism, the kingdom of
God is for and of the future. The extent to which this is true can be seen
in the way most dispensationalists of the Scofield-Chafer era handled

---

[31]Lesslie Newbigin, *Signs Amid the Rubble: The Purposes of God in Human History*, ed. Geoffrey Wainwright
(Grand Rapids, MI: Eerdmans, 2003), 103. Originally given as the Henry Martyn lectures at Cambridge University, 1986.

the Sermon on the Mount in Matthew 5–7.[32] Christ, this view argues, puts forth a kingdom ethic in these chapters. That is to say, the ethical demands of these chapters apply only during the millennial kingdom when Christ is reigning on his throne. Charles Ryrie writes that this is "clearly the view of the original *Scofield Bible* and of Chafer."[33] Ryrie himself argues that while the Sermon on the Mount "relates to life in the millennial kingdom," it is also "applicable and profitable to believers in this age."[34] Ryrie, however, like Scofield and Chafer, sees this current age as the church age, leaving talk of the kingdom for the age to come and not for this age.

Diametrically opposed to the dispensationalists, amillennialists tended to, in Russell Moore's vivid description, espouse a "crypto-Platonic" vision of eschatological hope.[35] In other words, when the Bible talks about grapes and wine and grain and bread it is *not* talking about grapes and wine and grain and bread, according to traditional amillennialists.

Then along came George Eldon Ladd. Immersed in the German wrangling over the kingdom of God during his doctoral studies at Harvard, Ladd found that the already/not yet construct could add a great deal of light to the heat generated by the debate. He had already seen how viewing the kingdom as both present (already) and future (not yet) had brought some equilibrium in Germany. Once he took up his post at Fuller Theological Seminary, Ladd thought the already/not yet concept could do the same for America.[36] He not only advocated for the already/not yet view of the kingdom; he argued it served well as the center, the guiding light, for all of New Testament theology.[37]

One further contribution from the Germans concerns the two words *Reich* and *Herrschaft*. *Reich* speaks of realm, the place where the kingdom is manifest. *Herrschaft* speaks of ruling, the act of reigning. Ladd used both of these to speak of the full-orbed nature of the kingdom of God. The

---

[32]Though it may be inappropriate to overdraw the differences within classical dispensationalism, there are some stages to its development. I would argue for three such stages of classical dispensationalism: (1) the Darby-prophecy conference era from 1880 to 1910s; (2) the Scofield-Chafer era from 1910s to 1950s; (3) the Walvoord-Ryrie era from the 1960s through the present day. The arrival of the progressive dispensationalists in the 1990s marked not so much a development as a change, and I would argue a substantive change. See Russell D. Moore, *The Kingdom of Christ: The New Evangelical Perspective* (Wheaton, IL: Crossway, 2004), 39–43.
[33]Charles C. Ryrie, *Dispensationalism* (Chicago: Moody Press, 1995), 99.
[34]Ibid., 100.
[35]Moore, *The Kingdom of Christ*, 51.
[36]See George Eldon Ladd, *Jesus and the Kingdom: The Eschatology of Biblical Realism* (New York: Harper & Row, 1964), 3–38.
[37]George Eldon Ladd, *New Testament Theology*, rev. ed., ed. Donald Hagner (Grand Rapids, MI: Eerdmans, 1993). I have spoken here of Ladd seeing the kingdom as the center of New Testament theology chiefly because that was Ladd's specialty. In reality, for Ladd the kingdom serves as the center of a theology of both Testaments, indeed, of theology itself.

kingdom, then, is a discrete place, a realm, and an activity. The kingdom, therefore, is both now, as God reigns, and in the future at the consummation of God's reign.[38]

These developments were not, however, merely owing to Ladd and the Germans. For as Ladd mediated German positions on the kingdom, so too Richard Gaffin mediated Dutch positions for Americans. The collective work of Geerhardus Vos (a Dutch theologian who taught biblical theology at Princeton) and Herman Ridderbos (a Dutch theologian who taught biblical theology in the Netherlands) stresses redemptive history, all from the center point of Christ's proclamation of the gospel of the kingdom understood as *inaugurated eschatology*. Inaugurated eschatology simply means that the kingdom, and eschatological promise, is in the beginning stages of fulfillment already, and will be fully consummated in the future. Inaugurated eschatology or the already/not yet view, in Gaffin's estimation, keeps the church from the danger of a too-realized eschatology on the one hand and a too-future eschatology on the other. This both/and construct has more merit, he argues, than either/or constructs. Gaffin further argues that to limit eschatology to a discussion of last things is a grave misstep, arguing instead that eschatology and one's discussion of the kingdom relate to "the present identity and experience of the Christian, and so too in the present life and mission of the church."[39] He, if pressed, would claim that eschatology is best understood from the perspective of christology. If pressed further, Gaffin would claim eschatology began and stems from Christ's resurrection.

In his work on the history of interpreting the kingdom, Russell Moore notes how this already/not yet construct has influenced the thinking of amillennialists like Gaffin and Anthony Hoekema on the one hand, and the progressive dispensationalists like Craig Blaising and Darrell Bock on the other hand. Moore further speaks of this inaugurated eschatology model as leading to a "consensus on the nature of the kingdom."[40] Moore is not alone in his assessment, because he is joined by Vern Poythress. Poythress sees the already/not yet effects on both sides of what had been a sharp dividing line between dispensationalists and amillennialists over the status of the kingdom. Would it be material and physical? Or would it be spiritual? Poythress sees both sides consenting to each other and giving

[38]See Ladd, *Jesus and the Kingdom.*
[39]Richard B. Gaffin, "The Usefulness of the Cross," *WTJ* 41 (1979): 229.
[40]Moore, *The Kingdom of Christ*, 53. Incidentally, Moore's book offers not only the most helpful survey on the kingdom in the twentieth century but also the best bibliography on the subject.

up formerly tightly held ground. He speaks of these "traditional millennial positions" being brought "closer to one another." And he speaks of
this movement as a "salutary advance."[41] Instead of the model of distinct
camps with high walls of separation between them, a newer model would
be more of a continuum sans the sharp divisions.

The already/not yet approach to the kingdom has also influenced German theologizing, most noticeably in the work of Wolfhart
Pannenberg. Pannenberg has had to recapture the future or "not yet"
side of the kingdom, surrounded as he is by those who want to stress
its "already" and realized nature. As Pannenberg puts it, "Our starting
point then is the Kingdom of God understood as the eschatological future
brought about by God himself. Only in the light of this future can we
understand man and his history." But then he immediately adds, "God's
rule is not simply in the future, leaving men to do nothing but wait qui-
etly for its arrival."[42] The question that Pannenberg took up in much of
his work concerned what to do while we wait. He argues that the trick to
understanding Jesus' proclamation of the kingdom is to see both future
and present as "inextricably interwoven."[43] Pannenberg declares, "Jesus
underscored the *present impact* of the imminent future."[44] Pannenberg
even sees the impact as extending to the question of addressing social
concerns and the church's agenda. He writes:

> We are not called to choose between concern for the Kingdom and con-
> cern for society. Rather, in concern for society we are concerned for its
> end and destiny, namely, for the Kingdom of God. To act for the sake of
> the Kingdom is to act for the sake of society, and, in so doing, we act to
> the benefit of the church.
>
> A concern for the church that is not first of all a concern for the
> Kingdom of God is inevitably inverted and leads, as we have seen, to the
> church's becoming superfluous.[45]

At the same time, Pannenberg admits that teasing out this interwoven relationship between present and future "is one of the most problematic questions in contemporary study of Jesus' teachings."[46] Perhaps,
given the far-reaching implications of one's understanding of the king-

---

[41]Vern S. Poythress, *Understanding Dispensationalists*, 2nd ed. (Phillipsburg, NJ: P&R, 1994), 47.
[42]Wolfhart Pannenberg, *Theology and the Kingdom of God* (Philadelphia: Westminster, 1969), 53.
[43]Ibid.
[44]Ibid., italics original.
[45]Pannenberg, *Theology and the Kingdom of God*, 84.
[46]Ibid.

dom of God, we could expand upon Pannenberg to claim that teasing out this interwoven relationship is one of the most problematic questions in contemporary theology. To put it another way, discipleship is learning how to live in between, to live in the "already" in light of and governed by the "not yet."

While there is an emerging consensus on the already/not yet paradigm of the kingdom of God—or, as Pannenberg has it, the inextricable interwoven nature of present and future—there remain significant differences as to what is already and what is not yet. And while there is a growing consensus, there are always holdouts. One further significant development on the current horizon concerns the view of the kingdom in emergent circles. Brian McLaren, for instance, seems at times to lose sight of the not yet in his zeal to see the already of the kingdom.[47] Time will tell where such thinking leads.

Behold, the End Has Come: Conclusions

It would be less than wise to ignore the history, as variegated as that history is, of the Christian tradition on the subject of the kingdom of God. Listening to the history of the tradition may prove wise as the church of today constructs its understanding of this all-encompassing, all-important phrase, "the kingdom of God"—and the full implications the phrase portends. What are we to make of the vast differences of interpretation of this phrase? Before the differences are addressed, however, we should first consider the similarities.

Two beliefs have remained constant in the orthodox strands of the Christian tradition. First, there is a firm belief in the physical, visible return of Christ. This is the doctrine of the second coming. Second is a firm belief in some form of a future, real kingdom in which the sum of all God's promises and covenants will be fully enjoyed by the righteous, as well as a future judgment visiting God's unmitigated wrath on the unrighteous. As Christ taught of the kingdom, there are sheep and there are goats (Matthew 25). There are those to whom the kingdom of God belongs, while there are those to whom it does not. These two constant beliefs find a home in the creeds of the early church and in the confessions and catechisms of the Protestant traditions.

So what are we to make of the differences on the kingdom of God?

---

[47]See Brian McLaren, *The Secret Message of Jesus: Uncovering the Truth that Could Change Everything* (Nashville: Thomas Nelson, 2007).

The vast differences over the centuries of the Christian tradition should at the least show the complexity and ambiguity of the subject of eschatology, of the complexity of the deceptively simple phrase, "the kingdom of God." The growing consensus, as Russell Moore spoke of it, of the already/not yet view of the kingdom helpfully avoids the negative polarity of the past. At the very least the various traditions and understandings of eschatology should be in dialogue, humbly seeking to learn from each other and exercising caution when it comes to understanding the end times.

Finally, we should consider the kingdom of God and the Christian life. This lodestone of the teachings of Jesus, the kingdom, has occupied the work of theology and biblical scholarship through the centuries, and well it should. But the phrase should also occupy our thinking on and living of the Christian life. Jesus reminded his followers that his kingdom was not of this world. Indeed, the kingdom's differences should startle us. We are far too easily consumed with contemporary agendas that are culturally conditioned and culturally situated. In Christ's day, his fellow Jews fully expected him to overthrow Rome. Even his closest disciples revealed their own susceptibility to being consumed with what was in front of them. Looking to Christ's teaching, we see a place to stand outside of our context, which brings clarity to the church's mission. There will still be debates and differences, to be sure. But sometimes merely asking the right question goes a long way. When the church of any age asks what the kingdom of God is and further asks how the kingdom should drive what we do—and even determine how we pray—the church is asking the right questions.

A sound doctrine of the kingdom of God also brings a great deal of comfort and assurance in times of distress. We saw this in the survey of perspectives on the kingdom in church history. The kingdom of God brought comfort to the martyrs of the patristic period. While the world order collapsed around him and an undetermined order loomed on the horizon, Augustine could rest in the God of the ages, who reigned supreme in the past, present, and future. Luther, in his most famous hymn, speaks of a devil-filled world. He tells of his impending death— "the body they may kill," but then in the last line triumphantly declares, "His kingdom is forever."

Luther's thinking impacted a later Lutheran musician, Johann Sebastian Bach. He put nearly every biblical theme to music, and eschatology and the kingdom were no exceptions. Jan Luth has argued that

Bach's view of the kingdom reflects the complexity, even the ambiguity, in the biblical teaching on the subject. Luth observes that Bach's music sometimes reflects the teaching of Jesus himself, noting, "Eschatology in Bach's compositions has many interpretations."[48] Bach could find harmony in the complexity and ambiguity. The mysteries of the kingdom represented for him something not to be excised but to be embraced. He put before the church the biblical teaching of the person of Jesus and his message of the kingdom, and he did so in the language of his vocation, the language of music. One of his hymns will prove the point, *"Herr Gott, Nun Schleuss den Himmel auf"* ("Lord, God, Now Open Wide Thy Heaven"). It is a hymn of hope.

And so Bach reminds the theologian how best to serve the church today in understanding the kingdom of God. There are things of which we are certain, and which we must believe and proclaim. There are things more ambiguous and complex concerning which we, like Jesus' original twelve disciples, will continue to inquire. There are things, maybe even more than we care to admit, which we will likely never fully know until the end has come. And all of these things lead us to worship the One whose kingdom has no end.

Finally, a sound doctrine of the kingdom of God teaches us how to pray, which in turn teaches us how to live. Jesus taught the disciples to pray, "Thy kingdom come, thy will be done, on earth as it is in heaven." During the Henry Martyn lectures at Cambridge University, Lesslie Newbigin called us all to think of these words from the Lord's Prayer. In fact, he declared, "Every concept of the Kingdom has to be continuously tested in the light of the revelation of the Kingdom given uniquely and once and for all in the ministry, death, and resurrection of Jesus."[49]

As we have seen throughout this essay, theologians and biblical scholars, as much as they would like to be driven solely by the text of Scripture in their work, tend to read Scripture through the lens of their own sociological and cultural circumstances. This seems to be particularly acute when it comes to understanding the kingdom of God and a theology of the end times. From Platonists who spiritualized the kingdom in the patristic period, to medieval visionaries identifying Muslim leaders as the Antichrist, to those today who buy local cable time in the middle of the night to explain how Daniel long ago prophesied current events in the

[48]Jan R. Luth, "Eschatological Expectation in J. S. Bach," in *Prophecy and Eschatology*, ed. Michael Wilks (Oxford: Blackwell, 1994), 223.
[49]Newbigin, *Signs Amid the Rubble*, 104.

Middle East, there is a long and winding train of defining the kingdom of God from the purview of where one stands and of what one prefers. We must guard against seeking the kingdom as we define it, as we construct it, and as we prefer it. The temptation to do so is all too strong. Instead, may we be reminded, as Jesus taught us, to pray—and to live:

Thy kingdom come.

2

THE KINGDOM OF GOD IN THE OLD TESTAMENT

Definitions and Story

BRUCE K. WALTKE

The phrase "kingdom of God" can often be used without a full awareness of its historical background or implications. This chapter and the following will introduce the important subject of the kingdom of God by reflecting upon the meaning of the kingdom of God specifically in the Old Testament, wherein it will be noted that there are two forms of the kingdom: the universal kingdom and the particular kingdom.

For our purposes, we will look closely at these two forms of the kingdom, which will be referred to as the external emerging kingdom of God (universal) and the internal emerging kingdom of God (particular). We will then reflect upon the irrupting or in-breaking of the particular kingdom of God into the social aspect of the universal kingdom, which rebelled against God and came under Satan's rule. The following chapter will reflect upon the concurrent and internal maturing particular kingdom of God, especially through the four covenants with which God has gifted her: the Abrahamic, the Mosaic, the Davidic, and the New.

Definition: Two Kingdoms

The Bible bears witness to two forms of God's kingdom: a universal kingdom and a particular kingdom. By God's universal kingdom is meant the activity of God (*'elohim*: "the transcendent, omnipotent Creator and Sustainer of all things") in exercising his sovereignty over all things. God parcels out to the nations their lands (Deut. 2:5, 9; 32:8), rules over their kings (2:30), and even gives them their gods (4:19; 29:25–26). Lester Kuyper comments:

> Yahweh [see below] was [*sic*! is] supreme over all gods, "he is God of gods, and Lord of lords" ([Deut.] 10:17). He is supreme to this remarkable degree that God has allotted to people these lower deities . . . (4:19). God has not allotted these gods to Israel (29:29). Worship, which is a normal function for mankind, falls under the providence of God. Even false religions are taken up in this world plan of God. This statement (rather startling) is to evidence the supreme rule of God. To allow pagan worship beyond the realm of God's sovereignty would make God less than he is.[1]

By God's particular kingdom is meant God's activity in exercising his authority over his subjects who, out of their faith in him and love for him, serve only him. It finds expression before the founding of the nation of Israel in the faith of men such as Abel, Enoch, and Noah. All of these men died in faith though their fortunes differed radically. Abel died a martyr, Enoch never died, and Noah experienced the death of the world around him, with the exception of his own family. What they had in common was their faith in God, to be rewarded with heavenly promises after earthly death, not their fates before earthly death (Hebrews 11).

After Adam and Eve rebelled against God to identify themselves with the subtle Serpent (i.e., Satan, "Adversary [of God and mankind]"), God sentenced Satan to certain death by realigning Eve's and Adam's religious affections to hate Satan and to wage war against him. God's death sentence against the Serpent reads: "I will put enmity between you and the woman, and between your offspring and hers; he will crush your head, and you will strike his heel" (Gen. 3:15).[2] Adam, by faith, responded to God's promise to change Eve's affection from allegiance to Satan to hatred of him by naming his wife "Eve," which means "life." He did so, he says, "Because she would become the mother of all the living" (v. 20). Satan's offspring, however, are all those who do not seek life; they do not bow their knees in sincere trust, love, and obedience to the God who reveals himself in sacred Scripture and above all in Jesus Christ.

---

[1]Lester Kuyper, "The Book of Deuteronomy," *Int* 6 (July 1952): 329.
[2]Unless otherwise indicated, Scripture quotations in this chapter are from *The Holy Bible, New International Version*.

Considering these two aspects of God's kingdom, we see that there is a twofold emphasis on God's kingship: he is King of all the earth (2 Kings 19:15; Isa. 6:5; Jer. 46:18; Pss. 29:10; 99:1–4) and of his chosen people in particular (Ex. 15:18; Num. 23:21; Deut. 33:5; Isa. 43:15). God allows Satan a limited, but powerful, rule over his universal kingdom to display God's own spiritual glory through his chosen people (Ex. 6:4). The cosmos, since its creation, displays God's incommunicable qualities—his eternal power and divine nature (Rom. 1:20)—but not his communicable attributes, such as his justice to all and his grace, mercy, patience, and reliable kindness to his chosen people (cf. Ex. 34:6). These sublimities are displayed on the stage of planet earth in the drama of *Heilsgeschichte*, a German term meaning "salvation history." The nation of Israel plays a center stage role in this salvation history.

True vs. Nominal Israel

God matures his saints in his particular kingdom by incorporating them within the nation of ethnic Israel. Ethnic Israel, the chosen nation, consists of nominal Israel and true Israel. The nations around Israel identified nominal Israel as the nation belonging to I AM, Israel's patron deity. Prior to the division of the kingdom between the North (Israel) and the South (Judah), nominal Israel was bound together externally by their common heritage of the Abrahamic covenant and their acceptance of circumcision, their verbal adherence to the Sinaitic covenant, their professed allegiance to the house of David, and their common memory. After the division of the kingdom, the nominal northern kingdom regarded itself as the offspring of the patriarchs, but they rejected the law of Moses, fabricating their own laws and ultimately rejecting the house of David (1 Kings 12:26–33). During the reign of Ahab son of Omri, they even recast the state religion to the worship of the Canaanite Baal (1 Kings 16:29–34). Nevertheless, despite the extreme religious apostasy of nominal Israel, and the political divisions between North and South, I AM's prophets regarded Israel as a unity, with the people representing I AM.

True Israel refers to those within nominal Israel who, in addition to being circumcised in their flesh, are also circumcised in their hearts and are set apart in truth to God. By their participation in the new covenant, whereby the Mosaic Torah is written on the heart, they keep the Mosaic covenant *ex animo*. True Israel says yes to Jesus; nominal Israel says no to him.

This chapter and the following will use the phrase "kingdom of God" to refer to the particular kingdom as it finds expression in ethnic Israel, the chosen nation/people, distinguishing between nominal Israel and true Israel only as necessary.

The External Emerging Kingdom of God

We begin reflecting upon the external emerging kingdom of God by considering (1) the plot tension between the rival kingdoms; (2) the meaning of "thy kingdom come" in the Lord's Prayer, a prayer for triumph of the particular kingdom when it becomes co-extensive with the universal kingdom; (3) the meaning and significance of the colossal war between the rival kingdoms as seen in God's name, I AM WHO I AM; (4) the developing trajectory of how the particular kingdom wages war; and (5) a bird's-eye view of the threefold expansion of the kingdom until all nations are blessed by the particular kingdom.

1) The Protagonists, Antagonists, and Plot

Salvation history is the great drama, the meta-narrative, of history from the divine viewpoint. A play or drama, in its most basic elements, consists of characters who are protagonists contended against by characters who are antagonists. The job of the play's plot is to develop an escalating tension between the two types of characters, peaking when the tension is resolved, followed by a denouement.

In the old dispensation the human protagonists of the particular kingdom are the heroes of faith such as those cataloged by the writer of Hebrews in chapter 11: Abel, Enoch, Moses, Noah, Abraham, etc. After the inauguration of the Davidic covenant God committed the political rule of his chosen people to the house of David. At the same time he committed her spiritual rule to the prophets, who represented God's sovereign moral rule of the kingdom. The human antagonists in the antediluvian period are men like Cain and his descendants, and in the postdiluvian period they are ethnic tribes such as the Canaanites. During the monarchy uncircumcised kings hostile to the Davidic monarchy represent the antagonists to the particular kingdom of God.

In the dispensation inaugurated by Jesus Christ and in conjunction with the Holy Spirit, the spiritual nature of the conflict is profiled more sharply by identifying the protagonists as the triune God (Father, Son, and Spirit) and Christ's church, assisted by ministering angelic spirits. Their antagonists are unmasked in the New Testament, revealing in the unseen world, Satan and principalities and powers, and on earth the "world" (*kosmos*), a social system (i.e., a world- and life-view) without faith in God, without hope in God, and motivated by love for self.

In the old dispensation, when the particular kingdom of God took the political form of Israel as a nation among the nations, the protagonists fought with physical swords, but in the new dispensation the physical sword is taken out of the church's hands. In all dispensations, however, the protagonists of the particular kingdom of God fight with spiritual armor, such as faith in the God of Abraham, Isaac, and Jacob; hope for a future in God's presence that outlasts clinical death; and divine love that is unquenchable. As for the antagonists, their faith is in their Goliath-like swords; their hope is only in this world; and their motive for love is self-love, which, even at its best, is no more than helping others out of enlightened self-interest.

The plot tension consists in pitting these spiritual forces of light and darkness against one another to demonstrate the prevailing and enduring nature of God's kingdom and so of his glory—the stronger the enemy, the greater God's glory. God's people put on God's eternal, spiritual armor (e.g., truth, faith, righteousness, Eph. 6:13–18) to vanquish Satan, whose spiritual weapons are lies and distortions; to put to death the deeds of their sinful bodies; and not to be conformed to the vain values of the world. The inspired psalmist sings:

> For the LORD takes delight in his people;
>   he crowns the humble with victory.
> Let his faithful people rejoice in this honor
>   and sing for joy on their beds.
> May the praise of God be in their mouths
>   and a double-edged sword in their hands,
> to inflict vengeance on the nations
>   and punishment on the peoples,
> to bind their kings with fetters,
>   their nobles with shackles of iron,
> to carry out the sentence written against them—
>   this is the glory of all his faithful people. (Ps. 149:4–9)

The faithful prayer and praise of God's people—not necessarily their eloquence—commence the work of slaying the foe. What majesty accrues to God when he brings on the field of battle the poor in spirit against the arrogant hordes of wickedness in order to slay their intolerable pride in the dust!

When, however, the chosen people fight with the weapons of the "world," such as dependence on arms, money, and human alliances (cf. Deut. 17:16), they go down in defeat, bringing disgrace on God and themselves. By contrast, when they fight with spiritual weapons (e.g., trust in God, which expresses itself in obedience to his Word; hope in his ultimate salvation; and love, even for the enemy)—not denying the use of such means—they prevail and bring glory to God.

This ongoing battle peaked in Christ's passion. Satan and his lackeys—the blaspheming Jewish high priest and the Roman legions—seemed to have won the battle when they crucified the Lord of Glory. In truth, however, they defeated themselves. Had they known that they were saving the kingdom of God from sin and death and sentencing themselves to death, they would not have crucified the sinless One. By his death Jesus Christ, the suffering servant of Isaiah's visions, atoned for the sins of God's kingdom, freeing them from sin and the fear of death (Isa. 52:13–53:12).

As Jesus Christ hung upon the cross, the Jewish leaders and the Roman soldiers mocked his faith in God. But even as Jesus Christ prudently fulfilled God's plan for the salvation of his elect people, God mocked the Jewish high priest by rending the veil through which theretofore only the high priest could enter the presence of God in the Holy of Holies, and so distinguish himself as better than others. With the veil rent, however, the high priest lost his unique privilege, for now all the faithful could enter boldly into God's presence.

God also mocked the Roman legion. The Romans revered Sol ("the sun," with various epithets, including *invictus,* "unconquered") and Terra Mater (goddess of land and earth). Moreover, they associated astronomical events with the birth and death of their emperors; astronomical anomalies, such as the appearance of a comet, played a part in the emperor's deification. The Roman Senate was serious enough about this to build a temple to the deified Caesar in Rome. When, then, the Roman centurion, who stood there in front of the crucified Jesus Christ, saw how Christ died, with the sun darkened and the earth shaken, he said, "Surely this man was the Son of God!" (Mark 15:39).

After Christ poured out his soul as a sin offering (Isa. 53:10), wicked hands could touch him no further. As the psalmist prophesied, "He protects all his bones, not one of them [was] broken" (Ps. 34:20; John 19:36). Isaiah's famous prophecy of the Suffering Servant predicted that the servant would be pierced for Israel's transgressions, be crushed for their iniquities, be punished to bring them peace, bear the iniquity of them all, and by his wounds they would be healed (Isa. 53:4–6). Isaiah began that song predicting that the insightful servant would rise from the dead, be lifted up in his ascension, and be highly exalted in his glorification (52:13). His triumph over the grave sealed the defeat and death of Satan's kingdom.

2) "Thy Kingdom Come": The End of Salvation History

Jesus taught the particular kingdom of God to pray: "Thy kingdom come." Paul Drake draws two conclusions about Jesus Christ's use of the phrase "the kingdom of God." First, it has a historical dimension: "The kingdom comes at the end of time as the culmination of everything that has happened from the creation until now."[3] Second, this eschatological reality has a legal dimension. As noted above, in this kingdom God exercises the authority of a sovereign in a realm where his subjects obey *ex animo* his commands.

Citing the Lord's Prayer, Drake defends the conclusion "that the synoptic tradition understands the kingdom of God as the establishment of God's sovereignty over the human race."[4] The Matthean version reads: "Your kingdom come, your will be done, on earth as it is in heaven. Give us today our daily bread" (Matt. 6:10–11). The Lukan version, however, reads, "Your kingdom come. Give us each day our daily bread" (Luke 11:2–3), lacking the petition, "your will be done on earth as it is in heaven." Matthew probably added that petition to explicate the petition for the coming of the kingdom.[5] Robert Henry Charles says, "The kingdom of God is defined as the regenerated community, in which the divine will should be realized."[6]

In light of the war between the particular kingdom of God under the direct rule of the triune God and of the universal kingdom under the restricted rule of Satan, the Lord's Prayer teaches the church to hope for a future when the particular kingdom will become coextensive with the universal kingdom. The concluding prayer in the "Prayers of David" likewise petitions God to crown his anointed king (Heb., *messiah*) as the universal ruler in time and space:

---

[3]Dale Patrick, "The Kingdom of God in the Old Testament," in *The Kingdom of God in 20th Century Interpretation*, ed. Wendell Willis (Peabody, MA: Hendrickson, 1987), 67–79.

[4]Ibid., 71.

[5]Robert G. Hamerton-Kelly, *God the Father: Theology and Patriarchy in the Teaching of Jesus* (Philadelphia: Fortress, 1979), 73–74.

[6]Robert Henry Charles, *A Critical History of the Doctrine of a Future Life in Israel, in Judaism, and in Christianity; or Hebrew, Jewish, and Christian Eschatology from Pre-Prophetic Times Till the Close of the New Testament Canon* (1899; repr. Whitefish, MT: Kessinger, 2003), 84.

May he endure as long as the sun,
  as long as the moon, through all generations.
May he be like rain falling on a mown field,
  like showers watering the earth.
In his days may the righteous flourish
  and prosperity abound till the moon is no more.
May he rule from sea to sea
  and from the River to the ends of the earth.
May the desert tribes bow before him
  and his enemies lick the dust.
May the kings of Tarshish and of distant shores
  bring tribute to him.
May the kings of Sheba and Seba
  present him gifts.
May all kings bow down to him
  and all nations serve him. . . .
May his name endure forever;
  may it continue as long as the sun.
Then all nations will be blessed through him,
  and they will call him blessed.
Praise be to the Lord God, the God of Israel,
  who alone does marvelous deeds.
Praise be to his glorious name forever;
  may the whole earth be filled with his glory.
Amen and Amen.
  This concludes the prayers of David son of Jesse. (Ps. 72:5–20)

Israel's prophets, during the dark days of Assyria's tyranny, envisioned God's response:

And it shall come to pass in the latter days that the mountain of the house of I am will remain established as the highest mountain, and it will remain lifted up [above] the hills, and nations will flow [to it and walk] upon it.

   And many nations will come and say, "Come, let us go up to the mountain of I am, to the house of the God of Jacob, that he may teach us his ways, so that we may walk in his ordained paths." For the law will go out from Zion, the word of the Lord from Jerusalem.

   And he will judge among many nations, and will reprove powerful [and] far-off nations. And they will beat their swords into hoes, and their spears into pruning knives. Nation will not lift up sword against nation, and they will no longer learn to wage war.

> And each one will sit under their own vine and under their own fig
> tree, with none terrifying them.
> For the mouth of I AM has spoken. (Mic. 4:1–4 AT)[7]

The kingdom of God is sometimes called the mediatorial kingdom of God because it mediates the will of God on earth as it is in heaven and is the locus through which the human race approaches God. As we saw earlier, the history of the irruption (the breaking in from without), not eruption (the breaking out from within), of God's kingdom on earth is often referred to as *Heilsgeschichte* ("salvation history"). In the Old Testament, God used his people Israel as the vehicle for accomplishing this breaking in of his kingdom on earth.

3) I AM WHO I AM: The Meaning of Salvation History
The history of the war between the rival kingdoms of God and of Satan, which Augustine called "the City of God" and "the City of Man," is written on a scroll that stretches out from the creation to the eschaton, from the *Urzeit* to the *Endzeit*. The war is costly: clinical death for the righteous; eternal death for the wicked. What's the point? Humans enjoy stories, but no one wants to hear a pointless story, especially this one, which is supposed to be the greatest story of all. Surely God's salvation history is not a story full of sound and fury, signifying nothing.

It was stated dogmatically above that the meaning of history, the point of this war, is to glorify God. That profound statement needs to be validated, which God does by giving his people the key to the meaning of *Heilsgeschichte*. He does this by self-disclosing the character of his name when he calls Moses to rescue the people of Israel out of the hostile womb of Egypt. Significantly, God reveals the meaning and significance of his name in connection with the founding of the nation he has chosen and for which he will be their patron deity. Israel will now fight to establish their kingdom as a nation among the nations under the banner bearing the name of their God and thereby bear witness to him. But what does his name mean and signify?

Self-disclosure #1. God's first self-revelation of the meaning and significance of his name as Israel's patron deity occurs when he calls Moses out of the burning bush to deliver his people from their slavery under Pharaoh's rule in Egypt. Moses, being only a shepherd at the time, objects

---

[7]For translation and commentary see Bruce K. Waltke, *A Commentary on Micah* (Grand Rapids, MI: Eerdmans, 2007), 191–220.

to the seemingly impossible task of leading of the Israelites and conquering the most powerful king of his world. He objects: "What is your name?" He asks not for a name of identification but for reassurance, for the meaning, the significance of God's name.[8] By this question, Moses seeks not only to assure himself of the success of his mission but also to know the name the Israelites should invoke (i.e., petition and praise) for their deliverance. That this is his intention becomes clearer in Exodus 3:15, where God says, "This is my name forever, the name by which I am to be remembered ["invoked," *irk*] from generation to generation." One cannot invoke without remembering, and one cannot remember well without invoking/proclaiming.

The name by which God wants to be invoked and remembered is *Yahweh* ("He will be/become"), a shortened form of the sentence name, which in God's own mouth means: "I AM WHO I AM" (Ex. 3:14–15). The sentence name Yahweh entails four notions: God (1) is eternal; (2) is before all things, and so the ground of all being; (3) is unlike anything or anyone else; and (4) must define who he is, what he is like, in the course of history.[9] By petitioning I AM for their victories over and restraint of their enemies and by praising I AM for answering their petitions, Israel glorifies God's name.

The sequence of the sandwiching of Psalm 8 between the concluding verse of Psalm 7 and the opening verses of Psalm 9 demonstrates this point:

> I will give thanks to the LORD because of his righteousness;
>   I will sing the praises of the *name of the LORD* Most High. (Ps. 7:17)

> LORD, our Lord, how majestic is *your name* in all the earth! (8:1)

> LORD, our Lord, how majestic is *your name* in all the earth! (8:9)

> I will give thanks to you, LORD, with all my heart;
>   I will tell of all your wonderful deeds.
> I will be glad and rejoice in you;
>   I will sing the praises of *your name*, O Most High. (9:1–2)

---

[8]Bruce K. Waltke and M. O'Connor, *An Introduction to Biblical Hebrew Syntax* (Winona Lake, IN: Eisenbrauns, 1990) sec. 18.2d, p. 320.

[9]Hilary of Poitiers (c. 320–367/8) is the earliest recorded bishop of Poitiers in Gaul. It is through Hilary's meditations on Ex. 3:14, showing Moses' experience of the revelation of God as the "I AM" in conjunction with Psalm 139, that brought Hilary into the Christian life, in seeking to pursue a life that was *"worthy of understanding that that* [his own mind] *had been given us by God."* That one single statement given to Moses, *I AM*—God the Creator *"testifying about himself"* as *I AM who I AM*—penetrated more deeply into Hilary's soul than anything he had ever heard or read from the philosophers.

In sum, God reveals the meaning of his name as the eternal and self-defining God, unlike anyone else, and Israel petitions and praises this name in their establishing God's universal rule, thereby bringing glory to God.

Self-disclosure #2. Moses reluctantly obeys God and sets out to deliver God's people but fails miserably in his first confrontation with Pharaoh. The dark king responds by hardening his own heart against Moses, against I AM, and against Israel. Instead of releasing God's people from his restraint, Pharaoh intensifies their harsh servitude to him, costing Moses the support of his own people. Within this context of defeat and despair, God then gives a second disclosure of his name. In this revelation God reassures Moses of victory over Pharaoh by promising that his chosen people—the particular kingdom of God—and Pharaoh—representing the universal kingdom of God under Satan—would experience the full significance of his name when he utterly destroys the dark kingdom of Egypt.

> God also said to Moses, "I am [the 'I AM,' or the 'HE IS,' or *Yahweh*, traditionally glossed 'LORD' or 'JEHOVAH,' which in Israel's mouth is the equivalent of 'I AM WHO I AM,' in God's mouth]. I appeared to Abraham, to Isaac and to Jacob as God Almighty [*El Shadday*], but by my name [the I AM, Yahweh, trad. LORD] I did not make myself known to them. I also established my covenant with them to give them the land of Canaan, where they resided as foreigners. Moreover, I have heard the groaning of the Israelites, whom the Egyptians are enslaving, and I have remembered my covenant. Therefore, say to the Israelites: 'I am the [I AM, Yahweh, trad. LORD], and I will bring you out from under the yoke of the Egyptians. I will free you from being slaves to them, and I will redeem you with an outstretched arm and with mighty acts of judgment. I will take you as my own people, and I will be your God. Then you will know that I am [the I AM, Yahweh, trad. LORD] your God, who brought you out from under the yoke of the Egyptians. And I will bring you to the land I swore with uplifted hand to give to Abraham, to Isaac and to Jacob. I will give it to you as a possession. I am the [I AM, Yahweh, trad. LORD].'" (Ex. 6:2–8)

Scholars refer to the formula, "You will know that I am the I AM," as the recognition formula. God does not immediately deliver his people from slavery because he has an agenda: to harden Pharaoh's heart so that his triumph over Pharaoh will be so stunning, so total, and so triumphant that his own people (6:7; 11:7; cf. 16:6), Pharaoh (7:17; 8:10, 22; 9:14, 29), and the Egyptians (14:4, 18) will know experientially that Israel's God is the *I AM*—the eternal, incomparable, and sublime God, and the ontological reality behind all things. Heretofore Israel knew *I AM*'s name, but God had not made himself known to them in such a way that the rival kingdoms would recognize and experience the full significance of his name.

In Israel's escape from Egypt, *I AM* lures Pharaoh and the Egyptian horde to the Red Sea for his climactic triumph over the dark kingdom. At the beginning of the book of Exodus, Pharaoh had ordered that all boys born to Israelite women be drowned in the Nile River. Now, in poetic justice, to complete Israel's exodus from Egypt *I AM* drowns all of the firstborn males of Egypt in the Red Sea. *I AM* explains his motive: "I will harden Pharaoh's heart, and he will pursue them. But I will gain glory for myself through Pharaoh and all his army, and the Egyptians will know that I am the LORD" (Ex. 14:4).

Reflecting on Israel's sufferings in Egypt, Paul Wright comments:

> Suffering is not to be viewed only in relation to the baser affections of man in opposition to God. It must also be comprehended in light of God's great work to bring glory to his name (Ex. 6:1; see also Isa. 66:18–19). And sometimes this great glorification entails the greater temporal suffering of the elect in order to increase the witness of God in the midst of the nations.[10]

Although we live for the present in a sinful and broken world, we must understand that, ultimately, God has already won the battle and will be victorious over all evil in the end. Indeed, this victory is part and parcel of his very identity, that he might bring glory to his name.

The recognition formula, "you will know that *I AM* the *I AM*," occurs in two clusters. At the beginning of Israel's history the formula is used in connection with *I AM* as a mighty Warrior, striking Egypt with blow upon blow (cf. Ex. 15:3). At the end of Israel's history, when the mighty Warrior goes to war against his own nation that has made a mockery of his name and lost its status among the nations by subjugating itself to their ungodliness, God's prophet Ezekiel uses the recognition formula in connection with God's prophecies, the sword of his Word, to validate his glory.

Continuing our reflections in the book of Deuteronomy, *I AM* further

---

[10]Paul A. Wright, "Exodus 1–24 (A Canonical Study)," unpublished PhD diss. (University of Vienna, Austria, March 1993), 191.

reveals himself as just, righteous, and moral, showing no partiality, and taking no bribes (Deut. 10:17), defending the cause of the widows and fatherless, and loving the resident alien (10:18). His moral purity calls for the extermination of the seven Canaanite nations (9:4–5) and for avenging the wrong of the Amalekites (25:17–19). His justice informs the standard for Israel's judges (16:18–20) and informs the threats against Israel (4:21–26; 6:14–15; 8:19–20). Ethics, not magic, divination, or chance, determines Israel's future. He is faithful to his word to the non-elect (2:5, 9, 19) and to the elect (1:8; 6:10; 9:5). His power sanctions his mercy and is seen in his past acts (3:24; 4:34; 7:21–23; 9:29; 10:22), in the creative power of his Word (28:2, 15; 30:1–10), and in holy war (7:17). His goodness is seen in his giving of four gifts to Israel: Torah (Deut. 6:24); land (9:4–5; 17:18–20; 26:5–10); prophets (18:22); and priests (18:6–7). He is loving, the attribute that is the basis of Israel's election (7:8; 23:5). He is angered by unbelief (1:34–36; 9:22) and breach of covenant (4:25). His wisdom is seen in his catechism (4:2–6). His jealousy is closely related to his uniqueness (4:24) and demands undivided loyalty (5:9; 6:5, 15) and the extermination of nations whose religions might corrupt Israel's loyalty (chapter 13). He has aesthetic appreciation (14:1–29; 22:4–11; 23:10–14). His holiness or "otherness" consists in the totality of all his sublime attributes and threatens human life (Deut. 5:22–27; 18:16). When Moses asked to see God's glory, he passed in front of Moses, proclaiming, "The LORD, the LORD, the compassionate and gracious God, slow to anger, abounding in love and faithfulness, maintaining love to thousands, and forgiving wickedness, rebellion and sin. Yet he does not leave the guilty unpunished; he punishes the children and their children for the sin of the parents to the third and fourth generation" (Ex. 34:6–7).

In sum, the Old Testament's story line represents the irruption of God's particular kingdom into his universal kingdom, which is under the rule of powerful hostile spiritual and political powers, to make himself known to all humanity as he is in himself.

4) Holy War: The Trajectory of How God's People Fight

The Bible is all about "Your [God's] kingdom come." The coming of that kingdom entails, as noted repeatedly above, holy war—a doctrine that changes and develops through the history of God's kingdom. This section sketches the trajectory of that history.

An old French oxymoron says, "The more things change, the more they are the same."[11] This is an appropriate aphorism for understanding the emerging kingdom of God. The Rainbow Bridge spanning the Niagara Falls cataract began with a kite. Those building the bridge flew a kite across the majestic waterway and, using weights, brought it down on the side of the gorge, linking the two sides with a thin string. Beginning with the string, the builders of the bridge pulled increasingly heavier strings, then ropes, and eventually steel girders across the gorge. The more the seemingly insignificant bridge changed, the more it became what it was always meant to be: a bridge to cross the Niagara River.

For our purposes the kite represents God's promise to Eve that her offspring from Adam's seed would crush the Serpent's head. In the progress of revelation the seed becomes more increasingly identified as the seed of Seth, not Cain; of Shem, not Canaan; of Abraham, not Nahor; of Isaac, not Ishmael; of Israel, not Esau. Likewise the leader of the nation of Israel is specified as coming from Judah, not Joseph, and then from David's house, and finally as Jesus Christ. The promised seed to Eve finds its final expression in the church, baptized into Jesus Christ (Rom. 16:20). Similarly, the Old Testament is pregnant with the truth that God is a Trinity, but that doctrine is not brought into the full light of day until the advents of Christ and of Pentecost. The Trinity of Father, Son, and Spirit is like a triadic musical chord (e.g., C-E-G); each note functions differently but is of the same substance and together they form a unity. Whereas God wanted to be proclaimed as I AM before the full disclosure of his triune being, in the new dispensation he wants to be known in and through his Son. The church prays in the Son's name, Jesus Christ (John 15:16), and proclaims the name of Jesus (Acts 2:38 passim).

Similarly the form of holy war in expanding the kingdom of God changes over the dispensations, from the pacifism of the patriarchs, to holy war with a sword from Israel's exodus to exile, to spiritual war with words in the exile and the New Testament.[12]

a. Patriarchal Narratives. The patriarchs do not take matters into their own hands by going to war to fulfill God's oath to make them a great nation. They lack the political power, the military might, and the divine authorization to conduct holy war. They do not fight to protect their matriarchs bearing the holy seed (Genesis 12 and 26), nor do they fight

---

[11]Sometimes credited to the French novelist and journalist Alphonse Karr (1808–1890) in *Les Guepes* (The Wasps, 1849).

[12]The following section is largely lifted from Bruce K. Waltke with Charles Yu, *An Old Testament Theology: An Exegetical, Thematic and Canonical Approach* (Grand Rapids, MI: Zondervan, 2007), 394–403.

for the land God promised them on oath. When strife develops between Abraham and Lot because the land could not sustain both, Abraham by faith gives up his rights (chapter 13). Isaac has to dig new wells to avoid conflict with his Philistine neighbors over property rights (chapter 26). When Levi and Simeon rashly draw the sword to uphold the honor of their sister Dinah, Jacob expresses disapproval (chapter 34). For their brutal and wanton act of violence, they are rejected from the line of kingship (chapter 49). In sum, the patriarchs refuse to realize the promise of becoming a great nation by the sword but rather trust in God to fulfill his promises, providing for both the seed and land. They root their reality in the spiritual hope of a future when God will make good on his word. Their hope is realized in the dispensation of Joshua's sword.

b. Exodus. God becomes the glorious Warrior King in the exodus. This radical change introduces a new dimension to God's name as I AM and is demonstrated with vividness in his showdown with Pharaoh. When Moses seeks to free his people in his own strength, God remains silent. But when Moses recognizes the limits of his own human strength, God calls him and uses him as an instrument for deliverance. In I AM's plagues inflicted upon Pharaoh, Moses battles with Pharaoh as a prophet with a staff, not as a warrior with a sword. The triumph over Egypt and the deliverance of the Israelites is entirely I AM's. The same is true in the Israelites' crossing of the Red Sea. Caught between the desert on either side, with the Red Sea ahead of them and Pharaoh's elite corps of chariots bearing down on them from the rear, Moses charges his own divisions: "[I AM] will fight for you; you need only to be still" (Ex. 14:14). He then raises his staff, stretches his hand out over the sea, and the waters divide, providing God's pilgrim nation passage through walls of water on dry ground. God does not fight with Israelite weapons; rather, he fights for his people on his own terms, above and apart from their arms.

A major change in the disposition of his kingdom's holy war occurs about a month later when, at Rephidim, Israel is attacked by the Amalekites. This time Moses does not direct the people to stand still and watch I AM fight for them. Instead, he commands Joshua to choose some mighty men and fight with swords. God demonstrates his new incarnation in real war by empowering Joshua to win only while Moses, symbolically on a hilltop, holds up his staff, which formerly had served to decimate the Egyptians. With this action, God makes the point that Israel's sword on behalf of justice depends fully on I AM. Israel must wield the sword, but they must do so through trust in I AM (Ps. 149:6–9). Like a true son, Israel must grow

out of the magic years of its infancy to the spiritual maturity of an adult
son who exercises his faith in the real world. In that world, the sword
effects I AM's justice, wrath, and grace without compromising the truth:
the battle belongs to I AM (Psalm 45).

c. Deuteronomy. The book of Deuteronomy provides the justification
for Israel's holy war against the Canaanites. As Moses explains to the people: "It is not because of your righteousness or your integrity that you are
going in to take possession of their land; but on account of the wickedness
of these nations, [I AM] your God will drive them out before you" (Deut.
9:5). As the Israelite army is poised to cross the Jordan River, I AM proclaims that the time of grace for the Canaanites is ended and the time for
Joshua's sword has arrived. Canaanite iniquities have ripened into rotten
fruit (cf. Gen. 15:16; Lev. 18:24–30).

Moses also anticipates the distant future when Israel's army will be
led by a king. To save the future king from the temptation to abuse his
power, Moses puts some parameters in place by limiting the number of
his warhorses, his treasury, and his political alliances through marriage.
All kingdoms strengthen themselves by increasing their armories, their
defense budget, and their international alliances. But the ideal king over
God's kingdom would be one who limits these well-known sources of
national strength (Deut. 17:16–20).

d. Judges. I AM aims through holy war not only to judge his enemies,
but to train his kingdom people to fight the fight of faith (Judg. 3:1–4).
Deuteronomy calls for restraint in the future king's accumulation of
power, a principle shared by Agur, who is well aware that he cannot handle much wealth without denying I AM as the true source of everything
(Prov. 30:7–9).

The book of Joshua fulfills the commands of Deuteronomy to enter
and inherit the Sworn Land and together with Judges supplements the
theme of I AM as warrior. Unlike Hitler's Third Reich, Israel's disposses-
sion of the Canaanites is not racial genocide or ethnic cleansing, as clearly
shown by the narratives of Rahab and Achan. Rahab, though a Canaanite
harlot, receives salvation along with her family when they prove faithful to
I AM (Joshua 6), while Achan, a circumcised Judahite, is executed for his
unfaithfulness to I AM (chapter 7).

In the battles recorded in the book of Judges, I AM fights by giving
his spirit to charismatic military leaders, imbuing them with daring and
strength. I AM uses people of faith regardless of their numbers. With
Moses and Joshua, God uses the forces of nature—earthquake and hail—

to defeat Israelite enemies; in the period of the judges he uses a rainstorm (cf. Judges 5). Gideon, one of the judges, has to learn to fight with only three hundred men (7:1–8). Moreover, God conducts psychological warfare by destroying the fighting spirit of the enemy, which Gideon realizes when he overhears Midianites talking about their dreams in which they are defeated.

However, God's kingdom is not relieved of its own obligation to make war in this formative period of its history. She is called to be faithful and to trust God. Israelites are to volunteer for war duty (there is no standing army during the time of tribal league). The Song of Deborah celebrates the tribes that go to war and castigates the tribes that stay home (Judg. 5:13–18). Israel's heroes continue to employ tactics such as ambush (chapter 20), night marches (Josh. 10:9), and other military maneuvers (Judg. 8:11). Faith and military shrewdness go hand in hand.

e. *United Monarchy and Prophets (1050–925 BC)—Samuel and Prophets.* In 1 Samuel 1:11, the term "[I AM] of hosts [*Seba'ot*]" (ESV) is used for the first time in the Bible. The title occurs in connection with the installation of Israelite kingship and serves as recognition that God is the Commander in Chief not only of his particular kingdom's army but also of all the hostile kingdoms and their armies that march against his nominal people. This comes as no surprise since, as pointed out above, God is sovereign over his universal kingdom.

Monarchy in the right hands blesses the kingdom, but in the wrong hands the kingdom is enslaved (1 Samuel 8–12). Thus, monarchy can prove to be a mixed blessing. The placing of a nation's full military might in the hands of one charismatic leader on the battlefield can lead to military effectiveness and political stability but also to the potential abuse of and rejection of I AM as the Warrior King. The temptation to usurp the role of the divine King is almost irresistible for any human king. To defend against this usurpation of the divine role, God gifts certain prophets to exalt his moral power over the king's military power. The prophet, armed with God's voice, has the authority to anoint, to rebuke, and finally to depose kings. Samuel, the first court prophet, anoints Saul, rejects Saul, and anoints David. In the scramble for succession after Saul, the prophet Nathan awards the crown to David, and faithful David obeys. This proper relationship between king and prophet is affirmed by Jesus, who is baptized by John the Baptist, the greatest of the prophets. As John the Baptist gives Jesus his prophetic anointing, he identifies Jesus as the greatest of the kings.

True prophets, like Samuel, subordinate the king to I AM's commandments and the covenant he mediated to Israel through Moses (see below).
Thus, the incarnation model of holy war from the time of the exodus continues. God fights for his kingdom through the sword, but only as the king
exercises the kind of faith David expresses in the Psalter: petition (Psalms
2–3), confidence (Psalms 11; 23), praise (Psalm 8), and obedience to the
covenant (Psalms 15; 24).

    f. Early Divided Monarchy and Prophecy (1050–925 BC)—Kings. The
commander of I AM's army made clear to Joshua by his drawn, unsheathed
sword that God is not on Israel's side unless Israel is on God's side (Josh.
5:13–14). We see this when I AM turns against Saul, Israel's first king and
an apostate one, from the very beginning of the monarchy. Samuel in turn
rejects Saul. Ahijah the prophet from Shiloh rends ten of Israel's tribes
from Solomon's kingdom to inaugurate the northern kingdom under
Jeroboam I (1 Kings 11:26–40). The book of Kings might more aptly be
titled the book of the Prophets, as it is the last of what the rabbis called
the "Former Prophets" in the canon. We continue to see in Scripture how
I AM's prophets install, rebuke, and depose Israel's kings throughout salvation history. The Lord of hosts begins to lead foreign armies against
his anointed king as early as Rehoboam son of Solomon. I AM abandons
Rehoboam to the Egyptian king Shishak, who plunders Jerusalem and
its temple until Rehoboam and his officials repent (2 Chronicles 12).
According to the true prophet Micaiah ben Imlah, I AM allows a lying
spirit from I AM's court to lure Ahab into defeat in Ramoth Gilead. Elijah
calls down fire on the first two of Ahaziah's three captains, each with
a company of fifty men (2 Kings 1), and Elisha misleads Jehoram and
Jehoshaphat into a defeat at the Moabite capital of Kir Hareseth (2 Kings
3:11–27, reading "attack," not "overthrow" in v. 19 [ESV]).

    With the installation of king and prophet there is a growing chasm
within the kingdom of God—between the political, nominal kingdom
represented by the king with military clout, and the spiritual realm,
represented by faithful prophets with moral clout. The preached word
of the prophet, which at first supplements the king's sword, eventually
replaces it entirely. The prophetic word gradually replaces Israel's army,
and reliance on the power of the word eventually overtakes the might of
the sword. Elisha's anguished and plaintive cry upon the ascent of Elijah
in a flaming chariot, "My father! My father! The chariots and horsemen
of Israel!" reflects his recognition that the security of Israel depends on

God's covenant-keeping prophets, not on the king's army (2 Kings 2:12). Kings cannot establish God's rule apart from the prophetic word.

This growing rift between the spiritual and political kingdoms is further evident in the Naaman incident (2 Kings 5). The spiritual kingdom, represented by prophets, their disciples, and the seven-thousand-strong remnant who refuse to worship the fertility deity Baal, and the apostate political state, represented by the king, his officials, and the masses, reaches a telling moment: Naaman, an Aramean general under Ben-Hadad II, has been plaguing Israel, but upon his healing by I AM through Elisha, he converts and becomes a worshiper of I AM. Prior to this episode, I AM worship is identified with the physical covenant community that resides within the boundary of the Sworn Land. Thus, there is an unspoken expectation that Naaman, having converted, will Josephus-like reside in Israel and offer his military genius to the service of Ahab and Israel. Shockingly, this does not happen. With the prophet Elisha's approval, Naaman returns to Aram, retains his post as the Aramean general in the service of Ben-Hadad II, and worships I AM while standing on a load of dirt from Israel within the temple of the Syrian storm god Raman. In other words, a worshiper of I AM, Israel's patron deity, heads the army that threatens Israel. Elisha's approval of this situation signals clearly that I AM has turned against his apostate nation. Naaman's first allegiance belongs to I AM's ethical rule, not to faithless Israel.

g. Late Monarchy and Writing Prophets (760–586 BC).
1) Day of I AM. In the late monarchy (760–686 BC) the term "Day of I AM" comes into prophetic parlance. The term emphasizes the experience of I AM's character and usually points to a future comprehensive judgment by I AM on his enemies, which means both war and I AM's accompanying theophany. According to Amos, for example, it is a day of darkness, not light. To counter Israel's jingoistic expectations, Amos (ca. 760 BC) turns the tables, proclaiming: "Woe to you who long for the day of [I AM]!" (Amos 5:18). In a funeral dirge he foretells I AM's death sentence against the instruments of Israel's theocracy: corrupt magistrates, unholy priests, and false prophets. The unholy alliance has positioned itself as I AM's enemies and stands in contrast to the faithful remnant that will experience I AM's salvation on that day when he wins glory for himself by defeating his enemies.

2) War and the Prophets. In the world of Israel's writing prophets every defeat of a nation involves the death of its national deity, or, at best,

the god's demotion to becoming a pawn in the temple of the victorious nation's patron deity. A patron deity that cannot protect its own people will not be worshiped as the supreme deity, as lord of lords. Thus, by the accepted standards of the ancient Near East, it would seem as though I AM attempts suicide by waging war against his nominal people. And yet, I AM does not work according to ancient standards. Rather, he makes himself known as God of gods and Lord of lords by waging war through the cutting words of his holy prophets, not through carnal war of unholy kings.

The writing prophets, giants of faith and passion, stand boldly before powerful kings, risking their very lives to do so. It is a new form of warfare against which kings' might cannot compete. Eschewing swords and arrows, these soldiers fight through their preached and written words—and what words they are! Sermons of judgment sear the souls of the hearers with fear and trembling. Sermons of compassion bleed the love of God for his wayward bride. The zenith of ethical monotheism is encapsulated in the magnificent words from these towering pillars of faith.

Near and remote future prophecies sanction the moral and spiritual power of their words. Ezekiel employs the "recognition formula" over fifty times for his amazing prophecies of Israel's immediate judgment and of her future salvation beyond the exile. Through the prophet Isaiah, against all expectations, I AM addresses the exiles in Babylon, foretelling that Cyrus will defeat Babylon, and even predicts how he will do it, viz. drying up rivers and opening gates (41:2; 44:27; 45:2). Normally the Euphrates runs through Babylon and, in battle, the gates under the city walls are shut to cause the river to run in a moat around the city. But, as Isaiah prophesies, Cyrus dries up the Euphrates by diverting it upstream into a swamp, leaving the gates under the city wall open and giving the Persians access into the city. Against all expectations Isaiah then predicts that Cyrus will return God's people to the Sworn Land in a second exodus (48:20–21; 51:9–11) and will rebuild I AM's holy city temple (44:26–28). No foreign political or spiritual power can begin to compete with I AM in this new form of battle (41:21–29). By the end of this historic period, God empowers the enemy to vanquish the apostate kings and nations of Israel and Judah; however, the worship of I AM survives because of the effectiveness of the prophetic word. God appoints prophets like Jeremiah "over nations and kingdoms to uproot and tear down, to destroy and overthrow, to build and to plant" (Jer. 1:10), demonstrating that kingdoms and nations may rise and fall but God's Word stands forever.

   h. Exile and Post Exile. The dissociation between the spiritual kingdom of God and the physical kingdom of Israel, which begins with the divided monarchy, reaches a new stage in the exile. The signal event of this period is God's election and anointing of Cyrus as messiah ("anointed [king]," Isa. 45:1). In this act, the external marks of kingship (anointing, political power, military power) are transferred to a non-Davidic, non–I AM–believing Gentile. Cyrus unwittingly—and so the more ironically—becomes I AM's slave/official to fight his wars for Israel's deliverance (v. 4). Instead of raising up a deliverer from within his covenant people, as in preexilic times, God hands the political fate of the people of Israel to the Gentile empires—Babylon, Persia, Greece, and Rome. But I AM continues to rule. By his prophets he eventually fells all of them (cf. Daniel 2 and 7). The same prophetic word also empowers the faithful remnant, preserving Israel and bringing salvation to the nations. Ironically, Jonah brings salvation to the Assyrians, who later become the rod in I AM's hand to smash his sinful nation (Isa. 10:5–27).

During the exile and postexilic periods, Isaiah outlines this new model of holy war: I AM hands over the military-political authority of kingship to Gentile emperors while investing spiritual authority in his prophets, culminating in his anonymous suffering slave/official, whose mouth is a sharpened sword (Isa. 42:1–7; 49:1–7; 50:4–11; 52:13–53:12). This model of holy war befits a spiritual, not political, kingdom—a kingdom that does not rely on territorial boundaries for its breadth, on military weapons for its security, and on law codes for its justice. This spiritual kingdom is moving toward a new kingdom that is administered by a new covenant, as described in Jeremiah (31:31–34).

5) Synopsis of Salvation History: Threefold Expanding Kingdom

Just as God revealed to Moses the meaning and significance of his name in connection with calling upon him to found Israel as a nation, so also he revealed to Abraham his threefold expanding kingdom in connection with calling him to father the people who would comprise that great nation and to go to the land that would sustain the nation.[13] Genesis 12:1–3, which summarizes the stages of the kingdom's expansion, may well be likened to the *TV Guide* of the Bible: "The LORD had said to Abram, 'Go from your country, your people and your father's household to the land I will show you. I will make you into a great nation, and I will bless you; I will make your name great, and you will be a blessing. I will bless those who bless

---

[13]This section is largely lifted from Waltke, *An Old Testament Theology*, 314–17.

you, and whoever curses you I will curse; and all peoples on earth will be blessed through you.'" The seven promises that accompany the command, "Go from your country, your people and your father's household to the land I will show you," pertain to three expanding horizons that *in nuce* present God's salvific program through his irrupting kingdom: individual (v. 1), national (v. 2), and universal (v. 3).

a. Individual (12:1). The salvific program begins within the narrow confines of God's election of Abraham. While the text assumes he exists with his family, including his wife Sarah and other relatives, the focus is on Abraham. In the same way that the unique, all-sufficient, self-sustaining God, who is an *aseity* ("from himself"), called the good creation into existence, he now calls Abraham to separate himself from his family for the benefit of the nations.

b. National (12:2). God promises to make Abraham into a great nation (i.e., a people with political control of its affairs and destiny). A nation or kingdom is typically comprised of a common people—the Israelites come into being in the book of Genesis; a common land—this land is specified in the book of Genesis and possessed in the book of Joshua; a common constitution/government—this is articulated in Exodus–Deuteronomy; and a common leader—this leadership is the theme of Judges–Kings.[14] This promise of nationhood is certified, refreshed, and defined more precisely by God through his covenants with Abraham defining the land as that of Canaan (Genesis 15) and defining his offspring as that from Sarah (chapter 17). Furthermore, as a reward for Abraham's radical obedience in offering to sacrifice his son Isaac, God swears by himself to make Abraham and his seed a universal blessing.

c. Universal (12:3). The climactic third element of Abraham's call expands the horizon of this blessing to the whole earth for all time. Hence, the flow of God's saving acts in history moves from blessing a particular, faithful individual and his family to blessing all people, the hope of the Lord's Prayer. The term "to bless" (*brk* with God as subject) denotes procreative largesse and victory, with a sense of loyalty to the future generations (Gen. 1:28; 26:24: 27:27–29). It also connotes redemption, as well as a relationship with God that transforms the beneficiary and provides security, safety, and victory. In the old dispensation "to bless" referred to physical offspring; in the new dispensation it refers to spiritual offspring.

---

[14]Israel during the time of exile was a common people with a common memory, but not a nation. Upon their return to the land with a leader, they were reconstituted as a nation subservient to the Persian Empire.

God promises to bless those who bless faithful Abraham and his family but "to curse" (*'rr*) whoever curses (*qll*) him. *Qll* means "to esteem lightly, to disdain." Those who bless Abraham refer to those who invoke God's blessing upon him and the nation he will father. In other words, in view are the peoples who recognize Abraham and his seed as the mediators of divine blessing and so pray for God's prosperity upon them. But none can disregard God's mediator without incurring the divine curse. Today those who curse and are cursed refers to people who treat Christ and his church with contempt. This is so because Jesus Christ is the quintessential seed of Abraham, and whoever is baptized into Christ is the seed of Abraham (Gal. 3:29). Today the Israel of God consists of a remnant of ethnic Israel and of Gentiles grafted into the holy root of the patriarchs (Romans 11).[15]

Conclusion

As we have seen thus far, the kingdom of God is a complex and weighty matter to unpack. The internal emerging kingdom, or particular kingdom, is continually bumping up against the external emerging kingdom, or universal kingdom, thus exposing the friction between the ways of a holy God and a corrupted world. While the two kingdoms are indeed at odds with one another, the reality is that God's purposes are far more complicated and gracious than we could ever imagine. That is to say, God uses his particular kingdom for the purpose of breaking into and having restorative impact on the universal kingdom, thus redeeming what has been corrupted. In the words of the prophet Isaiah, "As the heavens are higher than the earth, so are my ways higher than your ways and my thoughts than your thoughts" (Isa. 55:9). As we will see in the next chapter, God chooses to mature his particular kingdom using a covenantal approach, thereby accomplishing his purposes for the day when he will ultimately reign victorious over both kingdoms.

---

[15]See Waltke, *An Old Testament Theology*, 321–32.

3

THE KINGDOM OF GOD IN THE OLD TESTAMENT

The Covenants

BRUCE K. WALTKE

G od has called his people, the particular kingdom, to first and foremost bring glory and honor to himself. But he has also called his particular kingdom to be representatives of himself and instruments of change in the world at large, namely, the universal kingdom. This is a high calling and a lofty task. In the Old Testament, we see how God uses a covenantal approach to mature his people for such a purpose. And yet, as God's people fail time and again to keep one covenant after another, God continues to take them closer and closer to the ultimate fulfillment of those covenants: the new covenant.

All of the Old Testament covenants culminate in this new covenant, whereby every covenantal obligation is met in the person of Jesus Christ. In what follows, we will explore those covenants that God gave to his particular kingdom throughout the Old Testament and how they served to point God's people to Christ as well as display his character to the pagan nations around them.

The Internal Emerging Kingdom of God

This section reflects upon the maturing of the particular kingdom by considering: (1) founding moments during times of crisis and founding fathers that resolve the crisis, as well as epoch-making covenants made with the found-

ers; (2) the covenant of works versus the covenant of grace; (3) the unfolding of the covenant of grace in I AM's unfolding covenants; namely, (4) the
Abrahamic covenant involving the election of the chosen people and the
land sworn to them; (5) the Mosaic covenant that develops the holy nation;
(6–7) the Davidic covenant that gives the nation an enduring house; and
(8) the new covenant that empowers the nation to realize its holy destiny.

1) Founding Moments, Fathers, and Covenants

From a broad perspective, Israel's understanding of her identity and salvation history—the lenses through which the people of God are to understand themselves—is structured around several major events and key
moments: creation, fall, flood, patriarchs, exodus-conquest, monarchy,
prophecy, exile, and return. Epochal moments normally occur in connection with crises of faith—that is to say, historical moments when a person
or group of people encounters realities that conflict with their ideology.
When confronted with a crisis of faith, a group may either deny the present and retreat to the past, as fundamentalists tend to do; repudiate the
past with its interpretive ideology, as liberals and postmodernists tend to
do; or reconfigure and/or reinterpret the ideological schema in order to
demonstrate that the group's ideology can account for the present. The
third resolution to explain the previously unexplainable crisis advances
the group's understanding of its ideology.

In Israel's sacred history, I AM, not humans, takes the initiative to
advance his kingdom through those who respond to him by faith in his
refreshing promises. Those faithful few who respond are key figures of
the faith: Adam-Eve, Noah, Abraham, Moses-Joshua, David, Elijah, and
Elisha, followed by the writing prophets and Ezra-Nehemiah respectively.
All of these are founding fathers of the kingdom.

Moreover, I AM's refreshing initiatives and these faithful leaders are
usually associated with I AM's epoch-shaping covenants, wherein he obligates himself to his people, sometimes unconditionally and at other times
conditionally. The covenant relationship between God and his kingdom
people is unique. Moshe Weinfeld affirms that "the idea of a covenant
between a deity and a people is unknown to us from other religions and
cultures," and "the covenantal idea was a special feature of the religion

of Israel."[1] On the one hand, God's unconditional covenants assure the people of the kingdom of their destiny, filling them with faith and hope. To Eve he unconditionally obligated himself to give her an offspring who would crush humankind's Adversary. To Noah, because he proved himself faithful, God promised unconditionally never again to destroy the earth, assuring the faithful that the rug would not be pulled out from under them. To Abraham, because he too obeyed, God promised to give an eternal seed and land. To David, also because of prior demonstrations of faith, God covenanted to give an eternal house, kingdom, and throne. On the other hand, God's conditional covenants prompt the kingdom to love both God and humankind, putting the interests of others above their own. Through the mediation of Moses, God obligated himself conditionally to bless Israel. Although he covenanted never to dispossess the house of David, the blessings of that covenant were contingent on the king's obedience to the Mosaic Torah. In these conditional covenants we see the connection between the externally irrupting kingdom and the inwardly developing one. The kingdom escalates externally as it escalates inwardly in holiness.

God accompanied his foundational covenants with icons or symbols that revive the past even into the present and that serve as short, memorable symbols of the biblical message pertaining to the making of God's kingdom. The seed promised to Eve lays the foundation of all the other covenants and needs no other icon than the birth of covenant sons and daughters. The rainbow icon commemorates the Noahic covenant; circumcision, the Abrahamic; Sabbath, the Mosaic; the cup, the new. The Davidic covenant also needed no iconic augmentation, for David's continuing seed validated and sustained the covenant.

The covenants attached to the memorable, epochal events in the development of the kingdom of God are described in ways that bring out their continuity with the concerns, themes, and trajectories of the founding moments. The seed promised to Eve is foundational to all the covenants in the making of God's kingdom. The Noahic covenant guarantees a firm stage on which to play out the drama of salvation history to the final triumph of the kingdom. The Mosaic covenant articulates the teachings or law that will bind the kingdom together under God's rule. The

---

[1]Moshe Weinfeld, "berith," *The Theological Dictionary of the Old Testament*, ed. G. Johannes Botterweck and Helmer Ringgren, trans. John T. Willis (Grand Rapids, MI: Eerdmans, 1975), 2:278. For the decline, rise, and decline of covenant centrality in the history of Israel's religion studies, see Robert A. Oden Jr., "The Place of Covenant in the Religion of Israel," in *Ancient Israelite Religion: Essays in Honor of Frank Moore* Cross, ed. Patrick D. Miller Jr., Paul D. Hanson, and S. Dean McBride (Philadelphia: Fortress, 1987), 421–47.

Davidic covenant provides the nation with the unchanging political leadership necessary for God's theocracy to be firmly established. Eichrodt
believes that the concept of covenant expresses the basic tendency and
tenet of Israel's religion: "It enshrines Israel's most fundamental conviction, namely of its unique relationship with God."[2]

2) Covenant of Works versus Covenant of Grace

The interplay between God's character and human accountability is
important to understanding the so-called covenant of grace that provides
the spiritual foundation for the kingdom of God.[3] Theologians sometimes
contrast the covenant of works with Adam before his fall into sin (cf.
Hos. 6:7) with the eternal covenant of grace with the second Adam, Jesus
Christ. According to the covenant of works, God obliges himself to bless
Adam, the representative of humankind, if he obeys God's command not
to eat of the forbidden fruit (Gen. 1:28–30a) but to sentence him to death
if he disobeys (2:15–17). Adam fails and so receives death, not life. After
his fall into sin and the loss of the garden paradise, the covenant of works
is no longer a possibility. In his sovereign grace, however, God establishes
a covenant of grace on the basis of the benefits of Christ's active obedience and atoning death, validated by his resurrection from the dead, his
ascension into heaven, and his gift of the empowering presence of the
Holy Spirit to his church. Although the term "covenant of grace" is not
used, all of the elements that comprise this covenant are present throughout the Old and New Testaments and laid out most fully in Romans 3.

3) God's Historic Covenants with His Kingdom People

The rest of the covenants that progressively unfold in salvation history are
based on this covenant of grace. These later covenants divide the kingdom's history into three distinct dispensations, whereby God governs his
people differently (e.g., by conscience, law, and Spirit). He begins with the
covenant to the first representative mortals, giving them an elect seed
to defeat their archenemy (Gen. 3:15). The covenant of grace finds further expression in the Noahic covenant, which preserves the earth for
all people (9:9–17). In the Abrahamic covenant, God swears to give the
patriarchs an eternal seed and land so that they might bless all peoples

---

[2]Walther Eichrodt, *Theology of the Old Testament*, trans. J. A. Baker, vol. 1, The Old Testament Library (Philadelphia: Westminster, 1961), 17.
[3]This section is largely lifted from Bruce K. Waltke, *An Old Testament Theology: An Exegetical, Thematic and
Canonical Approach* (Grand Rapids, MI: Zondervan, 2007), 287–88.

(Genesis 15, 17, and 22). In the Mosaic covenant made with Israel at Sinai, Israel seals its relationship with I AM to be his holy people, mediating kingdom values by accepting his Torah (catechetical teaching), which guides the people to the realization of their elected destiny to be a priestly kingdom (Exodus 19–24). In his covenant with David, God promises to set his servant's house over his kingdom forever (2 Samuel 7; Psalms 89 and 132). In the new covenant, God openly proclaims the covenant of grace that makes these historic covenants possible. The Israel of God, the elect beneficiaries of these covenants, counts God trustworthy to keep his promises in his unfolding program of salvation history culminating in the second advent of Jesus Christ (Jeremiah 31; Luke 24:25–27; 1 Cor. 11:25; Heb. 8:8–13). Though these covenants initiate new epochs in the administration of God's kingdom, the enduring beneficiaries are unified by their common election to trust the God of Abraham, Isaac, and Jacob to make them heirs of the blessings of the covenant of grace and its unfolding expression in the historic covenants.

4) Abrahamic Covenant: Chosen Seed and Land

a. *Chosen Seed of Kingdom.* As noted above, the Bible is all about God revealing his sublimities to bring glory to himself through his irrupting particular kingdom breaking into the universal kingdom, which for the present is under the restricted rule of Satan. In Genesis, we learn about the elect "seed," a metaphor for the people of God who constitute his kingdom.[4] The narrator's use of key words such as "seed," "offspring," "descendants," and "blessings" (i.e., fertile and victorious) reinforces the book's theme that God elected the seed of Abraham, Isaac, and Jacob to be the people of his kingdom through whom he blesses the entire earth. They are the heirs of the promissory covenant God made with Abraham.

The narrator uses the refrain *toledot* ("this is the account of [Proper Name's] family line") to give the book of Genesis structure and meaning. In the first of the ten *toledot*, however, the representative man, succumbing to Satan's temptation, rejects God's rule for man's own rule and so loses the universal kingdom to Satan's rule. The results are catastrophic: chaos (the disruption of the creation to frustrate humankind's work) and human shame, alienating Adam and Eve from God's beneficent presence and from one another. Nevertheless, God intervenes by electing to change the woman's affection toward the Serpent from attraction to hate. Yet in

---

[4]This section is largely lifted from Waltke, *An Old Testament Theology*, 305–6, 317–20.

the promise that Eve will give birth to a seed that will crush the head of the Serpent, God warns that the Serpent will crush her seed's heel. In brief, salvation history tells the story of Eve's elect seed reversing the chaos Adam introduced by suffering for righteousness in the war against Satan's kingdom.

The breach between two seeds immediately becomes apparent at the end of *toledot* 1 in the conflict between the righteous Abel and the unrighteous Cain. The former approaches God with an acceptable sacrifice by bringing the best of what he has and so finds access to God and his blessing; the latter approaches God with an unacceptable token sacrifice. Cain's less-than-best, manipulative sacrifice dishonors God and wins God's wrath, not God's blessing. Cain's failure at the altar leads to his inability to master sin (Gen. 4:7, 11, 15). Out of envy toward his brother and anger against God, Cain irrationally kills the true worshiper, although earthly death only bruises Abel's heel. Cain's hubris results in God's banishing him from his presence. Like an infectious contagion, sin spreads and escalates in Cain's lineage. God blesses his lineage with talent in the arts and science, but they use their talent, we may assume, for their own glory, certainly not to bring God glory for they neither pray nor praise God.

God replaces childless Abel with the line of Seth (*toledot* 2). His lineage begins to call upon the name of I AM in its acceptable reconciliation to the forgiving God (Gen. 4:26). By *toledot* 3 (that of Noah) the yeast of sin spreads through the universal kingdom until it sours the whole human lump—all except righteous Noah and his family, the reduced kingdom of God. Universal sin merits God's universal flood. But in the ark that floats on top of the water covering the earth, God continues to rule and save the kingdom of his creation, small though it may be. At the end of *toledot* 3, it becomes obvious that Noah and his descendants still carry the gene of original sin (8:21). In *toledot* 4, sin's contagion is so rampant that the universal kingdom collectively revolts and seeks to usurp God's heavenly rule by building a tower into the heavens to overcome its restriction to earth. To minimize human hubris, God then divides humanity into warring nations using the barrier of language. But he still preserves a salvific seed through elect Shem, culminating in the birth of Abraham, as recounted in *toledot* 5.

The election and call of Abraham begins a new divine initiative, the forming of a new nation to bless the other nations. A nation, however, entails the possession of land. The holy nation needs sanctified space and sustenance. *Toledot* 6 (about Abraham) recounts that God entered into a promissory covenant, sworn to Abraham by God's own oath. The Abrahamic covenant promises that God will bless the patriarch with fertility and give his seed the land the Canaanites defiled. *Toledot* 8 and 10 narrow down the heirs of the covenant to Isaac, not Ishmael (*toledot* 7), and to Jacob and his twelve sons, not Esau (*toledot* 9). Ishmael and Esau sire nations that do not participate in the kingdom of God.

As recounted in *toledot* 10, providence leads the heirs of the covenant out of the land to escape Canaan's contagion by becoming aliens in racist Egypt until the iniquities of the Canaanites are fully ripe and ready to be cut down by Joshua's sword. Thus, the book of Genesis ends with the holy seed in Egypt awaiting the time when God will call them to realize his promissory covenant to give them land in which to dwell.

b. Covenanted Land of the Kingdom (Gen. 15:1–21). Through two covenants and an oath, God refreshes, expands, and clarifies his three promises that were dependent on Abraham's obedience to abandon his country and family and go to the land of Canaan.

Throughout *toledot* 6, Abraham slogs it out in the land of Canaan on the basis of God's promise to give him that land. He hangs on to this promise even though, when his honored wife dies, he has to buy an expensive cemetery plot as his first piece of real estate in the Promised Land (Genesis 23). God rewards Abraham's faith with the renewed promise of a seed and ratifies his promise regarding the land by making a unilateral, irrevocable covenant to give him the land of the Canaanites as his permanent fief (chapter 15). That land will extend from the "Wadi of Egypt to the great river, the Euphrates" (15:18).[5] God's later covenant to give Abraham and Sarah everlasting royal seed and God's climactic oath to make the nation they bear a universal blessing are reckoned as a single covenant, the Abrahamic covenant (Deut. 7:8; Neh. 9:32; Mic. 7:20; Luke 1:72–73; Heb. 6:13–20).

c. Covenanted Seed of Kingdom (Gen. 17:1–27). I AM's second grant to Abraham—this one in the form of a covenant by a legal grant—is marked out by the introduction "[I AM] appeared to him" (Gen. 17:1) and the conclusion "God went up from him" (v. 22). The scene's introduction emphasizes the impotency of Abraham to effect this covenant—a ninety-nine-year-old man cannot be exceedingly fruitful (v. 1). His body is a dried-up sap tree, and Sarah's womb at ninety years of age has become a

---

[5]Unless otherwise indicated, Scripture quotations in this chapter are from *The Holy Bible, New International Version*.

wilted flower. The promise of offspring clearly depends on the Author of
life, who even raises the dead (Rom. 4:18–25). This covenant distinguishes
itself by being an "everlasting covenant" between God and Abraham and
his offspring (Gen. 17:7). Nahum Sarna helpfully notes that the narrative
recounting this everlasting covenant has an alternating structure:

> A. Abraham the progenitor of numerous nations and kings; his name is
> changed from Abram to Abraham (17:1–8)
>> B. Law of circumcision set forth (17:9–14)
> A'. Sarah the progenitress of numerous nations and of kings; her
>> name is changed from Sarai to Sarah (17:15–22)
>> B'. Law of circumcision carried out (17:23–28)[6]

The parallel structure exposes the covenant's emphasis on expansion: to make Abraham and Sarah exceedingly fruitful and to bring forth
nations and kings. The covenant promises are trustworthy because I AM
will be their God, a promise guaranteeing them prosperity and protection. However, while the Noahic covenant depends totally on God to
fulfill its blessings and is displayed through his sign of the rainbow, the
Abrahamic covenant depends on the active faith obedience of the human
partner through the sign of circumcision. By initiating the sign of circumcision, a male activates the blessings of the covenant; without the
sign he forfeits his right to belong to the covenant community under
God's blessings. In the New Testament, however, this changes, and in
Christ we are now the new circumcision (Phil. 3:3).

5) Mosaic/Sinaitic Covenant

a. Introduction. Four centuries after I AM elects the patriarchs and
the twelve tribes of Jacob/Israel as his chosen people, he refreshingly
comes on to the scene again to accelerate his emerging kingdom both
externally and internally. The Egyptian threat to annihilate God's chosen people by drowning their boys in the Nile River prompts the new
initiative. God calls Moses, the next prominent figure in salvation history, to deliver his kingdom from Egyptian slavery. Out of gratitude for
I AM's deliverance, God's people are obligated to worship only him by
accepting the covenant with which he gifts them through Moses. This
covenant is called either "the Mosaic covenant," because Moses medi-

---

[6]Nahum M. Sarna, *Genesis*, JPS Torah Commentary 1 (Philadelphia: Jewish Publication Society, 1989), 122.

ated it, or "the Sinaitic covenant," because Israel ratified the covenant at Mount Sinai.

The Mosaic covenant is part and parcel of an unfolding covenant relationship between I AM and his chosen people.[7] By ratifying it, Israel sealed its covenant relationship with I AM rooted in the Abrahamic covenant. As we shall see, the house of David, the beneficiary of the Davidic covenant, realizes that blessings or curses are directly related to their faith in I AM as expressed in their obedience to his teachings. And, as we shall also see later, the *new* covenant assumes the content of the previous covenants.

The covenant's teachings (Torah) express and mirror God's holy and moral character. So by their very nature the teachings are eternal (James 2:10–11). Also, the Torah's substance is consistent with the order of creation. Jesus taught: "Not the smallest letter, not the least stroke of a pen, will by any means disappear from the [Torah]" (Matt. 5:18). Jesus rejected the legalism of Judaism (9:12–13; 23:27–28; Luke 16:15; 18:9) and abolished some ceremonial laws such as dietary restrictions (Mark 7:14–19), but he upheld the old covenant (Matt. 5:19, 21–24, 27–32, 43–48; Mark 7:1–13; 10:17–22), simplifying its complexities to two great commandments: love of God and love of neighbor (Matt. 22:37–40). By his obedient life and death, Jesus fulfilled the obligations of the Torah and the Prophets (5:18; Luke 24:44).

The Torah serves three purposes: pedagogical, civil, and moral. Pedagogically, it makes sinners realize how lost they are apart from God's saving grace through his Holy Spirit (Acts 15:10; Rom. 7:7–13; Gal. 5:1). Moses clearly states that the Torah requires perfect obedience to receive its blessings (Lev. 18:5). The Old Testament is a masterpiece of depicting the human heart that is bent on wandering from God. Proud people attempt to keep the Torah by their own resolve and efforts, failing to recognize from their own history their spiritual impotence. The lowly of heart recognize their spiritual impotence, cry to God to show them mercy, and look to God to empower them. They recognize their need of God's grace to regenerate their hearts to trust his promises, to love him, and to commit themselves to his provision of sacrifice to give them eternal life, not their own resolve and efforts to keep the Torah (Deut. 30:1–10; Josh. 24:19–24; Rom. 10:5).[8]

As for its civil value, the Torah is set up to restrain sin. Moreover,

---

[7] The section on the Mosaic law is largely lifted from Waltke, *An Old Testament Theology*, 406–9; 412–14; 435–37.

[8] Frank Thielman, *Theology of the New Testament* (Grand Rapids, MI: Zondervan, 2005), 368–70.

the human conscience approves its civil value. Conscience and law work together to produce the fear of God.

As for its moral value, the Torah gives true Israel understanding and is a lamp to their feet (Ps. 119:97, 103–5). Paul likewise upholds its moral content (Rom. 7:12). The apostle to the Gentiles regards his doctrine of justification by faith—not by Torah-keeping—as upholding and not annulling the Torah (3:31). In his inner man he delights in the Torah (7:22). Paul cites the Mosaic Torah as authoritative warrant for his ethical judgments (e.g., 1 Cor. 9:9; Eph. 6:1–2). Following his Lord, he holds that the Torah of love fulfills, not supplants, them (Rom. 13:10).

The Mosaic covenant is a concrete expression of what is meant by the prayer: "Thy will be done on earth as it is in heaven." In sum, the Mosaic covenant is an essential part of the emergence of God's kingdom without and her development within.

b. Form of Mosaic Covenant. The law given at Sinai (Exodus 20—Leviticus 27) and its renewal on the plains of Moab (Deuteronomy) is a mixture of forms of ancient Near Eastern law codes from the third and early second millennium BC and of treaties, initiated by a great suzerain with vassal kings, from the late second millennium. These treaties consist of: a preamble identifying the greatness of the author (cf. Ex. 20:1; Deut. 5:23–27); a historical prologue motivating the vassal to accept the treaty obligations out of appreciation for the suzerain's grace to him (cf. Ex. 20:2; Deut. 2:7; 4:32–38; 2 Kings 23:21–23; 2 Chron. 30:1–27; 35:1–3; Ezra 6:19–22); the stipulations to advance the kingdom, especially loving fidelity to the suzerain (Ex. 20:3–7; Deut. 6:5); provision for deposit of the text and for public readings (10:1–5; 31:9–13, 24–25); divine witnesses to the treaty (30:19–20); and blessings and curses for keeping or reneging on the covenant, respectively (Leviticus 26 and Deuteronomy 28).

c. Initiating the Mosaic Covenant (Exodus 19). I AM initiates the covenant in three cycles during Moses' ascending and descending Mount Sinai. In the first cycle, God instructs the people in the basis, motivation, and purpose of the covenant (19:3–8). Because of their patriarchal lineage, they have the unique privilege of entering into this covenant with none other than God himself. As for motivation, they are to accept the covenant out of gratefulness to God for redeeming them from Egypt and sustaining them as they wandered in the wilderness. With such a history, they are surely to know without a doubt that their God is wholly trustworthy. As for purpose, by trusting God and obeying his stipulations/teachings they will become: (1) the Creator's unique treasure; (2) the priestly nation through whom God mediates his blessings to the nations; and (3) a holy nation, mirroring to the world the holiness of their God.

After Israel formally accepts God's covenant in cycle 2, Moses is distinguished as the one worthy to mediate the law by God's invitation to join him on the mountain, and the people are consecrated to God (19:9–15). In cycle 3, Moses and Aaron, Israel's future high priest, are exalted by God's exclusive invitation for them to ascend the mountain (vv. 20–25).

d. Content of the Mosaic Covenant. Roughly, the Torah consists of: the Ten Commandments (Ex. 20:1–17); the book of the covenant (Exodus 21–23); liturgical regulations (Exodus 25—Leviticus 10); and miscellaneous other laws to sanctify God's kingdom (Leviticus 11–27). Of these the famous Ten Commandments are the most important. This can be inferred from several of its features.

(1) *Placement.* The Ten Commandments are given first. Hebrew syntax and rhetorical style commonly place the main concept first and then elaborate upon it, as in Genesis 1:1.

(2) *Better form of revelation.* Only the Ten Commandments are given directly by God; the rest of the Torah is mediated to Israel through Moses. Noteworthily, God's word mediated through Moses has priority over his words to other prophets because he spoke to Moses directly, face-to-face, and clearly; but to other prophets he spoke indirectly through visions that needed interpretation (Num. 12:1–8).

(3) *Deposited in the ark.* Only the Commandments are deposited in the ark, which resides in the Most Holy Place in the tent-sanctuary, which is a replica of the heavenly sanctuary (Deut. 10:1–5; Ex. 25:40; Heb. 8:5; 9:23).

(4) *Not limited to the sworn land.* Whereas the other laws were intended for Israel in the Promised Land (Deut. 5:31), the Ten Commandments are not restricted to geography or history, to time and space.

(5) *Called "the covenant" and the foundation of the canon.* The Ten Commandments by themselves are referred to as "the covenant" (4:13; 9:9, 11). With the people's acceptance of the Ten Commandments, we have the beginning of the canon of Scripture that gives the kingdom of God moral form, not immoral freedom; liberty within law, not lawlessness; and sex within marriage, not promiscuity. Scripture is self-authenticating to the kingdom of God. No human council decided the canon's content; the Holy Scriptures themselves commanded the kingdom's consent. Later councils merely authenticated the books that were already held to be canonical centuries earlier.

(6) *Addressed individually to the whole kingdom of God.* Contrary to the book of the covenant, which contains case law expressed in the impersonal third person pronoun, and contrary to the liturgy addressed to Moses, the Ten Commandments are addressed by the Creator and Ruler of all things personally to each individual of his kingdom. The legislative "you shall [not]" is second person singular, not plural. As such, the Ten Commandments establish intimacy between the King and each and every subject of his kingdom.

e. *Deuteronomy: A Covenant Renewal Document.* Deuteronomy receives its title from the Septuagint, which calls it *Deuteronomion* ("Second Law," or "Repetition of the Law"). More accurately, on a story level, it is a covenant renewal document written by Moses (ca. 1250 BC) and called "the book of the law"; on a plot level, it was written during the exile (ca. 550 BC) by an anonymous prophet and historian who added fifty-six verses to it, framing the book of the law within his history.[9] Presumably this prophet-historian, called "the Deuteronomist," wrote his history to engage the exiles with Moses' covenant renewal and encourage them toward their own personal renewal.

Deuteronomy is the most important book in the Old Testament. J. Gordon McConville calls it "one of the great theological documents of the Bible, or of any time." He says: "It . . . goes to the heart of the great issues of the relationship between God and human beings."[10] The book has had greater consequences for human history than any other single book. Its continuing influence is one of the major forces shaping the future of humanity. Its regulations are the first to establish universal education and health for all members of a nation and to establish the only welfare system that was in existence in ancient times. It first formulates the greatest command of all Scripture: to love God (Matt. 22:34–40). Moreover, it establishes a constitutional monarchy, a king subject to God's law.[11]

Deuteronomy's importance can be inferred from its cardinal role in the primary history (Genesis—2 Kings, excluding Ruth). That history calls upon the exiles to evaluate their failure to keep covenant with I AM. Each book in the Deuteronomistic history (Deuteronomy—Kings, apart from Ruth) has its own individuality and character, but Deuteronomy informs

---

[9]Waltke, *An Old Testament Theology,* 57.

[10]J. Gordon McConville, *Grace in the End: A Study in Deuteronomic Theology* (Grand Rapids, MI: Zondervan, 1993), 9.

[11]The book of the law comprises all but about fifty-six verses of the book of Deuteronomy (Waltke, *An Old Testament Theology,* 479).

all of them systemically in language and worldview, giving rise to the academic title for this collection of books as the Deuteronomistic history. Gerhard von Rad says, "We call these histories Deuteronomistic because they take as normative for their judgment of the past certain standards laid down either exclusively or chiefly in Deuteronomy."[12]

The book of the law provides the theological grist for the later prophets' interpretation (i.e., writing) of Israel's history in both their oracles of doom and of salvation beyond judgment. It first formulates the greatest command: to love God (Deut. 6:5; Matt. 22:34–40). Furthermore, it establishes a constitutional monarchy. Upon the human king's ascension to the throne over God's kingdom, he is to make a copy of this book under the tutelage of the priests and thereafter read it daily. Moreover, Jesus quotes Deuteronomy more often than any other book, suggesting its effect on shaping his theology. He resisted Satan's three temptations by three quotations from this book (Luke 4:1–13), implying the book's spiritual power.

f. Law of Moses and Words of the Wise. Presumably, then, Solomon son of David, king of Israel, copied the book of the law upon his ascension to the throne of God's kingdom and at first read it daily. David's deathbed charge to Solomon to keep the book of the Mosaic law assumes his knowledge of the book. Nevertheless, Solomon found his knowledge of the law insufficient for his responsibility as the supreme and final judge of God's kingdom on earth, so he asked God for a greater wisdom than he found in the Mosaic law, and God, delighting in his request, gave him "a wise and discerning heart" (1 Kings 3:4–14), enabling him to speak three thousand proverbs (4:29–34).

Solomon's proverbs take up those social and cultural issues that are too fine to be caught in the mesh of the law, too small to be hit by the broadsides of the prophets. The refinement of the law of Moses by Solomon's proverbs may be compared to learning to drive a car. A driver first learns the comprehensive rule: "Drive carefully." But that abstract rule needs to be defined more specifically, which is why we have such road signs as "Stop," "Yield," "Speed limit: 35 mph," and the signals of traffic lights. Before being granted a driver's license, the applicant must demonstrate his ability to follow these signs. But even knowing and following these more specific posted regulations do not qualify a driver for a driver's license. Many states also require the applicant to pass a written test before

---

[12]Gerhard von Rad, *Studies in Deuteronomy*, SBT 9 (London: SCM Press, 1963), 75.

granting the license. To pass this test the applicant must, for example, know to park at least fifteen feet [five meters] from a fire hydrant; to park at least fifteen feet from the corner of an intersection; to turn into the inside lane of a four-lane highway and to ease one's way over into the out-side lane through the use of mirrors; and so forth.

In this illustration the general rule "drive carefully" is like the com-prehensive commandments: "love God with all your heart, soul, mind and strength," and "love your neighbor as yourself." In the same way, these abstract commands need further definition. What road signs are to the driver, the Ten Commandments are to the chosen people. To love your neighbor means more specifically to bestow on others the right to life ("you are not to take innocent life"), home ("you are not to commit adul-tery"), property ("you are not to steal"), and reputation ("you are not to bear false witness"). But as essential as these commandments are, Solomon found them insufficient for taking to the road of life; they needed further refinement.

So then, comprehensive rules, such as "love your neighbor as your-self," or more specifically defined as "do not murder," become even more clear-cut when refined by Solomon and other sages in Proverbs. The com-mand not to murder becomes in the Proverbs a command to feed your enemy (25:21). The command not to commit adultery becomes the hus-band's standing up in his noble wife's presence to give her honor and to publicly give her verbal praise (31:28–31). "You shall not steal" becomes a proverb of exhortation to be generous (22:9). And the command not to bear false witness is sharpened by the proverb: "hatred stirs up conflict, but love covers over all wrongs" (10:12).

6) Davidic Covenant, Part 1

a. Introduction. As noted, a kingdom normally consists of a common people, on a common land, under a common law, and ruled by a common leader. The Deuteronomistic history is largely about the leadership of the nation from Joshua, Moses' handpicked successor (book of Joshua), to very flawed charismatic warlords (book of Judges), to a mixed bag of kings (books of 1—2 Samuel and 1—2 Kings [1—4 Kings, Septuagint]).[13]

The book of Samuel narrates three tectonic shifts in the structure of God's kingdom: (1) Israel's liturgical worship shifts from Shiloh to

---

[13]The section on the Davidic covenant is largely lifted from Waltke, *An Old Testament Theology*, 624–25; 660–61; 686–87.

Jerusalem; (2) Israel's leadership changes from episodic warlords to the eternal kingship of David; and (3) Israel is transformed from a tribal league to a unified kingdom capable of exercising imperial power over neighboring states. These tectonic shifts determine the contours of Israel's history for the next four centuries and lay the foundation for the next great tectonic transformation of God's kingdom from a people with a geopolitical identity to their true heavenly identity. In that shift the Jerusalem liturgy, David's kingship, and imperialism are types of the heavenly reality.

J. P. Fokkelman analyzes the book of Samuel's integrated structure as follows:

I. Section 1: Crossing of Fates Regarding Samuel (1 Samuel 1–12)
   A. Crossing of Fates of Eli and Samuel (1 Samuel 1–7)
   B. Crossing of Fates of Samuel and Saul (1 Samuel 8–12)
II. Section 2: Crossing of Fates Regarding Saul (1 Samuel 13–31)
   A. Saul Rejected as King (1 Samuel 13–15)
   B. Crossing of Fates of Saul and David (1 Samuel 16–31)
III. David (2 Samuel 1–20)
   A. Rise of David (2 Samuel 1–8)
   B. Decline of David (2 Samuel 9–20)
IV. Appendix (2 Samuel 21–24)

The crossing of the fates of Eli and Samuel and of Samuel and Saul trace the trajectory of the government in God's kingdom. Human rulership of God's kingdom shifts from the priest and warlord Eli (see 1 Sam. 4:18) to the prayerful prophet and warlord Samuel (7:16). "Crossing of Fates of Samuel and Saul (1 Samuel 8–12)" is framed by Samuel's antimonarchic speeches (1 Samuel 8 and 12), both of which conclude with God's thunderclap applause. Its plot develops from the people's demand for a king to the prophet's reluctant installation of Saul. The act is of exceptional importance, for its theme pertains to the demotion of Samuel from a prophet-warlord to only a prophet as he installs Saul as Israel's first king. Saul rises to power in this section by being privately anointed by Samuel (9:10–10:16) and publicly balloted at Mizpah (10:17–21) and by rescuing Jabesh Gilead from the Ammonites (1 Samuel 11).

After this victory the nation solemnly gathers around their prophet, Samuel, and their king at the holy palace of Gilgal to "renew the kingship"—that is, to restore and repair that which already exists between I AM and Israel and to adjust the relationship within the context of monarchy. An inclusive doctrine uniting the monarchy of I AM with that of his regent is formed; the new administration of the kingdom by monarchy will prove either good or bad according to the kingdom's fidelity to the Mosaic covenant (11:14–15). The king must serve under the rule of I AM, just as Samuel did; he is not above God's law. Whatever the political form of the kingdom's government, God never relinquishes control of his kingdom.

b. Desirability of Kingship. Source critics classically follow Julius Wellhausen, who divides the sources of 1 Samuel 8–12 into *koenigsfeindlich* (anti-monarchy) versus *koenigsfreundlich* (pro-monarchy). By allowing "+" and "-" in the following analysis to signify respectively pro-monarchy and anti-monarchy, one gains insight into the resolution of the tension:

A (-) Speech: People request a king; Samuel warns people
B (+) Story: Saul's providential meeting with Samuel and Saul's
    anointing
A (-) Speech: Samuel publicly flushes out a hiding Saul
B (+) Story: Saul's first victory at Jabesh Gilead
A (-) Speech: Samuel sets forth terms of the monarchy

Samuel's anti-monarchy speeches pertain to Israel's sin in choosing a king and God's punishment of Israel through their king. In the story of the warlords Israel rebelled against God's rule by turning to idols (Judg. 2:10–13). Facing the crisis of complete subjugation by the Philistines—an expression of the universal, rebellious system—the tribal league, failing to realize that their continued apostasy during this epoch brought them to their knees, commits the final sin of that period: asking for a king, not God, to save them from foreign oppression. It needs to be underscored that the people sin in their reason for desiring a king: their lack of faith in I AM's ability to lead them.[14]

God judges the apostate nation for requesting a human specimen to replace him by giving them a tyrannical king. Consequently, Samuel's speeches are all about the dangers of monarchy. In God's grace, however, he will use the same king who punishes the nation for her unbelief to deliver her from oppressors without in the hostile, universal kingdom.

---

[14]Gerald Gerbrandt, *Kingship According to the Deuteronomistic History*, SBLDS 87 (Atlanta: Scholars Press, 1986); J. Robert Vannoy, *Covenant Renewal at Gilgal: A Study of 1 Samuel 11:14–12:25* (Cherry Hill, NJ: Mack, 1977), 34–40, 149–80, 227–32; David M. Howard Jr. documents that within evangelical circles, a number of scholars have argued in the same direction. "The Case for Kingship in Deuteronomy and the Former Prophets," *WTJ* 52 (Spring 1990): 103 n. 8.

Saul, endowed with God's spirit, delivers Israel at Jabesh Gilead from the Ammonites (1 Sam. 11:11).

The books of Genesis and Numbers unequivocally anticipate kingship as God's good gift to the patriarchs and the nation. Humanity was created to rule the earth as God's regent. I AM unconditionally obligates himself to bless the patriarchs to sire kings (Gen. 17:6, 16; 35:11). The testament of Jacob (49:8–12) promises kingship to the line of Judah. This royal oracle begins with Judah's elevation above his brothers through conquest of his enemies, symbolized by his hand being on their neck and his being pictured as a fearsome lion, the king of beasts, returning from the prey (vv. 8–9). The main thrust of the oracle is that Judah's progeny will establish an everlasting dynasty. By striking hyperbole the oracle celebrates the prosperity of the kingdom. Wine, the symbol of prosperity and joy, will be so abundant that the affluent king will bind his hungry donkey to the precious vine and his voracious colt to the choice branch. He will use wine as scrub water; his eyes will sparkle like wine and his teeth will be whiter than milk.

Balaam builds on the testament of Jacob in his four oracles against Balak, king of Moab, by increasing specificity and intensity in his description of Israel's king vanquishing Moab. The book of Judges is an apology for kingship—more specifically, a monarchy from Judah, not Benjamin. The book of Samuel endorses God's choice of the house of David forever. The book of Kings endorses and rejects individual kings but never rejects monarchy itself as an institution or the house of David as the divine authorized ruler of Judah.

7) Davidic Covenant, Part 2

The book of Samuel peaks at the conclusion of section 3: God entrusts his kingdom forever to the house of David. The book's climactic scene opens with David in his palace at "rest from all his enemies" who had thwarted his rise to the throne. The statement "thus says [I AM]" divides God's oracular and pastoral response through his plenipotentiary messenger, the prophet Nathan, into three parts (2 Sam. 7:5, 8, 11). First, God turns down David as the king to build his temple. David is a warrior who sheds blood; a temple symbolizes peace without bloodshed (vv. 5–7). Second, I AM addresses David as "my servant," an accolade bestowed on such noteworthies as Moses and Joshua. I AM reminds David that he chose him while still a shepherd boy to be his *nagid* ("sacred leader") and cut off all his enemies. I AM now covenants with David that during David's own lifetime he will give: (1) David a great name (i.e., having an international dimension (v. 9b); (2) Israel a secure place from wicked oppressors (v. 10); and (3) David rest from all his enemies (v. 11a). These promises are realized in 2 Samuel 8.

The third part pertains to two sets of future blessings after David's death (2 Sam. 7:11b–16; cf. 1 Chronicles 17 and Psalm 89). The first set of future promises pertains to Solomon—I AM will (1) raise up offspring "who will come out from your own body," a reference to Solomon; (2) establish his kingdom (i.e., the sphere of his authority, v. 12b); (3) establish the throne of his kingdom (i.e., the symbol of his rule, v. 13); and (4) be his father and he will be God's son (vv. 14–15). That is, God will discipline David's son according to his son's covenant fidelity (v. 14), but I AM will never take his *hesed* (unfailing kindness) from him. Although the covenant is unconditional, the king's experience of its blessings depends on his obedience to the Mosaic covenant.

The second set of future promises pertains to the remote future: (1) David's house (i.e., his dynasty) will endure forever, (2) his kingdom will endure forever, and (3) his throne will be established forever (2 Sam. 7:16). In sum, the Davidic covenant contains a total of ten blessings: three fulfilled in David's lifetime, four in the lifetime of his son Solomon, and three in his remote future. David responds to the oracle with a long prayer of thanksgiving and praise (vv. 18–24) and a petition that God keep his promise "so that your name will be great forever" (vv. 25–29; esp. v. 26). God's renown is tied up with David's renown. To this day I AM and his chosen king remain famous through the fulfillment of the covenant promises in the eternal son of David, Jesus Christ, whose throne in heavenly Jerusalem rules an eternal kingdom that includes almost every nation on the earth.

8) New Covenant

a. Introduction. The Mosaic covenant, by which Israel sealed its relationship with I AM through the Abrahamic covenant and which is foundational to the Davidic covenant, has a glaring weakness: it led a proud, nominal Israel to attempt to keep the Mosaic covenant in their own strength and so to their condemnation. Had nominal Israel reflected upon salvation history, they should have realized that if Adam and Eve failed to keep the covenant of works in the garden of paradise, how much more would they fail by their own resolve to keep the Mosaic covenant in defiled Canaan? The Mosaic covenant was doomed to failure from the start, as foreseen by

Moses (Deut. 30:1–3) and Joshua (Josh. 24:14–27). The nation's founders knew from experience that Israel was stiff-necked and unfaithful by nature and therefore unable to keep their resolve. Throughout Israel's history, the broken covenant had to be ratified again and again (Deuteronomy 29; Joshua 23–24; 2 Kings 23; Nehemiah 9–10).

The prophets, beginning with Moses but especially those who experienced the exile, envisioned a new, not a replacement, covenant for all Israel, one that depended entirely on God, who by nature is eternally faithful.[15] Moses, in his final sermon in connection with the Mosaic covenant, predicted that after Israel returned from exile, "[I AM] your God will circumcise your hearts and the hearts of your descendants, so that you may love him with all your heart and with all your soul, and live. . . . You will again obey [I AM] and follow all his commands I am giving you today" (Deut. 30:6–8). The prophets of the exile labeled this anticipated new covenant in various ways, such as an "everlasting covenant" (Isa. 55:3; 61:8), a "covenant of peace" (Ezek. 34:25; 37:26), and a "new covenant" (Jer. 31:31–34). The text of Jeremiah is the longest Old Testament passage cited in the New Testament (Heb. 8:8–12), giving the two halves of the Christian canon their titles.

True Israel always depended on God for their salvation. For the regenerate heart the covenant's stipulations are a delight and joy gladly accepted (Josh. 1:8–9; Psalm 1; 112:1; 119:14, 16, 47–48, 113, 127–28, 163–67).

b. Continuities between the Old and New Covenants. The new covenant has significant continuities with the old:

(1) Both are given to the "house of Israel" and the "house of Judah" (Ex. 19:3; Jer. 31:31). Christ's apostles interpreted Israel as the church, which includes Jews and Gentiles, by their baptism into Christ, the true seed of Abraham (Eph. 2:11–22; Gal. 3:29; 6:15; 1 Pet. 2:9–10).

(2) Both are instituted after redemption from bondage: from Egypt and Babylon.

(3) Both took effect only after death: of bulls and of Christ (Ex. 24:4–8; Luke 22:20). In that sense the covenant is like a will, which takes effect only after the death of the one who makes the will (Heb. 9:16–17).

(4) Both have the same substance: "I will put my [Torah] in their minds and write it on their hearts" (Jer. 31:33).

c. Superiority of the New Covenant to the Old Covenant. The old covenant, which was glorious, has no glory now in comparison with the sur-

---

[15]This section is largely lifted from Waltke, *An Old Testament Theology*, 438–41.

passing glory of the new covenant (2 Cor. 3:10). Compare and contrast their glories:

(1) *Chronology.* Israel ratified the old covenant three months after their redemption from Egypt. But redemption from sin and death and the empowering of the new covenant administration occur synchronously with faith (Rom. 7:12; 8:9).

(2) *Mediators.* Moses, who mediated the old covenant, was highly exalted above the rest of Israel by his unique proximity to the holy God, but he was still only a faithful slave in God's house, whereas Christ, who mediates the new covenant, is God's faithful Son who rules over his house (Heb. 3:1–6). Moses built a replica of God's heavenly temple, but Christ ministers within the heavenly reality (8:5–6).

(3) *Medium.* God wrote the Ten Commandments on rock to establish the permanency of its stipulations, and it was later written on parchment with ink. But Christ, through his administration of the Holy Spirit, writes the new covenant on the "tablets of human hearts," thus changing human nature—and that makes all the difference when it comes to keeping laws. Saints with the Torah written on their hearts show to all that they are "letter[s] from Christ" (2 Cor. 3:3).

(4) *Obligees.* The old covenant depended on Israel's promise to keep the covenant's laws, but the new covenant is based on God's will to implant those laws on the heart.

(5) *Sanction.* The old covenant law was powerless because it was weakened by the human nature of nominal Israel. The new covenant is empowered in true Israel by the presence of the Holy Spirit (Rom. 7:8–8:9).

(6) *Duration.* The switching of the obligee from unfaithful Israel to the faithful God entailed that only the latter is eternal (Heb. 8:6–13; 2 Cor. 3:10).

(7) *Status.* The old covenant treated Israel, though God's heir, as a child in need of a tutor, making him, though a son, no better than a slave. But the new covenant treats God's son as an adult with the full right of being God's son (Gal. 4:1–7).

(8) *Sacrifice.* The old covenant was put into effect by sprinkling the blood of bulls on the altar and on the people, but the blood of bulls could never take away sin (Heb. 10:11). Their blood only foreshadowed the blood of Christ that truly takes away sin and effects the new covenant (Matt. 26:28).

Conclusion

The particular kingdom of God is by faith participating already in the fullness of that kingdom's destiny, but she will not consummately experience that destiny until the Lord Jesus returns a second time to usher in the eschaton. She already participates in making the particular kingdom coextensive with the universal kingdom, but she must live in hope for its consummation. Likewise, she is already participating in the covenant of grace and in its historic expressions, including the blessings of the old covenant through her identity with Christ, who by his perfect obedience fulfilled the law for her. But she must live by faith and in hope that all Israel will be saved, and what will that be but life from the dead (Rom. 11:15)?

4

THE KINGDOM OF GOD IN THE NEW TESTAMENT

Matthew and Revelation

ROBERT W. YARBROUGH

The New Testament bristles with theological terms and phrases: salvation, righteousness, forgiveness, grace, wrath of God, love of God, and many more. Among these we find the all-important "kingdom of God." What makes this particular expression so central? Why are so many books and articles devoted to this subject? A recent bibliography listed more than 10,000 publications pertaining to research on the kingdom of God in the twentieth century alone.[1]

Why Care about "Kingdom"?

Most treatments of the kingdom of God in the New Testament start with the beginning of the New Testament era—say, with John the Baptist, or Judaism prior to and during Jesus' lifetime, or perhaps with Jesus or the Gospels. This is understandable and eminently defensible. But another angle is possible. A look at the book of Revelation affords an impressive entree to our subject. We see immediately that "the kingdom of God" is definitive in at least five ways.

1) The kingdom of God is definitive for who God is with respect to the ultimate order of all things. The last and climactic vision of God and

---

[1]See Lesław Daniel Chrupcała, *The Kingdom of God: A Bibliography of 20th Century Research* (Jerusalem: Franciscan Printing Press, 2007).

Christ ("the Lamb") in Scripture is kingdom-connected—a regal God with the Lamb sits in splendor at the place where kings preside: a throne.

> Then the angel showed me the river of the water of life, bright as crystal, flowing from *the throne of God and of the Lamb* through the middle of the street of the city; also, on either side of the river, the tree of life with its twelve kinds of fruit, yielding its fruit each month. The leaves of the tree were for the healing of the nations. No longer will there be anything accursed, but *the throne of God and of the Lamb* will be in it, and his servants will worship him. (Rev. 22:1–3)

This is clearly kingdom imagery. Since Christian teaching affirms the ontological priority of the future,[2] this vision of "what must take place" (see Rev. 4:1) is foundational for understanding Scripture and this world in the present age—whether in the New Testament era or today. Father and Son are shown in Revelation to mean (in addition to much else) "royal ruler" or "king." The final scene of Scripture, a scene consummative of our world and suggestive if not descriptive of the age to come, is a portrait of the identity of Father-Son (with Spirit implied) in majestic reign. All reality through all time and eternity is presented as standing under the aegis of God's "kingdom," his royal precedence in and over all conceivable domains.

2) The kingdom of God is definitive for who God's people are. Scripture's climactic apocalyptic vision describes believers as "a kingdom" (surely a subsidiary of "the" kingdom) ruled from the heavenly throne by Jesus Christ, "the ruler of kings on earth."

> John to the seven churches that are in Asia: Grace to you and peace from him who is and who was and who is to come, and from the seven spirits who are before his *throne*, and from Jesus Christ the faithful witness, the firstborn of the dead, and the *ruler of kings* on earth. To him who loves us and has freed us from our sins by his blood and made us a *kingdom*, priests to his God and Father, to him be glory and *dominion* forever and ever. Amen. (Rev. 1:4–6, kingdom language emphasized):

God's people have been appointed subjects of the divine reign. This consciousness was integral to apostolic perseverance: "I, John, your

---

[2]That is, from the standpoint of human understanding, the ultimate meaning of things in this age will only be fully known in the light of what God finally reveals them to be. See, e.g., Gen. 50:20; Mark 4:24; Acts 4:24–28. God can be trusted as Lord of the present because he has continually proven to be Lord of the future. See Isa. 45:20–21 (the gods of the nations cannot declare the future); 46:8–10 (only Yahweh sees the end from the beginning).

brother and partner in the tribulation and *the kingdom* and the patient endurance that are in Jesus" (Rev. 1:9). As Bruce Chilton has observed, in early Christian communities a view of the kingdom "provided motivation to persist, in the face of often trying circumstances."[3] John was conscious of the ultimately victorious status of the kingdom to which he was loyal, despite his banishment to Patmos at the time. And he could be just as confident of the demise of his (and his royal Lord's) opponents. In that light, because of kingdom considerations, Jesus' followers know like John that they are subjects under his sovereign protection and rule. They concur with John that "tribulation and the kingdom and the patient endurance that are in Jesus" form the nexus in which they live out their lives.

3) The kingdom of God is definitive for the doxological conviction of the church. The prophetic vision of Revelation 4—5 culminates in a vision of the heavenly throne (4:1–2) with the Lamb in proximity (5:6) lauded by the host of heaven because his sacrifice constituted sinners into a kingdom (vv. 9–10) who will one day share in God's reign. Both God and the Lamb are the object of eschatological praise.

> Then I looked, and I heard around *the throne* and the living creatures and the elders the voice of many angels, numbering myriads of myriads and thousands of thousands, saying with a loud voice, "Worthy is the Lamb who was slain, to receive *power* and wealth and wisdom and *might* and honor and glory and blessing!" And I heard every creature in heaven and on earth and under the earth and in the sea, and all that is in them, saying, "To him who sits on *the throne* and to the Lamb be blessing and honor and glory and *might* forever and ever!" And the four living creatures said, "Amen!" and the elders fell down and worshiped. (5:11–14)

This is praise that is rightly offered only to God because his reign alone is supreme:

> I, John, am the one who heard and saw these things. And when I heard and saw them, I fell down to worship at the feet of the angel who showed them to me, but he said to me, "You must not do that! I am a fellow servant with you and your brothers the prophets, and with those who keep the words of this book. Worship God." (22:8–9)

---

[3] Bruce Chilton, "Kingdom of God, Kingdom of Heaven," in *NIDB*, ed. Katharine Sakenfeld (Nashville: Abingdon, 2008), 3:513.

In view of God and the Lamb and their glorious kingdom, the church lives in readiness to praise its Lord and in conviction that as eternal King he, and he alone, is eminently worthy of that praise.

4) The kingdom of God is definitive for the martyrological readiness of the church. This means readiness to be God's *martys* (Gk. "witness") at all times and in all places and ways God calls for. In the midst of proleptic[4] proclamation of God's victory over the kingdoms of earth (11:15–19), vision is granted of the Devil's fall to earth. "Now" (12:10) is the hour of God's salvation through the Lamb's death and his emulation by his "testifiers" (witnesses) which guarantee that Satan's time is short (vv. 7–12), as he will eventually be demoted even more drastically (20:10). Jesus himself glimpsed and "witnessed" to this (Luke 10:17–18; John 12:31). "The kingdom of God" positions Jesus' followers to attest (witness) to the Lord and the excellence of his ways in all times and places whatever challenges and assaults this life may confront them with.

5) The kingdom of God is definitive for the fundamentally "tensive"[5] fabric of current existence under the rule of God's kingdom. The whole book of Revelation assumes that creation is presently subject to two conflicting realities, one that is not eternal and one that is.[6] Evil in its tyranny is real and destructive but fleeting. However robust its manifestation in past or current history, its days are numbered. God in his regal activity is inexorably bringing evil to an end.

Revelation's victorious regal depictions are given doctrinal basis in other Scripture passages that note, e.g., how God subjected the Son to death in order that he might be crowned with glory and honor (Heb. 2:6–9) in defeating death (vv. 14–15). Being "crowned" is coronation language—this is how the Son comes to occupy the throne of which Revelation speaks. Paul writes to similar effect—note the italicized regal language:

> Then comes the end, when he delivers *the kingdom to God* the Father after destroying every *rule and every authority and power*. For he must *reign* until he has *put all his enemies under his feet*. The last enemy to be

---

[4] That is, "anticipatory." There is much in Scripture that anticipates things that have not yet fully occurred, as when Jesus said, "I saw Satan fall like lightning from heaven" (Luke 10:18). This did happen, to an extent, as Jesus sent out his disciples and they preached, healed, and cast out demons. But Satan's ultimate demise lay in the future, as it still does at the present time.

[5] = under tension. Cf. R. T. France, "Kingdom of God," in *DTIB*, ed. Kevin Vanhoozer (London: SPCK, 2005), 422: "As long as God continues to allow his world to resist his rule, so long will there be tension and paradox built into the language of the 'kingdom of God.'"

[6] Paul concurs: see, e.g., Rom. 8:19–23, 35–39.

destroyed is death. For "God has *put all things in subjection under his feet*" [Ps. 8:6]. But when it says, "all things are *put in subjection*," it is plain that he is excepted who *put all things in subjection* under him. When *all things are subjected to him*, then the Son himself *will also be subjected to him who put all things in subjection under him*, that God may be all in all. (1 Cor. 15:24–28)

More will be said about Paul's view of the kingdom below. But we may already note that the tensive, "already/not yet" structure of this age as Christians experience it is a primary point of orientation and hope in the midst of the conflicted cosmos into which they have been thrust. Virtually no sphere of our lives or service is untouched by this overlap of two ages and kingdoms, one fading, the other gaining gradually in grandeur, however hidden: "the darkness is passing away and the true light is already shining" (1 John 2:8). "The night is far gone; the day is at hand" (Rom. 13:12). Christ himself lived and died fully engaged in this tension. Although he was a royal Son, he was willingly subject to the inexorable ravages of sin and death (without committing sin), even to the point that he "learned obedience through what he suffered" (Heb. 5:8). Yet he fulfilled his mission so that he might reign by the Spirit "already" in the current age, to the present and eternal benefit of believers (see also Rom. 8:1–4, 12–14).

The importance of "kingdom" in the New Testament is confirmed in Table 4.1, which tallies all New Testament references to that word.

Table 4.1

New Testament book or division	Number of occurrences of "kingdom" (ESV)
Gospels	124 in 116 verses
Matthew	54 in 52 verses
Mark	20 in 18 verses
Luke	45 in 43 verses
John	5 in 3 verses
Acts	8 in 8 verses
Paul (Romans—Philemon)	14 in 14 verses
General Epistles	4 in 4 verses
Revelation	7 in 6 verses
Entire New Testament	157 in 148 verses

Another, more focused look at the data is required, however. Table 4.2 tallies the times "kingdom of God" (and in Matthew "kingdom of heaven") appears.

Table 4.2

New Testament book or division	Number of occurrences of "kingdom of God" (ESV)
Gospels	53
Matthew	5 ("kingdom of heaven" 53 times)*
Mark	14
Luke	32
John	2
Acts	6
Paul (Romans—Philemon)	8
General Epistles	0
Revelation	0
Entire New Testament	67

*"Kingdom of heaven" occurs in no other New Testament book.

Between the high volume of references evident in Tables 4.1 and 4.2, and the strategic importance of "kingdom" evident from our glimpses of Revelation and elsewhere, it would be hard to deny that "the kingdom of God" is a central New Testament theme. "It is . . . at least one possible theme by which biblical theology can be integrated."[7] That is, we could conceivably array all of biblical theology along an axis entitled "kingdom of God." That is how frequent and central reference to it is in Scripture, as sections below will show in some detail.

Recent Scholarship

What the book of Revelation highlights—the centrality of God as king presiding over all reality at all times as his kingdom, with redemption unfolding through a people he has chosen, a people dignified and ennobled by regal benefits he delegates to them—numerous scholarly studies seek to probe and clarify. A glance at a range of recent publications will yield a feel for the current state of discussion.

Some of these studies seek to be comprehensive in scope. However

---

[7]Graeme Goldsworthy, "Kingdom of God," in *New Dictionary of Biblical Theology*, ed. T. Desmond Alexander and Brian Rosner (Leicester, England: Inter-Varsity, 2000), 620.

difficult, there is need to characterize the kingdom of God as a whole. Hence Gottfried Vanoni and Bernhard Heininger, for example, have collaborated to investigate the kingdom of God in Old Testament writings, in the world at the time of the New Testament, and in the writings of the New Testament itself.[8] What stands out most perhaps is the complexity of the kingdom concept and the diversity of its implications for both ancient and modern times, particularly for those who seek to take it seriously and align their existence with its movement. Arthur Glasser has canvassed not only the New Testament but the whole of Scripture to relate the kingdom of God to missiological concerns and priorities.[9] Not all studies of "kingdom of God" are comprehensive, of course; most subordinate kingdom considerations to broader topics, like Jesus himself and the hope that moved him,[10] or the place of contemporary readers in the story line of the Bible.[11]

How did the notion of "kingdom" used by Jesus and New Testament writers mesh (or not) with other uses of that term in antiquity? Margaret Barker contends that New Testament usage grows out of hidden tradition regarding the Most Holy Place and the high priesthood in Judaism.[12] This view has not found deep resonance with others working in the field. Mary Ann Beavis argues that "kingdom of God" takes its place among other utopian visions of the Roman world, though with many Jewish distinctives and a center found in Jesus, who did not call followers away from the world to form separatistic communes (like the Essenes) but modeled a vigorous engagement with the wider world.[13] Anne Dawson finds a key for understanding the kingdom of God in Mark's Gospel by focusing on passages that speak of *exousia*[14]—a word connoting "freedom" of one kind in Roman understanding, but of a very different kind, Dawson argues, for Jesus as Mark presents him.[15] Dawson's work is a reminder that "kingdom" issues may be present where the word itself is not.

Bruce Malina draws lines of connection between the kingdom of God in the Social Gospel movement of modern times, on the one hand, and the

---

[8]Gottfried Vanoni and Bernhard Heininger, *Das Reich Gottes* (Wurzburg: Echter, 2002).

[9]Arthur F. Glasser, *Announcing the Kingdom: The Story of God's Mission in the Bible* (Grand Rapids, MI: Baker, 2003). Cf. Gordon Fee, *Listening to the Spirit in the Text* (Grand Rapids, MI: Eerdmans, 2000), 165–80.

[10]See Jonathan Knight, *Jesus: An Historical and Theological Investigation* (New York: T&T Clark International, 2004).

[11]See D. A. Carson, *The God Who Is There: Finding Your Place in God's Story* (Grand Rapids, MI: Baker, 2010), chap. 5: "God Reigns."

[12]Margaret Barker, *The Hidden Tradition of the Kingdom of God* (London: SPCK, 2007).

[13]Mary Ann Beavis, *Jesus and Utopia: Looking for the Kingdom of God in the Roman World* (Minneapolis: Fortress, 2006).

[14]The word is found in Mark 1:22, 27; 2:10; 3:15; 6:7; 11:28, 29, 33, 34.

[15]Anne Dawson, *Freedom as Liberating Power: A Socio-political Reading of the Exousia Texts in the Gospel of Mark* (Fribourg: Universitaetsverlag; Goettingen: Vandenhoeck & Ruprecht, 2000).

Mediterranean world, on the other.[16] He thinks that political and kinship convictions fundamental to Mediterranean social life and consciousness are key to understanding Jesus' view of kingdom of God then and now. Jacob Neusner, however, finds the background to lie in "kindred systems" found in other cultural settings.[17] Robert Rowe finds a key in the Psalms more elemental than either social setting.[18] It is here that the foundation is laid for the two-tiered kingship idea found in the New Testament. There Jesus is "Messiah" ("king"), yet also Son of David, Son of Man, and Son of God. And even as "king" of sorts, Jesus points to a heavenly king and rule. This raises the question of the connection between Jesus and his earthly kingdom and the transcendent, ultimate reign of God. The message and ministry of Jesus in Mark grow out of this linkage, Rowe contends.

A theme of some scholarship is how "kingdom" in Jesus' understanding and preaching should lead his followers today to bring about universal peace and justice. For Andre Trocmé (1901–1971), a French pastor whose church rescued Jews from the Nazis, and Charles Moore this will be through revolutionary nonviolence.[19] Elliott Maloney draws on Latin American scholarship and Markan eschatology to furnish insights for current efforts to extend God's power and will into earthly domains.[20] John Crossan finds inspiration in Jesus' nonviolent resistance to the brutal machinations of Pilate and the Roman empire.[21] Bernard Scott turns to the parables to show how Jesus "reimagined" his world in kingdom terms and sought to mobilize his followers to do likewise.[22] The contrarian nature of kingdom convictions as Jesus announced and modeled them is the theme of Donald Kraybill's study,[23] which focuses on how out-of-step and counterintuitive many of Jesus' ways and teachings were in their day and time—and continue to be today. Paul Wadell makes a similar point in briefer compass.[24]

---

[16]Bruce Malina, *The Social Gospel of Jesus: The Kingdom of God in Mediterranean Perspective* (Minneapolis: Fortress, 2001).
[17]Jacob Neusner, "The Kingdom of Heaven in Kindred Systems, Judaic and Christian," *BBR* 15 (2005): 279–305.
[18]Robert Rowe, *God's Kingdom and God's Son: The Background to Mark's Christology from Concepts of Kingship in the Psalms* (Boston: Brill, 2002).
[19]Andre Trocmé and Charles Moore, *Jesus and the Nonviolent Revolution*, rev. ed. (Maryknoll, NY: Orbis, 2003).
[20]Elliott Maloney, *Jesus' Urgent Message for Today: The Kingdom of God in Mark's Gospel* (New York: Continuum, 2004).
[21]John D. Crossan, *God and Empire: Jesus against Rome, Then and Now* (San Francisco: Harper, 2007). On Jesus and government more broadly see, e.g., Johnny Awwad, "The Kingdom of God and the State: Jesus' Attitude to the Power and Governing Structures of His Day," *Near East School of Theology Theological Review* 22 (April 2001): 35–60. Awwad thinks Jesus critiqued the abuse of governmental power rather than that power itself.
[22]Bernard B. Scott, *Re-Imagine the World: An Introduction to the Parables of Jesus* (Santa Rosa, CA: Polebridge, 2001).
[23]Donald Kraybill, *The Upside-Down Kingdom*, 3rd ed. (Scottsdale, PA: Herald, 2003).
[24]Paul Wadell, "The Subversive Ethics of the Kingdom of God," *Bible Today* 41 (2003): 11–16.

Other studies relate the kingdom of God in the New Testament to the relation between Paul's doctrine of justification and Jesus' kingdom teaching,[25] to the church's self-understanding and mission,[26] to the convention and imagery of eating as depicted in numerous New Testament passages,[27] to the teaching of Paul,[28] to the cross of Christ and Jesus' prediction of the kingdom's imminent coming,[29] to the miracles in Matthew's Gospel (and their meaning for the Nigerian church today),[30] to the relation of "Spirit" and "kingdom" in Luke's writings and Paul,[31] to eschatology,[32] and to the view of God held by Jesus, Paul, and John.[33] "Kingdom of God" also looms large in the study of modern scholars (primarily though not exclusively of the New Testament) for whom the concept was central in their research and writing, like Albrecht Ritschl and Johannes Weiss (whose influence continues in, e.g., Rosemary Ruether and Stanley Hauerwas),[34] Albert Schweitzer,[35] Hans-Joachim Kraus,[36] and Rudolf Bultmann.[37]

This glance at contemporary publications confirms that "kingdom of God" in its New Testament usage is a focal point for discussion by scholars working in an almost dizzying array of fields. To distill all the nuances of

---

[25]Eberhard Jüngel, *Paulus und Jesus: Eine Untersuchung zur Präzisierung der Frage nach dem Ursprung der Christologie*, 7th ed. (Tübingen: Mohr Siebeck, 2004).

[26]John Fuellenbach, *Church: Community for the Kingdom* (Maryknoll, NY: Orbis, 2002). See also, e.g., Bertil Ekstrom, "The Kingdom of God and the Church Today," *Evangelical Review of Theology* 27 (October 2003): 292–305.

[27]Peter-Ben Smit, *Fellowship and Food in the Kingdom: Eschatological Meals and Scenes of Utopian Abundance in the New Testament* (Tübingen: Mohr Siebeck, 2008). From another angle see Gary Shogren, "Is the Kingdom of God about Eating and Drinking or Isn't It? (Romans 14:17)," *NovT* 42, (2000): 239–45.

[28]See Karl P. Donfried, *Paul, Thessalonica, and Early Christianity* (Grand Rapids, MI: Eerdmans, 2002), chap. 12.

[29]Michael F. Bird, "The Crucifixion of Jesus as the Fulfillment of Mark 9:1," *TJ* 24 (Spring 2003): 23–36. For a different reading of Mark 9:1, see Thomas R. Hatina, "Who Will See 'The Kingdom of God Coming with Power' in Mark 9,1—Protagonists or Antagonists?" *Bib* 86, no. 1 (2005): 20–34.

[30]Asahu-Ejere Kingsley, *The Kingdom of God and Healing-Exorcism (Mt 4:17–5:12)* (New York: Lang, 2003). On Matthew and kingdom more broadly see Andreas B. du Toit, "The Kingdom of God in the Gospel of Matthew," *Skrif en Kerk* 21, no. 33 (2000): 545–63. On exorcism see Craig Evans, "Inaugurating the Kingdom of God and Defeating the Kingdom of Satan," *BBR* 15, no. 1 (2005): 49–75. On the implications of Matthew's kingdom teaching for Ghana, see Opoku Oyinah, "Matthew Speaks to Ghanaian Healing Situations," *JPT* 10, no. 1 (2001): 120–43; for South Africa, see Nicholaas Vorster, "Transformation in South Africa and the Kingdom of God," *Hervormde Teologiese Studies* 62, no. 2 (2006): 731–53.

[31]Youngmo Cho, *Spirit and Kingdom in the Writings of Luke and Paul: An Attempt to Reconcile These Concepts* (Milton Keynes, UK: Paternoster, 2005). See also by the same author "Spirit and Kingdom in Luke–Acts: Proclamation as the Primary Role of the Spirit in Relation to the Kingdom of God in Luke–Acts," *Asian Journal of Pentecostal Studies* 6, no. 2 (2003): 173–97.

[32]David W. Baker, *Looking into the Future: Evangelical Studies in Eschatology* (Grand Rapids, MI: Baker, 2001), especially chapters by Bruce Waltke and Darrell Bock.

[33]Jean Zumstein, "Das Gottesbild bei Jesus, Paulus und Johannes," *TZ* 62, no. 2 (2006): 158–73.

[34]Annette Ahern, "Social Justice: Now, later or never? The contribution of Albrecht Ritschl and Johannes Weiss to social justice theology," *SR* 32, no. 3 (2003): 281–97.

[35]James Brabazon, *Albert Schweitzer: Essential Writings* (Maryknoll, NY: Orbis, 2005), 21–57.

[36]Bertold Klappert, "Reich Gottes—Reich der Freiheit: Hans-Joachim Kraus (1918–2000) und sein Weg zur Gesamtbiblischen Theologie," *TBei* 33, no. 4 (2002): 220–31.

[37]D. J. C. van Wyk, "Die probleem van hoe die Verkondiger die Verkondigde geword het: Die bydrae van Rudolf Bultmann (The problem of how the Proclaimer became the Proclaimed: The contribution of Rudolf Bultmann)," *HvTSt* 57/1–2 (2001): 649–75.

their proposals is impossible within the scope of these two book chapters. Strictly speaking, there can hardly be said to be a consensus on exactly how "kingdom of God" should be understood. R. T. France, however, has noted by way of summary that we are dealing with the "broad concept of God implementing his eternal sovereignty in the affairs of this world."[38] He recommends replacing "kingdom" with terms like "kingship" or "reign" to express "the basic biblical conviction that God is king" along with

> the central concern of Jesus that divine sovereignty . . . be fully imple-
> mented and acknowledged, not only by those who have chosen to "enter
> the kingship of God," but also by the wider world, which has yet to bow
> the knee.[39]

Ben Witherington III makes the case for "dominion" to replace the word "kingdom," since in the New Testament the Greek word translated "kingdom" sometimes "refers to a divine saving activity resulting in a reign, and sometimes to a realm where that reign takes place."[40] "Dominion" is broad enough to cover both senses. However one chooses to translate the term—and there are probably pros and cons with all the options—it makes sense now to turn to Scripture, and the history within which it took shape, to observe for ourselves some of the various facets of what language of the kingdom represents and demands.

Foundation of God's Kingdom: Old Testament Promises

Two previous chapters have thoroughly explored the kingdom of God in its Old Testament dimensions. The task here is merely to touch once more on the fact that New Testament outlooks and claims grow out of Old Testament passages believed to carry prophetic authority and to be informed by God-given foresight.[41]

From the standpoint of Old Testament writers, God's kingdom had been and always would be sovereign over all: "The LORD has established his throne in the heavens, and his kingdom rules over all" (Ps. 103:19). He "does according to his will among the host of heaven and among the inhabitants of the earth; and none can stay his hand or say to him, 'What have you done?'" (Dan. 4:35). He is not a local deity or the ruler of merely

[38]R. T. France, "Kingdom of God," in *DTIB*, 422.
[39]Ibid.
[40]Ben Witherington III, *The Indelible Image*, vol. 1: *The Individual Witnesses* (Downers Grove, IL: InterVarsity, 2009), 80.
[41]On Jesus' high regard for Scripture, and what that may mean for followers of Jesus, see John Wenham, *Christ and the Bible*, 3rd ed. (Eugene, OR: Wipf & Stock, 2009).

this or that tribe or people. While "kingdom" is of special interest to those who know and bow to the King, "kingdom" is relevant to every creature on the earth and every square inch of this world's domains.

God made known his kingly status, character, and reign through a people of his choosing. From this people came heavenly oracles (Rom. 3:2) written down not only for their sake but also for the sake of future generations (15:4). In these Scriptures we learn that the God of Abraham, Isaac, and Jacob established his ruling and saving presence particularly through the patriarchs (9:5), among whose descendants Judah was pictured in lion-like terms: "Judah is a lion's cub. . . . He stooped down; he crouched as a lion and as a lioness; who dares rouse him?" (Gen. 49:9). But one of his descendants would transcend by far the status of his forebear: "The scepter shall not depart from Judah, nor the ruler's staff from between his feet, until tribute comes to him; and to him shall be the obedience of the peoples" (49:10).

In the course of time, the Judean monarchy came to symbolize and particularize the kingdom of God in its earthly manifestation. The throne of David (from the tribe of Judah) was prophesied to foreshadow an eternal throne and reign, as God through Nathan spoke these words to David, with implications for his immediate son Solomon as well as for future descendants (2 Sam. 7:12–16):

> When your days are fulfilled and you lie down with your fathers, I will raise up your offspring after you, who shall come from your body, and I will establish his kingdom. He shall build a house for my name, and I will establish the throne of his kingdom forever. I will be to him a father, and he shall be to me a son. When he commits iniquity, I will discipline him with the rod of men, with the stripes of the sons of men, but my steadfast love will not depart from him, as I took it from Saul, whom I put away from before you. And your house and your kingdom shall be made sure forever before me. Your throne shall be established forever.

Thereafter other prophecies promised the restoration of David's throne when it languished (Amos 9:11–15) and a "great light" (Isa. 9:2) on whom all governance would rest. His names point to his splendor, as he would be called "Wonderful Counselor, Mighty God, Everlasting Father, Prince of Peace" (v. 6). Moreover, "of the increase of his government and of peace there will be no end, on the throne of David and over his kingdom, to establish it and to uphold it with justice and with righteousness" (v. 7). This would be effected by nothing short of the "zeal of the LORD of hosts" (v. 7). These and other prophecies form a nexus for understanding why in future centuries descendants of Abraham and David like Joseph of Arimathea were "looking for the kingdom of God" (Mark 15:43) when the New Testament era arrived.

In "the fullness of time" when God sent his Davidic Son (Gal. 4:4; Rom. 1:3), there seems to have been consensus that the present age, and God's present mode of administering it, were about to be done away with. A new age would arrive, and with it a modified and intensified manifestation of God's dominion. God is already Lord of all, and in that sense king, but his reign is presently obscured and the full exertion of his public dominance held in abeyance. Yet the day is coming when he will assert his kingship explicitly and universally. The "kingdom of God" will have arrived!

Different subgroups among the Jews held different conceptions of the kingdom. The Zealots sought to usher in divine intervention by military and political resistance against the Roman overlords. Some Jews were of apocalyptic persuasion and viewed the kingdom strictly as a future intervention of God that he would bring about in his own way and timing; humans could not force it as the Zealots appeared to suppose. The Essenes show evidence of acknowledging the futurity of God's kingdom, yet they also stressed its presence in the form of study and adherence to the Torah.[42] The Sadducees appear to have taken a dim view of any existence beyond the current one; they stressed the demands and prospects of life in the here and now.

In sum, there were variations on two broad options: an imminent, political-military manifestation of God's kingdom, perhaps through the restoration to power of the house of David; or an eschatological manifestation, in which the kingdom would be revealed in opposition to all that is merely political and historical. The eschatological outlook could draw especially on Danielic prophecy appealed to by Jesus himself (Dan. 7:13–15; see also Mark 14:62):

> I saw in the night visions, and behold, with the clouds of heaven there came one like a son of man, and he came to the Ancient of Days and was presented before him. And to him was given dominion and glory and a kingdom, that all peoples, nations, and languages should serve him; his dominion is an everlasting dominion, which shall not pass away, and his kingdom one that shall not be destroyed.

---

[42]Preceding lines of this paragraph draw on Hans Bayer, "Reich Gottes," *Evangelisches Lexikon für Theologie und Gemeinde*, ed. Helmut Burkhardt and Uwe Swarat (Wuppertal/Zürich: R. Brockhaus, 1994), 3:1676.

In both political and eschatological formulations, Jews in Jesus' time felt that the outcome of these matters would be favorable most of all with respect to the Jews.[43] Specifics were hazy and often contradictory, as is generally the case when mere humans seek to divine the future, even with the aid of biblical revelation. The Jewish writer Josephus does not even make explicit reference to "the kingdom of God," suggesting it was a notion that at least some Jews in some situations had decided they could live without. Yet it is fair to say that most scholars acknowledge the kingdom of God to have been an almost universally held (if variously construed) concept in the Jewish world of Jesus' time.

A long-standing discussion among scholars is whether the biblical words translated "kingdom" in English speak primarily of a territory or other geographical location. Or, is "kingdom" more apt to be about the dominion or reign of some royal figure? Recent lexicography suggests that in the Bible of the early church, the Septuagint, *basileia* (in the New Testament usually translated "kingdom") refers less frequently to "territory ruled by" someone. More commonly, *basileia* refers to:

- "dominion, reigning, supreme authority"
- "act or manner of ruling and controlling"
- "period of reign"
- "position of supreme rulership"[44]

This might suggest that to the extent that Jesus' view of the kingdom is informed by the Old Testament, he is less apt to be speaking about a geographically bordered region and more apt to be speaking about a "reign" or "supreme authority" that exists without any particular physical or political boundaries.

Craig Keener summarizes first-century Jewish conviction, as well as the outlook of Gospel writers growing out of Jewish (and Old Testament) conviction, like this:

> The Jewish people recognized that God ruled the universe in one sense now, but they prayed daily for the day when his kingdom, or rule, would be established over all peoples of the earth. Then, they believed, everyone would submit to God. Because the Gospels affirm that Jesus must

---

[43]See Otto Merk, "Reich Gottes," *Calwer Bibellexikon*, ed. Otto Betz, Beate Ego, and Werner Grimm (Stuttgart: Calwer Verlag, 2003), 2:1123–24.
[44]See Takamitsu Muraoka, *A Greek-English Lexicon of the Septuagint* (Louvain-Paris-Walpole, MA: Peeters, 2009), 114.

come twice, they recognize that the kingdom comes in two stages: God's future rule is established in the lives of those who obey him in the present, and over all the world when Jesus returns.[45]

It is now time to determine what we find in the New Testament writings themselves.

Jesus and the Kingdom: The First Gospel

It can be said at the outset that Jesus signified and conveyed a great deal regarding God's kingdom—which he often conflates with his own exercise of authority—in the Gospel of Matthew. Its canonical placement as a sort of bridge from the Old Testament to the New makes it all the more telling that Old Testament promises touched on above come to fruition precisely here. In fact, in our overview of the kingdom of God in this chapter and the next, we will devote more attention to this Gospel than to any other New Testament writing. This is justified because its kingdom pronouncements are so numerous and pregnant with meaning. Below we make nine major observations:

1) Regal Overtones Frame the Entire Gospel

Matthew opens with the words, "The book of the genealogy of Jesus Christ, the son of David, the son of Abraham" (Matt. 1:1). There are two explicit kingly reverberations here. First, Jesus is called son of David, in the train of Abraham's descendants. We have already seen in the previous section how the house and throne of David provide the framework for one who would come in fulfillment of prophetic promises. Second, Jesus is called "Christ." This means "messiah" or "king." The word *christos* (Christ) preserves a tie "to the ceremony of anointing a king . . . for office in recognition of God's approval (Ex. 28:41; 1 Sam. 9:15–16; 10:1; 16:3, 12–13; 1 Chron. 29:22)."[46] Matthew begins by giving the genealogy of "King Jesus." This title is repeated in 1:18: "Now the birth of Jesus Christ took place in this way." Divine agency and presence are immediately in force, because before Mary and Joseph had relations, "she was found to be with child from the Holy Spirit." In the typical Jewish outlook of the time there is only one God, and only one Spirit of God; in being named "king," Jesus is being identified as bearer of the one eternal God's dominion, his

---

[45]Craig Keener, *The IVP Bible Background Commentary: New Testament* (Downers Grove, IL: InterVarsity, 1993), 138.

[46]David Turner, *Matthew*, BECNT (Grand Rapids, MI: Baker Academic, 2008), 57.

kingdom. When the same Gospel reaches its end, it is fitting that Jesus' final commission to his disciples begins with the words, "All authority in heaven and on earth has been given to me" (28:18). Of course it has: he is Jesus the king, the one sent from God to usher in a definitive forward movement of his dominion over and in this world.

Here a surprising fact should be noted. While "Jesus Christ" is common in the New Testament, appearing 139 times, in addition to 88 occurrences of "Christ Jesus," *the term "Christ Jesus" never occurs in the four Gospels. "Jesus Christ" occurs only five times.* Two are in the Matthew passages just noted (1:1, 18). In addition, Mark opens his Gospel with the words, "The beginning of the gospel of Jesus Christ, the Son of God" (1:1). "Jesus Christ" is found twice in John's Gospel: (1) "For the law was given through Moses; grace and truth came through Jesus Christ" (1:17); (2) "And this is eternal life, that they know you the only true God, and Jesus Christ whom you have sent" (17:3). There are no other occurrences in the Gospels. The paucity of references to "King Jesus" confers special significance on passages where the rare term does occur, as it does twice in Matthew 1. Jesus is an explicitly regal, kingdom-ruling figure in Matthew from beginning to end.

2) "Kingdom" Is a Central Motif from the Start in the Preaching of Both John the Baptizer and Jesus

The first recorded words of John's preaching run, "Repent, for the kingdom of heaven is at hand" (Matt. 3:2).

It is commonly affirmed that "heaven" was used among Jews in biblical times as a means of hallowing the very name of God himself; a word other than "God" (like "heaven") was used to avoid cheapening the name of God by frequent or casual reference. "For this reason, no fixed difference . . . can be assumed" between the phrases "kingdom of God" and "kingdom of heaven."[47] This view, attributed to nineteenth-century German scholar Gustav Dalman, was refuted long ago.[48] In addition, recent scholarship pointedly challenges this, arguing that "kingdom of heaven" has a peculiar place and meaning in Matthew's Gospel. Namely, it highlights the tension

---

[47]Bruce Chilton, "Kingdom of God, Kingdom of Heaven," in *NIDB*, 3:513. Chrys Caragounis concurs and adds that Matthew's usage "has stylistic value" in *The Development of Greek and the New Testament* (Grand Rapids, MI: Baker Academic, 2006), 242 n. 34.

[48]See G. Gilbert, "Kingdom of God (or Heaven)," in *DCG*, ed. James Hastings (Edinburgh: T.&T. Clark, 1906), 1:933. Gilbert remarks, "It is impossible to suppose that the man who called God his Father, and who felt that God was always with Him, the man who brought God near to His disciples and convinced them that He numbered the hairs of their heads, that they could approach Him at any time without priest or outward sacrifice—that such a man shared the superstitious regard for the Holy Name."

that currently exists between heaven and earth, or God and humanity, while anticipating eschatological resolution of that tension.[49]

In either case, the overlap between the terms is substantial. While Jesus is rightly credited with highlighting the kingdom of God in his preaching, this kerygmatic pinpointing of "kingdom"—it is somehow "at hand" in John's proclamation of it—did not start with Jesus but with John, who himself fulfilled Old Testament prophecies by serving as forerunner for the Lord (3:3; cf. Isa. 40:3). The Lord God who will come "with might" to judge and rule, in Isaiah's formulation (Isa. 40:10), turns out to be Jesus for John, who highlights this by identifying him as the sin-bearer for the world (John 1:29). John was forerunner for the transcendent, invisible God's kingdom and his now present-in-history king.

"Kingdom" is where Jesus' preaching starts, as well. After John was arrested, and Jesus had shifted residence to Galilee from Nazareth (Matt. 4:12–13), he "began to preach, saying, 'Repent, for the kingdom of heaven is at hand'" (v. 17). God's kingdom is highlighted in Matthew by serving as the opening and prominent theme of both John's and Jesus' preaching.

The prominence of "kingdom" continues as Jesus' ministry gets underway: "And he went throughout all Galilee, teaching in their synagogues and proclaiming the gospel of the kingdom and healing every disease and every affliction among the people" (4:23). Here we see that there is a "gospel" associated with the kingdom. What is the relationship between "gospel" and "kingdom"? First, it is "good news," a "favorable announcement," which is the basic meaning of the original (euangelion). Jesus sounds this note repeatedly throughout his ministry. Some months after his public ministry began, Matthew records that "Jesus went throughout all the cities and villages, teaching in their synagogues and proclaiming the gospel of the kingdom and healing every disease and every affliction" (9:35). There is a dogged consistency here. And as Jesus' earthly course nears its end, he looks to the future and states that his gospel/kingdom message will be carried forth until the world as we know it comes to an end: "And this gospel of the kingdom will be proclaimed throughout the whole world as a testimony to all nations, and then the end will come" (24:14). He relates this epochal gospel good news not only to the nations and to the whole world but also to individuals: of the woman who anoints his feet for burial, Jesus notes, "Truly, I say to you, wherever this gospel is pro-

---

[49]See Jonathan Pennington, *Heaven and Earth in the Gospel of Matthew* (Grand Rapids, MI: Baker Academic, 2009). For helpful summation of Pennington's important work, see http://thegospelcoalition.org/blogs/justintaylor/2007/01/09/interview-with-jonathan-pennington/, accessed February 10, 2011.

claimed in the whole world, what she has done will also be told in memory of her" (26:13). In the context of Matthew, this can be no other "gospel," no greater good news, than that of the kingdom.

Second, it transmits kingdom tidings. It announces that the reign of the God of Abraham, Isaac, and Jacob, a reign never totally rejected among the Jews over the pre-Christian centuries but often obscured, is now present in a new way, to a new extent, and for a new purpose. Synagogue teaching is being updated and upgraded. Sick and sorrowing are being restored. Third, it is inextricably bound to Jesus the king, as Matthew has already established. Therefore it is not only the placement of "kingdom" language in Matthew (beginning and end) but also what it signifies that makes it such an important term.

3) Kingdom Affliction in the Present with Future Compensation
Defines the Addressees of the Matthean Beatitudes (Matt. 5:1–12)
An analysis of Jesus' message to his disciples may be depicted as follows in Table 4.3: "Blessed are . . .

Table 4.3

Identity Marker of a Disciple	Promised Benefit
the poor in spirit, because	theirs is **the kingdom of heaven.**
those who mourn, because	they *shall be comforted.*
the meek, because	they *shall inherit* the earth.
those who hunger and thirst for righteousness, because	they *shall be satisfied.*
the merciful, because	they *shall receive mercy.*
the pure in heart, because	they *shall see* God.
the peacemakers, because	they *shall be called* sons of God.
those who are persecuted for righteousness' sake, because	theirs is **the kingdom of heaven.**"

Additional explanation (5:11–12), with an eighth emphatic "Blessed are" follows the seventh beatitude, perhaps because Jesus' whole utterance was (and remains) so counterintuitive: "Blessed are you when others revile you and persecute you and utter all kinds of evil against you falsely on my account. Rejoice and be glad, for your reward is great in heaven, for so they persecuted the prophets who were before you." How can such maltreatment be regarded as blessing?

The answer lies in the constitution of God's reign, which Jesus here endorses at the beginning of his treasured pronouncement (5:3) and again at the end (v. 10; note bold type in chart above). In the Beatitudes Jesus affirms a future state of affairs (note the italicized future tense verbs in the chart above) that casts present trying circumstances in a different and favorable light. Theirs *is* the kingdom (present tense), because of what God *shall do* in the future to make their present discomfort and exposure to danger worthwhile, both now and then. There is both a present and a future dimension to the kingdom Jesus announces.

Jesus underscores this point later in interchange with detractors, to whom he states, "But if it is by the Spirit of God that I cast out demons, then the kingdom of God has come [*ephthasen*] upon you" (Matt. 12:28; cf. Luke 11:20). Last century C. H. Dodd argued that the aorist verb used here (see the italicized word in the quote) proved that Jesus viewed the kingdom as already fully present. Dodd called this "realized eschatology." There is no future fulfillment of "kingdom"; the royal eternal has already broken into time and changed the world forever. This seems to downplay the evil still rampant in our world, plus to ignore other statements of Jesus in which the kingdom is clearly future. Caragounis has shown decisively that on the contrary the aorist *ephthasen* is used here, first, to refer "to an event that is viewed as both certain and imminent."[50] Second, Caragounis points out that throughout the history of the Greek language, the aorist indicative has been used "in place of the future indicative to enhance vividness and animation in discourse, by describing actions that strictly belong to the future as though they had already transpired."[51] The kingdom is "at hand" in Jesus' ministry, but there is a future dimension that will affect all persons, to the good for his disciples (as in the Beatitudes), and unto woe for detractors and skeptics. As Caragounis concludes, "The force of the saying . . . is one of warning, almost a threat."[52]

4) Kingdom Disciples Are Appointed to Public Influence and Testimony

Immediately after assuring his disciples of future consolation despite being hammered in the present (Matt. 5:1–12), Jesus states a purpose in their blessed duress. First, they are "the salt of the earth" (v. 13). Just as Jesus brought a tang into personal relationships and social situations, so will his followers, due to their association with him. Second, Jesus terms

[50] *The Development of Greek and the New Testament*, 278. See also Chrys Caragounis, "Kingdom of God/Heaven," in *Dictionary of Jesus and the Gospels*, ed. Joel B. Green and Scot McKnight (Downers Grove, IL: InterVarsity, 1992), 420–24.
[51] Ibid., 277–78.
[52] Ibid., 278.

them "the light of the world" (v. 14). Following Jesus makes them beacons of the same heavenly life and message their master delivered to them. To this indicative Jesus adds an imperative: "Let your light shine before others, so that they may see your good works and give glory to your Father who is in heaven" (v. 16). There will be obvious temptation to bottle up the "blessedness" because as Jesus describes it, it so often brings disadvantage and discomfort with it. But disciples of "the kingdom of heaven" (vv. 3, 10) are called to honor their "Father who is in heaven." Kingdom priorities, specifically flavoring (salt) and lighting up the world, become central necessities and goals for Jesus' followers.

5) The Kingdom Is Central in the Sermon on the Mount

It is fair to say that the Sermon on the Mount in its entire sweep is suspended on a kingdom cord. Jesus' kingdom orientation does not diminish as he moves from the Beatitudes to subsequent divisions of this rightly hallowed discourse.

First, with respect to the all-important written Word of God, Jesus warns he has not come to abolish "the Law or the Prophets" (5:17), likely a term inclusive of what we know as the Old Testament. For us, by analogy, it would include the New. To any who might be tempted to attenuate the written revelation of the God of Israel, Jesus admonishes regarding that person's loss or gain in terms of status as judged by kingdom standards: "Therefore whoever relaxes one of the least of these commandments and teaches others to do the same will be called least in the kingdom of heaven, but whoever does them and teaches them will be called great in the kingdom of heaven" (v. 19).

Jesus then pushes a step further. It is well known that he accused the Scripture experts of his time of setting aside God's Word in favor of their own traditions that obscured or distorted it (see, e.g., 15:1–9). He warns his disciples against this drift: "For I tell you, unless your righteousness exceeds that of the scribes and Pharisees, you will never enter the kingdom of heaven" (5:20). Those who assume Moses' seat of authority in that society (see 23:2) may tamper with God's Word, but his disciples dare not. For to do so would bar them from kingdom entrance, the very thing their master is announcing and inviting them to accept.

Second, Jesus' kingdom orientation continues with the prayer he teaches his disciples. Following respectful address of "our Father in heaven" and the request that his name be hallowed, a petition fundamental to that request is set forth: "Your kingdom come, your will be done, on earth as it is in heaven" (6:10; cf. Luke 11:2). Foundational to the Lord's Prayer and by implication all Christian prayer is recognition of God's reign, the yearning to see it come to pass, and an understanding of his reign as God's very will being done on this earth precisely as we know it is in his transcendent dwelling place. For the disciple who has learned to pray from Jesus, kingdom consciousness is integral to prayerful effectiveness.

Third, kingdom is central in the Sermon on the Mount in terms of priority. Life for sinners on this earth (which is to say: all of us) is full of woe and uncertainty. It is easy to be anxious and fearful. Jesus calls for perspective here. He refers to the animal world as well as to plants and how in general God sustains them (Matt. 6:26–28). Humans are much more valuable than them all (v. 26). Instead of endorsing the phobias of people at large, when in fact our "heavenly Father knows that you need" all these things (v. 32), Jesus gives kingdom counsel: "But seek first the kingdom of God and his righteousness, and all these things will be added to you" (v. 33). Here is a foundation for liberation from the tyranny of worry over what God alone controls. Here also one notes a correlation between "kingdom" and "righteousness," a link that will become important when we take up Paul.

Fourth, the kingdom is central at the climax of the Sermon on the Mount. In the closing section as Matthew records it, Jesus describes the elusiveness of entering the kingdom, first in Matthew 7:13–14 ("Enter by the narrow gate"), where "kingdom" is not explicitly mentioned, and then in 7:21–27, where it is (v. 21: "Not everyone who says to me, 'Lord, Lord,' will enter the kingdom of heaven, but the one who does the will of my Father who is in heaven"). This is "kingdom" with an edge. Many claim kingdom affiliation, but only those who comply with its conditions actually possess it (v. 21). Jesus urges hearing his words and doing them to avoid calamity at the end (vv. 21, 24). That is the message of the well-known children's song about "the wise man who built his house upon the rock," or in the foolish man's case "upon the sand." Children understandably think of the rain, the wind, and the respective houses standing firm or collapsing with a resounding crash (often signified by their clapping and shouting). In the larger context, however, this is a song not about storms and construction technique but about the kingdom and entering it . . . or not. The urgency of Jesus' words is underscored by his assertion that "the gate is wide and the way is easy that leads to destruction, and those who enter by it are many" (v. 13). Kingdom entrance is not the human norm: rather, kingdom evasion is. Conversely, "the gate is narrow and the way is hard that leads to life, and those who find it are few" (v. 14). Jesus could hardly be clearer that it behooves listeners to give utmost attention to the kingdom of God, its implications, and the conditions under which its door swings open to earnest seekers.

The kingdom emphasis throughout the Sermon on the Mount helps account for the astonishment the discourse created (7:28–29). Jesus projected "authority," the prerogative of a ruler. And he cast the entirety of human existence under the jurisdiction and eschatological verdict of himself as the gatekeeper of his domain. Unless he recognizes a person "on that day" (v. 22), they will suffer eternal kingdom exclusion.

6) Jesus' Parables Frequently Relate Directly to "Kingdom"

Under his leadership and instruction in parabolic form, Jesus' followers were equipped from the start to pursue kingdom existence, which is to say life under his lordship. Following are gleanings from a dozen kingdom-connected parables as presented in Matthew's Gospel. The first eight of them are grouped in chapter 13.

a. The parable of the sower (Matt. 13:1–23). "Kingdom" is at the center of this well-known story (13:1–9), interchange with the disciples (vv. 10–17), and dominical[53] interpretation (vv. 18–23). In discussion with his disciples, Jesus asserts that recognition of kingdom realities is a divine gift: "To you it has been given to know the secrets of the kingdom of heaven, but to them it has not been given" (v. 11). Like recognition of Jesus' messiahship (16:16–17) and other aspects of Jesus' message (11:25), divine initiative necessarily stands behind human appropriation of kingdom tidings.

In the same parable discourse, Jesus terms his saving message "the word of the kingdom" (13:19). Whether it is snatched away by the evil one, falls on rocky ground or among thorns, or meets fruitful reception, at issue is the kingdom and hearers' relationship to it.

b. The parable of the weeds (Matt. 13:24–30, 36–43). Here "kingdom" is portrayed as the whole world. The gospel message goes forth everywhere. The "sons of the kingdom" (13:38) accept it. Around them however are the weeds, "the sons of the evil one" (v. 38). At the end evildoers and the righteous alike will receive their reward: "The Son of Man will send his angels, and they will gather out of his kingdom all causes of sin and all law-breakers, and throw them into the fiery furnace" (vv. 41–42). In

---

[53]In this chapter "dominical" means "of or pertaining to Jesus." His title "Lord" is *dominus* in Latin.

contrast to the weeds, the good seed are "the righteous" who "will shine like the sun in the kingdom of their Father" (v. 43). When Jesus concludes with "He who has ears, let him hear" (v. 43), it is the kingdom message he has in mind.

c. *The parable of the mustard seed (Matt. 13:31–32).* Jesus draws an analogy between a tiny garden seed and "the kingdom of heaven." Like the towering mustard plant in a garden of smaller herbs, that kingdom will assume gigantic proportions despite small beginnings. This parable is recounted in Luke's Gospel too (Luke 13:18–19), except that in Luke Jesus speaks of "the kingdom of God."

d. *The parable of the leaven.* Jesus said, "The kingdom of heaven is like leaven that a woman took and hid in three measures of flour, till it was all leavened" (Matt. 13:33). The kingdom's progress may be gradual and imperceptible, but in the end it has its intended comprehensive effect. Following this parable, Matthew observes that Jesus' parabolic style of communication was a fulfillment of Old Testament prophecy (v. 35). Jesus' kingdom disclosure is not clever innovation on his part but a strategy foreordained by God long before the incarnation took place. Luke records this parable in similar words, though again Jesus says "kingdom of God" instead of the Matthean "kingdom of heaven" (Luke 13:20).

e. *The parable of the hidden treasure.* Jesus states, "The kingdom of heaven is like treasure hidden in a field, which a man found and covered up. Then in his joy he goes and sells all that he has and buys that field" (Matt. 13:44). This kingdom, its benefits, or both are worth everything that one might glimpse and risk one's entire livelihood to procure. Jesus makes this same point in a different parable that follows immediately.

f. *The parable of the pearl.* Instead of a nondescript man and real estate, Jesus now speaks of a merchant and pearls. "Again, the kingdom of heaven is like a merchant in search of fine pearls, who, on finding one pearl of great value, went and sold all that he had and bought it" (13:45–46). In this parable as in others, Jesus interprets his ministry in terms of "kingdom" and implies that nothing of greater value is conceivable in this life.

g. *The parable of the net (Matt. 13:47–50).* The kingdom is like a net tossed into the sea. When hauled in, a net may pulsate with all kinds of fish. Jesus' point relates to eschatology: as men sort netted fish, culling out the worthless ones, so at the end of the age "the angels will come out and separate the evil from the righteous and throw them into the fiery furnace. In that place there will be weeping and gnashing of teeth" (13:49–50).

h. The parable of the household manager. As Matthew recounts the lengthy line of discourse found in Matthew 13, Jesus now takes a break from the relentless progression from parable to parable. He inquires of his hearers, "Have you understood all these things?" (13:51). Would they know if they had not? They gamely answer in the affirmative. Jesus is evidently pleased, for he seems to praise his hearers by likening them to a scribe ready for kingdom realities: "Therefore every scribe who has been trained for the kingdom of heaven is like a master of a house, who brings out of his treasure what is new and what is old" (v. 52). Discipleship consists of many things and might be depicted with many metaphors, but here Jesus associates it with kingdom readiness in the form of remembrance of the past ("what is old") and simultaneously access to "what is new." Kingdom living can be content with neither reactionary conservatism alone nor breathless fixation with the present and future alone. The wisdom Jesus promulgates calls for integration of the two. "Kingdom" involvement requires shrewdness, discernment, creativity, and daring.

i. The parable of the unforgiving servant (Matt. 18:23–35). In the wake of Jesus' teaching on forgiving those who sin against us, Peter pressed the issue by trying to put some finite limit on the number of forgiving acts that might be expected. Jesus sets before him a kingdom principle in the form of this parable. The story has a grim ending, as the servant who was forgiven so much chokes a fellow slave who owed him much less, resulting in his return to his master. The master consigns him to jail to pay off the debt formerly forgiven him. Jesus' application of this parable may have struck Peter as grimmer still: "So also my heavenly Father will do to every one of you, if you do not forgive your brother from your heart" (18:35). Here an ethical imperative is connected to "kingdom," namely, the ethic of forgiveness of others as God has forgiven those to whom he grants kingdom entrance and membership.

j. The parable of laborers in the vineyard (Matt. 20:1–16). In this celebrated parable, an employer hires day laborers at various times, then pays each a full day's wage at the end. How is the "kingdom of heaven" (20:1) like the actions of this master? In the kingdom, God does what he chooses with what belongs to him (see v. 15). Here kingdom benefit amounts to grace writ large. God defines the metrics of compensation, not human expectation or convention. Moreover, "the last will be first, and the first last" (v. 16). Kingdom ethics as God models them (cf. 5:48) often invert what humans might implement or approve. It would be a mistake to begrudge God's generosity (20:15) based on human convention.

k. The parable of the two sons (Matt. 21:28–32). To the chief priests' and elders' questioning of Jesus' authority, Jesus replied in terms of John's baptism (21:23–27). Notwithstanding their cultivated appearance of support for God's kingdom as John announced it, in reality they said no to him. Meanwhile, society's "sinners," whose lives were a default "no" to God, repented. Jesus' response to his interlocutors is scathing:

> Truly, I say to you, the tax collectors and the prostitutes go into the kingdom of God before you. For John came to you in the way of righteousness, and you did not believe him, but the tax collectors and the prostitutes believed him. And even when you saw it, you did not afterward change your minds and believe him. (vv. 31–32)

Kingdom entrance and blessing call for willingness to rethink, to be called in question, to be humbled to repentance, and even to undergo inner rebirth (as Nicodemus in John 3 learned). It also calls for believing or faith, a fact that only gains in clarity as one moves from the Gospels to Acts and the Epistles.

l. The parable of the wicked tenants (Matt. 21:33–45). This parable with its vineyard motif calls attention to the Jewish hierarchy who opposed Jesus, as the last verse of the pericope makes clear: "When the chief priests and the Pharisees heard his parables, they perceived that he was speaking about them" (21:45). The story line is familiar. The master of the estate planted a vineyard, leased it to tenants, and went to another country. When he sent servants to collect payment, the tenants repeatedly abused them. They even killed the master's own son (v. 39).

What will the master do?, Jesus asks his listeners. They rightly respond, "He will put those wretches to a miserable death and let out the vineyard to other tenants who will give him the fruits in their seasons" (v. 41).

With this, Jesus' listeners have condemned themselves. Jesus underscores this by referring to the kingdom: "Therefore I tell you, the kingdom of God will be taken away from you and given to a people producing its fruits" (v. 43). Jesus makes his judgment based on Psalm 118:22–23, which he chides his listeners for not heeding (v. 42). In terms of the kingdom of God, we may infer from this parable the centrality of the Son as affirmed in Old Testament prophecy as the norm for kingdom inclusion. Further, fruitfulness is a criterion by which God confers (or withdraws) kingdom blessing. Specifically, at this particular juncture in the history of God's dealing with his people, Jesus telegraphs the divine intent to shift the locus of the kingdom from those who had long enjoyed it in an almost exclusive way "to a people producing its fruits." This surely makes reference to the more multiethnic collage of subgroups that came to make up the church within a few decades of its initial rise in the Jerusalem-Judea-Galilee region.

m. *Other kingdom parables.* Jesus illustrates the kingdom with three other parables set in the closing days of his earthly ministry. In the parable of the wedding feast (22:1–14) he warns against failing to heed God's invitation to enter his kingdom. Those who spurned the invitation met a bitter end (v. 7). In a sort of addendum (vv. 11–14) he extends the story to warn against phony presence in the kingdom—symbolized by "a man who had no wedding garment" (v. 11). He is summarily cast out. Those affecting to have entered the kingdom had better be appropriately arrayed—New Testament epistles speak of "putting on Christ" (Rom. 13:14; Gal. 3:27) and spiritual armor (Rom. 13:12; Eph. 6:11; 1 Thess. 5:8) and qualities like love (Col. 3:12, 14) and the new self (Eph. 4:24; Col. 3:10). They dare not enter as merely gawking, freeloading spectators.

The parable of the ten virgins (Matt. 25:1–13) illustrates multiple ways of failure to respond adequately to the kingdom's presence. The five indolent virgins exhibit ditzy traits like sloth, presumptuousness toward others who were not slothful ("Give us some of your oil" [v. 8]), and even presumptuousness toward the master, who however is not bound to cover up their negligence: "The other virgins came also, saying, 'Lord, lord, open to us.' But he answered, 'Truly, I say to you, I do not know you'" (vv. 11–12). Jesus himself furnishes the major lesson of this parable: "Watch therefore, for you know neither the day nor the hour" (v. 13). As fateful as present implications of the kingdom may be, there remains an outstanding future aspect that is perilous to overlook.

Jesus underscores this lesson with the parable of the talents (25:14–30). It becomes clear that Jesus' notion of eschatological readiness is not, say, a minutely detailed projection of specific future events. It is rather making full use of what one has been given. For there will be a final day of reckoning, illustrated parabolically by the master's declaration that "to everyone who has will more be given, and he will have an abundance. But from the one who has not, even what he has will be taken away" (v. 29).

So much for the parables in Matthew. Jesus' parables are one of the most celebrated and familiar components of the New Testament record. "The parables of the kingdom have been regarded as the most authentic element in Jesus' teaching."[54] This makes it all the more significant that so many of them are calculated to promote, clarify, or otherwise publicize "the kingdom of God/heaven."

*7) "Kingdom" Epitomizes the Gravity and the Promise of
Jesus' Ministry and Saving Message in Matthew*

Turning now from parable back to narrative, the first Gospel's final two mentions of "kingdom" draw attention to its eschatological aspect. In Jesus' depiction of the final judgment (Matt. 25:31–46), where the sheep are separated from the goats, the sheep receive this welcome pronouncement: "Then the King will say to those on his right, 'Come, you who are blessed by my Father, inherit the kingdom prepared for you from the foundation of the world'" (v. 34). This parable, of course, highlights ethical kingdom credentials like caring for the hungry, thirsty, lonely, desolate, and sick. Those who failed on such counts hear a crushing verdict at the end: "Then he will answer them, saying, 'Truly, I say to you, as you did not do it to one of the least of these, you did not do it to me.' And these will go away into eternal punishment, but the righteous into eternal life" (vv. 45–46).

Just a few days after this, Jesus makes his final kingdom declaration in Matthew's Gospel. As he and his disciples finish up what came to be known as the Last Supper, a cup of wine marks the end of the meal. Jesus has already immortalized the normally routine festal act of filling the cup by stating, "Drink of it, all of you, for this is my blood of the covenant, which is poured out for many for the forgiveness of sins" (Matt. 26:27–28). But now, after three years of teaching them about kingdom, he wraps it all together by declaring, "I tell you I will not drink again of this fruit of the vine until that day when I drink it new with you in my Father's kingdom" (v. 29). Luke records similar words on this occasion: "I tell you that from now on I will not drink of the fruit of the vine until the kingdom of God comes" (Luke 22:18). But in Luke's account Jesus utters analogous words with respect to the bread he broke and shared: "I will not eat it until it is fulfilled in the kingdom of God" (v. 16).

The kingdom of God is as much a central motif at the Last Supper as it is in the Beatitudes or the Lord's Prayer. Jesus' kingdom orientation and focus remain consistent as he approaches the direst straits of his life. His disciples would have remembered that occasion not only for its atone-

---

[54]Chrys Caragounis, "Kingdom of God/Heaven," 424.

ment imagery (stressed in many churches today) but also for its kingdom associations (largely absent, it seems, from contemporary consciousness when the Lord's Supper is commemorated).

8) Kingdom Ethics May Controvert Conventional Wisdom

Jesus' disciples, hearing him speak so frequently on God's kingdom, no doubt wondered how they measured up to that kingdom's demands. Accordingly, one day they asked him, "Who is the greatest in the kingdom of heaven?" (Matt. 18:1). In reply Jesus stressed, first, that true entrance is key. This involves a "turn" (repentance), followed by the ready trust (in Jesus and what he brings) that children properly exhibit toward authority figures like parents. Jesus goes beyond mere information dissemination here to issue an ultimatum: "Truly, I say to you, unless you turn and become like children, you will never enter the kingdom of heaven" (v. 3; cf. Luke 18:17). And to the disciples' question about greatness, Jesus' answer was no doubt as unexpected in that social setting as it would be in most: "Whoever humbles himself like this child is the greatest in the kingdom of heaven" (Matt. 18:4). Jesus reiterates this later as people bring children to him for blessing and the disciples rebuke them (19:13). Jesus is of another mind: "Let the little children come to me and do not hinder them, for to such belongs the kingdom of heaven" (v. 14; so also Luke 18:16).

If Jesus' promotion of childlikeness to a criterion of greatness in the kingdom seems counterintuitive, so does his insistence on self-sacrificial service. When the mother of the sons of Zebedee asks for preferential treatment for her sons in Jesus' kingdom (Matt. 20:20–21), he prescribes not privileged power but servanthood: "Whoever would be great among you must be your servant, and whoever would be first among you must be your slave" (vv. 26–27). This is not an armchair dictate; rather, Jesus himself serves as the model, as he adds, "Even as the Son of Man came not to be served but to serve, and to give his life as a ransom for many" (v. 28). Participation in the kingdom of God calls for humility in the form of hard work in serving others. Jesus knows that this cuts against the grain of public perception of what political oversight typically entails: "You know that the rulers of the Gentiles lord it over them, and their great ones exercise authority over them" (v. 25). The kingdom Jesus ushers in exalts contrasting priorities in calling for self-denigrating, altruistic lives.

9) Kingdom in Matthew: Final Observations.

The numerous relevant passages and lessons found in Matthew defy facile summation. Jesus' ministry was not one-dimensional. It was not simplistic in its demands. Even his kingdom teaching is not monolithic but variegated. We can however observe that the kingdom of God (most frequently "the kingdom of heaven" in Matthew) may be past, present, future, or a combination of all three. Ethics are frequently on Jesus' mind in his parabolic discourse. Even futuristic parables call for behavior change in the present; one scholar speaks here of "eschatological inversion," with things to come turning common notions of behavior upside down.[55] Most kingdom parables in Matthew call for diligence in discipleship, which is to say, in following Jesus. This places a premium on personal relationship with him; kingdom ethics are relational, not an abstract, moralistic code of conduct. From the beginning of Matthew's Gospel to its end, urgency attends Jesus' kingdom references, because the reward for kingdom entrance is heavenly, and the penalty for kingdom negligence is calamitous.

At stake in "the kingdom of God" in Matthean definition is not some literary or conceptual "center" of early church teaching. It is rather the short- and long-term destiny of every individual soul and indeed of the entire world with Jesus, or personal faith commitment to him, as decisive criterion, and with Jesus also the ultimate judge.

Conclusion

The kingdom of God is enigmatic in nature, and yet we have seen that in spite of this mystery it still communicates something about the way things are meant to be. It points us to who God is as Ruler over his realm, who his people are as participants in his kingdom, who his church should be in giving praise to their King, what the readiness of the church should be as she witnesses for him, and how the already/not yet tension should cause us to anticipate his coming in a world still marred by sin. This kingdom is an all-encompassing force, meant to point God's people to their ultimate King. In short, the kingdom of God tells us where true life is to be found—and requires a response.

The book of Matthew enhances the weightiness of this kingdom message, showing us how Jesus himself focused on the kingdom of God through his numerous proclamations about it. These proclamations serve not only as a bridge connecting Old Testament promises to their fulfill-

---

[55]Craig Keener, *The Historical Jesus of the Gospels* (Grand Rapids, MI: Eerdmans, 2009), 208–12.

ment in Jesus, but they also emphasize what was most important to Jesus, the Ruler of this kingdom: making disciples, a people who would follow him no matter what the cost. The Matthean narrative, then, faithfully and compellingly presents the redemptive, albeit anti-cultural, message of Jesus, thus paving the way for subsequent "kingdom" discussions in the New Testament, to be explored in the following chapter.

5

THE KINGDOM OF GOD IN THE NEW TESTAMENT

Mark through the Epistles

ROBERT W. YARBROUGH

The kingdom of God, present throughout Scripture in past, present, and future form, is a complex reality grappled with throughout biblical history. Whether symbolized through the earthly manifestation of the Davidic rule in the Old Testament or the hoped-for upheaval of the Roman Empire in the New Testament, some form of belief in the kingdom of God was continually present among Jewish culture. Everyone believed that there would be a day when the old order would pass away and a new order would arrive. And arrive, indeed, it did in the person of Jesus, though not in the way people had envisioned.

Taking the lead from Matthew, the following New Testament books directly or indirectly build off the gospel reality that Jesus is King—a King who demands all or nothing, a King who will be victorious in the end. As subjects of his rule and reign, God's people have the privilege of participating in his coming kingdom in the here and now.

Jesus and the Kingdom of God in Mark

Mark's Gospel does not refer to the kingdom of God as frequently as Matthew's. But the term is still a fixture of both narrative and discourse from beginning to end. The reference to Jesus as "Christ" in Mark 1:1 starts the Gospel off on a note of recognition that he holds the status of "messiah" or "king." The good news of Mark is the good news of the arrival of God's co-regent, Jesus the Christ.

The Centrality of the Kingdom

Explicitly, this Gospel's references to the kingdom of God are as follows. The kingdom involves God's superintendence over history—"the time is fulfilled"—and the necessity of human response: "repent and believe in the gospel" (Mark 1:15). These are Jesus' words as his public ministry begins, just after his temptation and John the Baptizer's arrest. Jesus' words also constitute "the gospel of God" (v. 14). Kingdom news is at least provisionally "good news." Yet the need to repent is a reminder that the promise of benefit is conditional and contains within it a threat should the promise be spurned. Jesus' preaching, like that of his prophet predecessors, demanded a verdict. Hearers and indeed the world's inhabitants generally were confronted with claims that demanded decision. A sense of the kingdom's "intrusive imminence compels an immediate response."[1]

"Kingdom" comes into view in the dispute over Jesus' exorcism activity, which drew accusations that he was colluding with demons. Jesus takes up kingdom imagery in pointing out that a kingdom divided against itself cannot stand (Mark 3:24). The implication is that while his detractors are out of step with God's kingdom purposes, to the extreme extent that they flirt with blaspheming the Holy Spirit and eternally forfeiting forgiveness (v. 29), Jesus is subject and responsive to that kingdom. He thus calls on all to do "the will of God" so as to enter into a discipleship connection with him (v. 35).

There is a cognitive dimension to kingdom. Jesus tells parables that tend to mystify audiences at large. He says nothing explicit about "kingdom" on one particular such occasion (Mark 4:1–9), but in his explanation alone with his disciples he makes it clear that kingdom was at the forefront of his meaning: "And he said to them, 'To you has been given the secret of the kingdom of God, but for those outside everything is in parables'" (v. 11). Kingdom discernment is a gift from God, evidently. Also evident is that the spread and growth of the kingdom, in Jesus' view, are intertwined with the sharing of "the word" (v. 14). This is presumably the word that he has been proclaiming about God's kingdom and the imperative to respond to it. He goes on immediately to show how the growth of that word is a function of the kingdom: "And he said, 'The kingdom of

---

[1]Craig Keener, *The Historical Jesus of the Gospels* (Grand Rapids, MI: Eerdmans, 2009), 198.

God is as if a man should scatter seed on the ground'" (v. 26). The seed sprouts and grows, and the farmer just watches. Then comes the time of harvest. The farmer is not in control; he simply responds to the growth of the crop he sowed. In this same context Jesus likens the kingdom of God to "a grain of mustard seed" (vv. 30–31). What seems infinitesimal in size grows to be dominant and to serve important purposes.

Mark makes it clear that Jesus' preferred didactic method, at least in this phase of his ministry and on reported occasions, was to announce the kingdom by the oblique means of parable: "With many such parables he spoke the word to them, as they were able to hear it. He did not speak to them without a parable, but privately to his own disciples he explained everything" (vv. 33–34). There is both a hidden and a revelatory dimension to the kingdom of God.

"Kingdom of God" continues to flicker across Mark's narrative screen as his Gospel account unfolds. The imminent arrival of the kingdom, or at least a fresh infusion of its vigor, is announced just prior to the transfiguration: "And he said to them, 'Truly, I say to you, there are some standing here who will not taste death until they see the kingdom of God after it has come with power'" (Mark 9:1). Is this kingdom arrival the appearance of Elijah with Moses and Jesus' heavenly radiance bestowed by the Father at the transfiguration? Is Jesus speaking proleptically of the Son of Man's suffering and ultimate vindication (vv. 9–13)? Is it a look ahead to his resurrection and his realized mission in the church in decades to come? In any case, "the kingdom of God" is central in Jesus' consciousness and pedagogy.

The kingdom's centrality for Jesus in Mark is confirmed, additionally, in connection with apocalyptic warning: "And if your eye causes you to sin, tear it out. It is better for you to enter the kingdom of God with one eye than with two eyes to be thrown into hell" (9:47). Whereas some passages treat kingdom as imminent or even present, here it is plainly future. When Jesus' disciples try to ward off troublesome parents with their children, Jesus rebukes them for kingdom reasons: "Let the children come to me; do not hinder them, for to such belongs the kingdom of God. Truly, I say to you, whoever does not receive the kingdom of God like a child shall not enter it" (Mark 10:14–15). Here kingdom has both present and future dimensions: it already "belongs" to those who receive it like children in some sense, yet it "shall not" be entered at some point in the future by those who hinder children from drawing near to Jesus.

Mark's Gospel draws a close analogy between "eternal life" and "kingdom of God" (this is significant for understanding John's Gospel) with its account of the rich young man who asks, "Good Teacher, what must I do to inherit eternal life?" (Mark 10:17). After this man retreats sorrowfully, Jesus comments to his disciples, furnishing the densest collection of kingdom references in this entire Gospel:

> And Jesus looked around and said to his disciples, "How difficult it will be for those who have wealth to enter *the kingdom of God*!" And the disciples were amazed at his words. But Jesus said to them again, "Children, how difficult it is to enter *the kingdom of God*! It is easier for a camel to go through the eye of a needle[2] than for a rich person to enter *the kingdom of God*." (vv. 23–25)

In rapid succession several truths about the kingdom are affirmed. The first italicized phrase speaks of kingdom in its future dimension. The second seems to shift focus more to the present. The third, like the first, underscores the ethical dimension of kingdom entrance—turning away from earthbound focus in renunciation of sin and opening up to God in pursuit of his righteousness is required. The rich young man's kingdom interest, yet kingdom refusal, offers a telling portrait of how Mark's Gospel understands "kingdom of God" in an individual application with implications for all would-be Jesus followers.

More "Kingdom" References

Four more references to "kingdom of God" are found in Mark:

1) When the throng cries out on what we know as Palm Sunday, "Blessed is the coming kingdom of our father David! Hosanna in the highest!" (11:10), popular faith in God's kingdom is in view.[3] David's kingdom is a proleptic manifestation of the divine reign that the Davidic dynasty dimly foreshadowed.

2) God's kingdom in its personal implications comes into view when an erstwhile scribe answers wisely in a memorable exchange with Jesus over the great(est) commandment. Jesus honors him, and silences onlook-

---

[2]On the explanation for this expression, see Keener, *The Historical Jesus of the Gospels*, 207. He notes that "an elephant passing through a needle's eye" was a figure used by Jewish teachers in Babylonia where the elephant was the largest land animal. The expression denoted a matter that was difficult or even impossible. In Palestine, a large and visible cargo animal was the camel. Jesus may have been using in Jerusalem a figure of speech like that known to have been used by rabbis at that time elsewhere.

[3]Cf. *Psalms of Solomon* 17, a pre-New Testament Jewish document in which David's kingdom is at the same time God's kingdom.

ers, with the pronouncement, "You are not far from the kingdom of God" (12:34).

3) When Jesus declares at the Last Supper, "Truly, I say to you, I will not drink again of the fruit of the vine until that day when I drink it new in the kingdom of God" (14:25), he refers to kingdom in its radically future dimension. That time will not come until he returns and the new age has arrived in full.

4) Anticlimactic, but redolent of the same sentiment voiced on Palm Sunday in 11:10 (see above), is the allusion to one of several figures who distinguished themselves following Jesus' death: "Joseph of Arimathea, a respected member of the Council, who was also himself looking for the kingdom of God, took courage and went to Pilate and asked for the body of Jesus" (15:43). Luke links Joseph's kingdom focus with the fact that he had not been in favor of Jesus' crucifixion to begin with: Joseph "had not consented to their decision and action; and he was looking for the kingdom of God" (23:51). No less than Jesus promised and signaled the kingdom's arrival, and many of Abraham's descendants in that day wistfully longed for it, however hazy or imperfect their conception may have been. Scholars today may debate the origin and meaning of the kingdom concept, but it was "in the air" among Jews of that era. "Palestinian Jews were quite familiar with the concept of kingdom."[4]

In sum, Mark's Gospel from start to finish serves to fuse kingdom fulfillment through Jesus' person and work to the kingdom desire that God had cultivated in his people over many centuries leading up to the moment when the Markan Jesus appears and announces, "The time is fulfilled, and the kingdom of God is at hand; repent and believe in the gospel" (1:15).

Jesus and the Kingdom of God in Luke–Acts

References to "kingdom" occur almost as many times in Luke's Gospel (forty-five) as in Matthew's (fifty-four). The Lukan passages will be examined below. But first, should we perhaps consider Acts for a moment? Even though Acts is, essentially, part two of Luke's Gospel, it contains only eight references to "kingdom" or "kingdom of God." It could be asked whether the Acts passages actually might constitute a diminution of the importance of kingdom for the story Luke–Acts tells. Was "kingdom of God," so central for Jesus, a fading concern as the early church

---

[4]Keener, *The Historical Jesus of the Gospels*, 197.

took shape and matured during the three decades covered by Acts? In fact, in the Acts passages we see the kingdom emphasis of Luke's Gospel continued, not abandoned.

Acts

The kingdom of God is a central teaching point of Jesus right up to the last hours of his earthly life. The risen Jesus "presented himself alive to [his disciples] after his suffering by many proofs, appearing to them during forty days and speaking about the kingdom of God" (Acts 1:3). The message Jesus announced from the start of his public ministry remains his theme as he prepares to return to his heavenly station at the Father's right hand (cf. 7:56).

It is of no less concern for Jesus' disciples. This is understandable since they had listened to Jesus teach and preach about "kingdom" for some three years. As Jesus was about to ascend, "when they had come together, they asked him, 'Lord, will you at this time restore the kingdom to Israel?'" (1:6). Graham Twelftree has observed, "Luke never explains the phrase the kingdom or reign of God."[5] Perhaps Jesus did not either, using it extensively but allusively and

> in a multivalent way, sometimes referring to the eschatological saving activity of God breaking in and changing a person's life, sometimes referring to the eschatological reign of God in some place, and sometimes referring to a condition or even a place that believers would one day enter, inherit, or obtain.[6]

Whatever Jesus meant by it, at the beginning of Acts Jesus teaches about it, and the disciples want to know more. This has at least the potential effect of making what follows in Acts relevant to the question of the meaning and the future of "the kingdom of God."

Jesus as King. Jesus "the Christ" or king is prominent in the preaching of Acts' early chapters ("Christ" appears in 2:31, 36, 38; 3:6, 18, 20; 4:10; 5:42). As the regally rich gospel message begins to spring the confines of Jerusalem, Philip takes it to Samaria, where we catch a glimpse of how the gospel and the kingdom coalesce: "But when they believed Philip as he preached good news about the kingdom of God and the name of Jesus Christ, they were baptized, both men and women" (8:12). "The kingdom

---

[5]Graham H. Twelftree, *People of the Spirit: Exploring Luke's View of the Church* (London: SPCK, 2009), 193.
[6]Ben Witherington III, *The Indelible Image*, vol. 1: *The Individual Witnesses* (Downers Grove, IL: InterVarsity, 2009), 81.

of God" was central to the message of those who Jesus promised would be his witnesses in Jerusalem, Judea, Samaria, and beyond (see 1:8). "The kingdom of God," along with "good news" and "the name of Jesus Christ," was part of the mix of the saving message first received by the Samaritans who responded to Philip.

It could be asked whether there is a subtle affirmation of Jesus' kingdom power in his implied triumph over Agrippa I. This is the King Herod who "laid violent hands on some who belonged to the church," killed John's brother James, and then arrested Peter when he saw how pleased many Jews were at the mayhem he was unleashing (12:1–3). The Acts narrative has already established that to persecute the church is to persecute the risen Jesus himself (9:5). King Herod basks in political acclaim for a season but then is struck down "because he did not give God the glory" (12:23). His kingdom terminates abruptly, while in the very next verse Luke's laconic observation is, "But the word of God increased and multiplied" (v. 24). Without using the word "kingdom," in its way this incident trumpets the triumph of the kingdom of God as represented by the early church and opposed in vain by earthly powers.

The church: an expression of the kingdom. "The kingdom of God" summarizes the sphere of the churches founded by Paul and Barnabas on the first missionary journey (Acts 13–14). When at the end of that two-year circuit they "returned to Lystra and Iconium and Antioch, strengthening the souls of the disciples, encouraging them to continue in the faith," the watchword they left with the enclaves of new believers was: "through many tribulations we must enter the kingdom of God" (14:21–22). While church planting was in some ways a culmination of the kingdom movement Jesus announced, in Luke's view church establishment is not the terminus of kingdom but an ongoing expression of its reality. Church is subordinate to kingdom; kingdom is not simply a synonym for church.

There must have been a strong sense of the kingdom of God that attached to Paul's preaching as the second missionary journey got underway. For early in those months, at Thessalonica, Paul proclaims that Jesus "is the Christ" (17:3). This foments a mob action. The charge: "These men who have turned the world upside down have come here also, and Jason has received them, and they are all acting against the decrees of Caesar, saying that there is another king, Jesus" (vv. 6–7). Even if the charge is trumped up, it is bound to have some basis in the social, political, and religious ramifications of the message Paul delivered with its kingdom implications and associations.

The kingdom of God is in the foreground of Paul's ministry at Ephesus, where after Paul administered the Holy Spirit to a fledgling group of believers (19:1–7), "he entered the synagogue and for three months spoke boldly, reasoning and persuading them about the kingdom of God" (v. 8). Ephesus is the site of Paul's lengthiest known consecutive ministry venue, and he kicked things off echoing Jesus' own signature stress, "the kingdom of God." A couple of years later as Paul looks back on his time at Ephesus, and indeed the whole of his third missionary journey, he summarizes his work with these retrospective words to the Ephesian elders, "And now, behold, I know that none of you among whom I have gone about proclaiming the kingdom will see my face again" (20:25). Paul's own blanket expression for his missionary, pastoral, evangelistic, and apostolic work is "proclaiming the kingdom" of God.

Finally, just as Acts began with mention of the kingdom of God, so it ends. Paul's epic voyage to Rome, in the wake of a couple of years of imprisonment in Caesarea, is capped by an audience with the Jews at Rome (28:17–22). Their leaders request a full accounting from Paul, because they have heard of him and "this sect . . . that everywhere it is spoken against" (v. 22). When Paul has occasion to explain himself, "the kingdom of God" looms large in his presentation:

> When they had appointed a day for him, they came to him at his lodging in greater numbers. From morning till evening he expounded to them, testifying to the kingdom of God and trying to convince them about Jesus both from the Law of Moses and from the Prophets. (v. 23)

This note of emphasis on the kingdom of God is repeated a few verses later in Acts' closing lines. As Paul languished awaiting trial for two years, welcoming visitors of various persuasions, Luke summarizes Paul's activity this way: he was "proclaiming the kingdom of God and teaching about the Lord Jesus Christ with all boldness and without hindrance" (v. 31).

The kingdom of God, far from being muted in Acts, furnishes an axis from which the whole narrative and its animating message are suspended.

The scales are tipped in the direction of kingdom having decisive significance in Acts when we think in both literary and historical terms of Acts being part two of Luke's Gospel. Most if not everything that Luke presents regarding Jesus has connection with the kingdom of God or, occasionally and synonymously, Jesus' own kingdom. Kingdom references may taper off in frequency in Acts, but given the deep and broad basis that is established in Luke, it is of paramount importance for Luke's two-volume work overall.

Luke

We will now group and describe some relevant passages in Luke's Gospel in the nine sections that follow. In Luke's Gospel:

1) *The kingdom of God is eternal.* Gabriel tells Mary, "He will be great and will be called the Son of the Most High. The Lord God will give to him the throne of his father David, and he will reign over the house of Jacob forever, and of his kingdom there will be no end" (1:32–33). Here is an example of "kingdom" being used to signify its tie both to God (who grants it to the Son) and Christ (whose kingdom will have no end). Gabriel hails this reign as without temporal termination, in obvious distinction from any earthly or merely historical regime. Its coming will be fateful for many, first of all among God's own people, as we read shortly thereafter, "Behold, this child is appointed for the fall and rising of many in Israel, and for a sign that is opposed" (2:34).

2) *The kingdom of God is disputed by rivals.* While "kingdom of God" contains in it the notion of God's sovereignty, this is not to say it is dominion untouched by competition and conflict. At Jesus' temptation, "the devil took him up and showed him all the kingdoms of the world in a moment of time" (4:5). Jesus preached that God's kingdom was at hand, but he knew Satan's dominion was lurking in the shadows to trip him up if that were possible. This comes to the fore after a particular exorcism at which "people marveled" (11:14). But precisely on that occasion, some scoffed and theorized that Jesus was in league with Satan. Jesus cast his response in kingdom terms: "But he, knowing their thoughts, said to them, 'Every kingdom divided against itself is laid waste, and a divided household falls. And if Satan also is divided against himself, how will his kingdom stand?'" (vv. 17–18). Answer: it will not and cannot. Instead, Jesus observes that "if[7] it is by the finger of God that I cast out demons, then the kingdom of God has come upon you" (v. 20). Jesus may be challenged and buffeted by God's archenemy, but the outcome only serves to underscore how complete and unilateral God's dominion turns out to be despite temporal and temporary appearances to the contrary.

3) *The kingdom of God is at the center of Jesus' agenda.* In Luke as in

---

[7]The Greek suggests this "if" affirms that Jesus does believe himself to be casting out demons by God's "finger" (i.e., his power and/or commission).

the other Gospels, Jesus is explicit from early on about his consciousness of kingdom purpose and his resolve to further and eventually fulfill it. After preaching (and narrowly averting personal attack [4:29]) in
Nazareth and ministering in Capernaum, Jesus sets about visiting synagogues and preaching there (v. 44). This sudden activity, a break with
nearly thirty years of apparently quiet life as a tradesman, is driven by
kingdom conviction: "I must preach the good news of the kingdom of God
to the other towns as well; for I was sent for this purpose" (v. 43). Luke
indicates that this awareness was not only an initial but also a continuing driving force: several chapters later, after numerous notable events
and discourses (like the Sermon on the Plain [6:20–49]), Jesus' activity is
summarized with the words, "Soon afterward he went on through cities
and villages, proclaiming and bringing the good news of the kingdom of
God" (8:1). By now not only Jesus but also various men and women are
engulfed in kingdom pursuits:

> And the twelve were with him, and also some women who had been
> healed of evil spirits and infirmities: Mary, called Magdalene, from
> whom seven demons had gone out, and Joanna, the wife of Chuza,
> Herod's household manager, and Susanna, and many others, who pro-
> vided for them out of their means. (vv. 1–3)

Some time later, after the twelve have been sent out "to proclaim the
kingdom of God and to heal" (9:2; see below), Jesus' continuing focus on
this theme is confirmed. He withdraws with the apostles to Bethsaida but
cannot shake the crowds. Where one might expect pique on Jesus' part,
instead "he welcomed them and spoke to them of the kingdom of God
and cured those who had need of healing" (v. 11). It is therefore not surprising that when Jesus lays down the basics of prayer for his inquiring
disciples, "kingdom" is front and center in the formula: "And he said to
them, 'When you pray, say: "Father, hallowed be your name. Your kingdom come"'" (11:2).

4) *The kingdom of God is paradoxical in splendor.* Regarding paradox
in Jesus' kingdom teaching, Chilton comments, "Paradox can be used as
an occasion to see things in a new way, to break through habits of thought
that are not appropriate to the apprehension of a new reality."[8] Jesus was a
master of this technique. In the course of praising John the Baptizer, Jesus

---

[8]Bruce Chilton, "Kingdom of God, Kingdom of Heaven," in *NIDB*, ed. Katharine Sakenfeld (Nashville: Abingdon, 2008), 3:522.

exalted the high privilege of kingdom entrance and involvement: "I tell you, among those born of women none is greater than John. Yet the one who is least in the kingdom of God is greater than he" (7:28). There is no reason to suppose this is some slight or denigration of John or the quality of his faith (shaky though it might have been at this point in the narrative, with messengers from John asking whether Jesus really is "the one who is to come"; see 7:18–23). Rather, Jesus is surely highlighting the glorious gravity of the shift that has occurred in salvation history, a shift John was central in heralding. The Lukan narrative takes pains to record popular response to Jesus' praise of John, yet greater praise of kingdom: "When all the people heard this, and the tax collectors too, they declared God just, having been baptized with the baptism of John" (v. 29). There are wheels within wheels in the wonder of God's kingdom-coming-to-pass in that day and time. It exceeds facile grasp.

5) *The kingdom of God is paradoxical with respect to its presence.* On one occasion when some Pharisees seemed to be banking on a future kingdom, they asked Jesus "when the kingdom of God would come" (17:20). Jesus' reply was, surprisingly, that in a sense it is already here: "The kingdom of God is not coming in ways that can be observed, nor will they say, 'Look, here it is!' or 'There!' for behold, the kingdom of God is in the midst of you" (vv. 20–21). Craig Blomberg explains that here, "in Jesus' person, God's reign appears even in the midst of his enemies."[9] The Pharisees wonder when they will see the kingdom, and Jesus replies (no doubt opaquely in their view) that in a sense they are looking right at it. The kingdom is already here.

On the other hand, Jesus moved decisively to correct people who "supposed that the kingdom of God was to appear immediately" (19:11). Jesus told the parable of the ten minas (vv. 11–27). The point here with respect to the kingdom's coming seems to be that Jesus foresaw an era when "minas" (talents, resources) would be distributed for servants of the kingdom to employ for their master's benefit. Woe to the servant who sits on what he receives as if there will be no future day of reckoning (v. 24)! The kingdom in its final implications is not here, after all, but lies in the future.

This same paradoxical tension shows up elsewhere in Luke. Not until unmistakable signs of impending eschatological doom will disciples "know that the kingdom of God is near" (21:31). Here the kingdom

---

[9]Craig L. Blomberg, *Jesus and the Gospels: An Introduction and Survey*, 2nd ed. (Nashville: Broadman, 2009), 449.

is future, as it is also shortly after the Last Supper, when Jesus tells the Eleven, "I assign to you, as my Father assigned to me, a kingdom, that you may eat and drink at my table in my kingdom and sit on thrones judging the twelve tribes of Israel" (22:29–30). Yet when the criminal hanging next to Jesus' own cross says, "Jesus, remember me when you come into your kingdom" (23:42), Jesus envisions immediate advent of the kingdom, at least in terms of its benefit for the penitent criminal who trusts in him: "Truly I say to you, today you will be with me in Paradise" (v. 43).

6) *The kingdom of God is revelatory in terms of human recognition of its presence.* We have already touched on this with reference to Matt. 13:11 and Mark 4:11 above. When Jesus' disciples ask him to explain the parable of the sower, Jesus replies, "To you it has been given to know the secrets of the kingdom of God, but for others they are in parables, so that 'seeing they may not see, and hearing they may not understand'" (Luke 8:10). The disclosure of kingdom claims and realities was at one level a matter of public record. As Paul states in Acts, "This has not been done in a corner" (Acts 26:26). Later in Luke's Gospel, Jesus' detractors will complain before Pilate, "He stirs up the people, teaching throughout all Judea, from Galilee even to this place" (Luke 23:5). Jesus did not operate in the dark. Yet only those to whom vision was "given" could see his work in its messianic implications. In Jesus the kingdom of God is both revealed (to some) and concealed (to most).

7) *The kingdom of God is at the core of the disciples' ministry.* Not only Jesus but also his followers are commissioned to publicize God's kingdom. Jesus "sent them out to proclaim the kingdom of God and to heal" (9:2). This is at the initial commissioning of the Twelve. Later Jesus "appointed seventy-two others" (10:1). Among the instructions he gave them was to "heal the sick in it and say to them, 'The kingdom of God has come near to you'" (v. 9). Even if the towns they evangelize reject their message, so that the disciples must say, at Jesus' direction, "Even the dust of your town that clings to our feet we wipe off against you," they are also to declare, "Nevertheless know this, that the kingdom of God has come near" (v. 11). In a discourse addressing life's anxieties and cares over daily needs, Jesus advised that "your Father knows" what they need, so that rather than fret or throw in the towel, "Instead, seek his kingdom, and these things will be added to you" (12:30–31).

Precisely here Jesus underscores what he takes to be a consoling dimension to the kingdom: "Fear not, little flock, for it is your Father's good pleasure to give you the kingdom" (v. 32). Paradoxically, however, this assurance of kingdom possession is coupled with an expectation that could be viewed as exorbitant:

> Sell your possessions, and give to the needy. Provide yourselves with moneybags that do not grow old, with a treasure in the heavens that does not fail, where no thief approaches and no moth destroys. For where your treasure is, there will your heart be also. (vv. 33–34)

The price of kingdom consolation, it appears, was kingdom commitment, however costly. Disciples who opted for kingdom riches in exchange for earthly abundance would perhaps recall what Jesus had already declared, according to Luke, "Blessed are you who are poor, for yours is the kingdom of God" (6:20). One of the reasons for the poverty Jesus had in mind could have been compliance with his call to place one's own livelihood at the service of others.

Jesus' prioritizing of kingdom was not only for those committed to his leadership, like the Twelve and the seventy-two. Prospective followers at large, too, heard a similar summons. In a Lukan pericope typically entitled "The Cost of Following Jesus" (9:57–62), he told the person who asked for funeral leave before joining the disciples' ranks, "Leave the dead to bury their own dead. But as for you, go and proclaim the kingdom of God" (v. 60). To the person who wanted to say farewell to those at home before following Jesus, he admonished, "No one who puts his hand to the plow and looks back is fit for the kingdom of God" (v. 62).

8) *The kingdom of God has a narrow door.* As Jesus journeyed toward Jerusalem, preaching as he went, he was questioned regarding the stringent demands of his call to discipleship, "Lord, will those who are saved be few?" (13:23). It is hard to say how satisfying Jesus' reply was, for his answer ran, "Strive to enter through the narrow door. For many, I tell you, will seek to enter and will not be able" (v. 24). On the one hand, Jesus' kingdom proclamation was public and magnanimous. In this period of his ministry, "great crowds accompanied him" (14:25). But in his reply Jesus pictures a household master who excludes those claiming to have entered, saying, "I tell you, I do not know where you come from. Depart from me, all you workers of evil!" (13:27).

Jesus' final words in this episode show that he has viewed the entire exchange in terms of kingdom membership. He speaks of a miserable place to which these deluded kingdom claimants will be relegated, and he describes it not once but twice:

> In that place there will be weeping and gnashing of teeth, when you see
> Abraham and Isaac and Jacob and all the prophets in the kingdom of
> God but you yourselves cast out. And people will come from east and
> west, and from north and south, and recline at table in the kingdom of
> God. And behold, some are last who will be first, and some are first who
> will be last. (13:28–30)

Kingdom specifications may run counter to public ones. People may
presume to have entered it on their terms. But the "eschatological inversion" noted above in Matthew's account is a feature of Jesus' outlook in
Luke's Gospel, too. There is a wideness in God's mercy that moves Jesus to
lament just a few verses later as he contemplates his arrival in Jerusalem:
"O Jerusalem, Jerusalem, the city that kills the prophets and stones
those who are sent to it! How often would I have gathered your children
together as a hen gathers her brood under her wings" (v. 34). But because
of people's recalcitrance ("You were not willing!" [v. 34]), he characterizes
the door to that mercy as narrow.

Perhaps it is this very recalcitrance that Jesus senses when he makes a
prickly response at a banquet hosted by "a ruler of the Pharisees" a short
time later. It was a Sabbath day, and others at the banquet "were watch-
ing him carefully" (14:1). This is not a setting friendly to Jesus. As they
witnessed him heal a man with dropsy and heard him discourse on the
need for humility and hospitality toward the disenfranchised who cannot repay (vv. 2–14), one of those present sought to break the tension by
exclaiming, "Blessed is everyone who will eat bread in the kingdom of
God!" (v. 15). Jesus' reply is a parable (vv. 16–24) that echoes his "narrow
door" teaching: "I tell you, none of those men who were invited shall taste
my banquet" (v. 24). Many who glibly extol kingdom benefits have no idea
what they are talking about.

Shortly after this account, when money-loving Pharisees (16:14) ridi-
cule Jesus for his teaching that "you cannot serve God and money" (v. 13),
Jesus observes that "the Law and the Prophets were until John; since then
the good news of the kingdom of God is preached, and everyone forces
his way into it" (v. 16). This would seem to refer to those who rejected
Jesus' kingdom teaching because they believed they already possessed the
divine favor that Jesus claimed to mediate. Jesus, whose reading of the
Old Testament did not favor the self-justifying approach to it of his opponents, concludes: "But it is easier for heaven and earth to pass away than
for one dot of the Law to become void" (v. 17). Those who "force their way

into" the kingdom—who think they have entered it under terms different from those espoused first by John and then later by Jesus—are entering under false pretenses encouraged by their misreading of Scripture. Jesus' insists that this very Scripture justifies his representation of the kingdom of God in which he is central, not theirs according to which he misleads the people. The door is narrow since it is Jesus. Because his opponents with their own hermeneutic and political stature disagree, that door remains for them closed. In actuality they have not entered the kingdom at all.

9) *The kingdom of God costs everything but rewards handsomely.* To a rich ruler's query about eternal life, Jesus responds with a call to all-out personal commitment to following him, symbolized by sale of his estate and distribution of the proceeds to the poor (18:22). Luke's account says only that when the man heard this, "he became very sad, for he was extremely rich" (v. 23). Jesus interprets this encounter in kingdom terms: "Jesus, seeing that he had become sad, said, 'How difficult it is for those who have wealth to enter the kingdom of God!'" (v. 24). He adds, "For it is easier for a camel to go through the eye of a needle than for a rich person to enter the kingdom of God" (v. 25). This does not mean it was impossible, for "what is impossible with man is possible with God" (v. 27). But Jesus' point remains that his call to discipleship is synonymous with entrance to the kingdom, and this entrance makes imposing demands on those who answer the call.

Jesus' own disciples felt the radicalness of this, for Peter immediately seeks assurance that Jesus thinks he and the other disciples have responded adequately: "Peter said, 'See, we have left our homes and followed you'" (18:28). Jesus confirms that they will not be disappointed to have made such sacrifice: "Truly, I say to you, there is no one who has left house or wife or brothers or parents or children, for the sake of the kingdom of God, who will not receive many times more in this time, and in the age to come eternal life" (vv. 29–30). Kingdom discipleship is total in its demands, but it is also generous beyond description in its benefits both in the present and the final age.

Jesus and the Kingdom of God in John

"The kingdom of God plays no significant role in John's Gospel."[10] The phrase "kingdom of God" appears only twice. This is when Jesus speaks with Nicodemus:

---

[10]Chrys Caragounis, "Kingdom of God/Heaven," in *Dictionary of Jesus and the Gospels*, ed. Joel B. Green and Scot McKnight (Downers Grove, IL: InterVarsity, 1992), 429.

> Jesus answered him, "Truly, truly, I say to you, unless one is born again he cannot see the kingdom of God." (John 3:3)

> Jesus answered, "Truly, truly, I say to you, unless one is born of water and the Spirit, he cannot enter the kingdom of God." (v. 5)

Nicodemus as a leading Pharisee would probably have harbored some nationalist associations in his view of the kingdom. "The kingdom of God" should in some way displace the hated rule of Rome and all other Gentile powers over the land promised to Abraham and his descendants. Perhaps it was Jesus' (and before him John the Baptizer's) kingdom claims that spurred Jerusalem suspicion about this new message (see 1:19). The buzz surrounding "kingdom" preaching (particularly under Roman rule that could regard such claims as seditious) may have been an impetus for Nicodemus' nocturnal visit to the person he appears to acknowledge as a God-blessed teacher and miracle worker (3:2).

Jesus' reply dashed any political hopes. To see the kingdom of God requires an inner transformation (v. 3). It requires spiritual rebirth (v. 5). This does not square easily with known Pharisaic soteriology; Nicodemus's seeming sarcasm (v. 4) and claim not to comprehend (v. 9) are appropriate to the purported historical setting. By "water and Spirit" Jesus could have been challenging Nicodemus to take another look at John's baptism, which Pharisees as a party seem to have rejected. To see and enter the kingdom, Nicodemus needs to repent and receive that baptism. This will open him up to reception of the Spirit which, John states, Jesus will eventually mediate (see 1:33).

John's Gospel, then, does not tell us here what the kingdom is. It merely points to conditions necessary for Nicodemus (and by extension others since) to glimpse and enter it.

Later, Jesus speaks of his kingdom three times in the only other verse in John's Gospel where the word "kingdom" appears: "Jesus answered, 'My kingdom is not of this world. If my kingdom were of this world, my servants would have been fighting, that I might not be delivered over to the Jews. But my kingdom is not from the world'" (18:36). At the very least, this statement to the Roman governor Pontius Pilate expresses that Jesus is not a political or national messiah à la common conceptions of the era. This cannot be pressed to mean that following Jesus carries no this-worldly implications for those who trust in him; John's Gospel is rich in its suggestions for the beliefs and behavior of those who believe in the Son of God.

The Eternal Life of the Kingdom

Scholars commonly note that in John's Gospel, "kingdom of God/heaven" as found in the other Gospels is replaced by John's references to "eternal life" (seventeen times) or simply "life" (nineteen times). These terms are closely associated, even interchanged, in the Synoptics: in Mark Jesus speaks of entering "life" and entering "the kingdom of God" synonymously (9:43–47). Again in Mark, when a man asks Jesus how to inherit eternal life (10:17), Jesus interprets his question as referring to entrance into the kingdom of God (vv. 23–25). Similarly, in Matthew Jesus equates "the kingdom prepared for" his followers with the "eternal life" they will receive in the end (Matt. 25:34, 46). In that sense, John's Gospel speaks extensively about "the kingdom of God." It simply does so under a different label.

It can be said that by shifting Jesus' accent from "kingdom of God" to "life" or "eternal life," John may be accomplishing three things: (1) mapping out a new perspective on Jesus' teaching about himself and his call to discipleship rather than simply repeating just what the other Gospels have already concretized; (2) reflecting the post-resurrection setting of John and his readers, in which "the kingdom" is now about faith in Jesus and receiving the grace he offers; and (3) avoiding Jewish nationalist associations that may have inhered in the language of "the kingdom of God" for Gentile audiences (tradition says that late in life, when he wrote his Gospel, John was resident in Ephesus, which would have been a region of predominately Gentile church membership).

In any case, while this chapter is about the kingdom of God and not about life or eternal life, since John uses the latter for the former, it is important to note some of the central truths found in John's Gospel pertaining to "life" or "eternal life." For these truths are also, in the end, pointers to New Testament understanding of the kingdom of God, its benefits, and entrance into it.

"In him was life" (1:4). The opening verses of John assert that the Word that was to become incarnate (v. 14), preexistent with the Father (v. 2), was God's agent in creation of the material world (v. 3). All "life" has its origins and basis in the Word who "became flesh and dwelt among us" and showed the "glory as of the only Son from the Father, full of grace and truth" (v. 14).

John's Gospel furnishes, then, the christological basis upon which the Son in the Synoptics announces the kingdom. In John's Gospel the Son is presented as the one who "gave his life" so that "whoever believes in him should not perish but have eternal life" (3:16). "The wrath of God remains on" those who do not obey the Son (v. 36), grave language reminiscent of Jesus' frequent warnings about eternal punishment in the Synoptics. Jesus gives spiritual refreshment, he tells the Samaritan woman at the well, which is "a spring of water welling up to eternal life" (4:14). In keeping with Synoptic images of sowing and reaping in connection with the kingdom, in John "the one who reaps is receiving wages and gathering fruit for eternal life" (v. 36). In the Synoptics, the one who hears Jesus' words and does them enters the kingdom; in John "whoever hears [Jesus'] word and believes him who sent [Jesus] has eternal life" (5:24). Just as in Matthew Jesus speaks of a final judgment of the just and the wicked (Matt. 25:31–46), in John Jesus speaks of the resurrection of the just and the wicked, "those who have done good to the resurrection of life, and those who have done evil to the resurrection of judgment" (John 5:29).

In the Sermon on the Mount Jesus warns against undue care about food and clothing; his followers should "seek first the kingdom of God" (Matt. 6:25, 33). Near-equivalent words are found in John's Gospel, with "eternal life" promised in lieu of the kingdom: "Do not work for the food that perishes, but for the food that endures to eternal life, which the Son of Man will give to you" (6:27). In Matthew the one who brings the kingdom "will baptize you with the Holy Spirit" (3:11); in John Jesus states, "The words that I have spoken to you are spirit and life" (6:63). In Luke Jesus says, "Fear not, little flock, for it is your Father's good pleasure to give you the kingdom" (12:32); in John the Good Shepherd of the flock promises, "I give them eternal life, and they will never perish, and no one will snatch them out of my hand" (10:28).

This is not a comprehensive comparison between John and the Synoptics, but even a cursory survey shows that kingdom language in the Synoptics and "life" language in John's Gospel correlate closely. One overarching message of Matthew, Mark, and Luke is that to become Jesus' disciple is to enter the kingdom of God; John writes his Gospel "so that you may believe that Jesus is the Christ, the Son of God, and that by believing you may have life in his name" (20:31). "A careful reading of both the Synoptic Gospels and the Gospel of John does not lead to soteriological disparity,"[11] or other disparities either (apart from style, word choice, and selection of material), but to a unified message regarding "kingdom

---

[11]David Johnson, "Life," in *Dictionary of Jesus and the Gospels*, 471.

of God" (in the Synoptics) and the saving visitation of the Son through believing, which the fourth Gospel calls "(eternal) life."

This is not to mention the dramatic and consistent degree to which John's Gospel highlights Jesus' messiahship[12]—his status as the promised king of God's chosen people and by extension, as the Son of God, God's co-regent over all creation. It is not necessary for John's Gospel to speak of "the kingdom of God" announced by Jesus, because all that Jesus says and does are acts of a king sent by and from God. All of Jesus' words and deeds are self-evidently kingdom manifestations. In the end, the differences between the Synoptics and John's Gospel with respect to "the kingdom of God" are, first, semantic—different words, substantially equal meaning when seen in their respective full sweep. And they are second, perspectival. That is, the Synoptics may well highlight the *ipsissima verba Jesu* (very words of Jesus) on numerous occasions, while John unrelentingly confronts readers with both the salvation and judgment present in the presence and preaching of "the King of Israel" (John 1:49), whose Johannine profile constitutes a sovereign and unmistakable messianic—which is to say "kingdom"—claim.

Jesus and the Kingdom of God in the Epistles

From Romans to Jude, the New Testament contains about eighteen references to the kingdom of God or of Christ:

Romans 14:17	2 Thessalonians 1:5
1 Corinthians 4:20; 6:9, 10; 15:24, 50	2 Timothy 4:1, 18
Galatians 5:21	Hebrews 1:8; 12:28
Ephesians 5:5	James 2:5
Colossians 1:13; 4:11	2 Peter 1:11
1 Thessalonians 2:12	

What the New Testament letters share is emphasis on Jesus as Lord, with "Lord" understood as the Christ who is central to salvation, life in the Spirit, last things, and all other aspects of both church life and the world at large. Is this consistent with Jesus' representation of the kingdom of God? Bertold Klappert answers positively, at least for Paul:

> By tying salvation to the person of Jesus and by developing Christology along the lines of soteriology, pneumatology, and eschatology, Paul has

---

[12]See especially Larry Hurtado, "Christ," in *Dictionary of Jesus and the Gospels*, 114–17.

maintained a consistent and legitimate extension of Jesus' preaching of
the kingdom of God, although he has adapted this to the post-resurrection situation as regards the cross and the resurrection.[13]

In other words, in Paul's letters (and in the other letters too) the term
"kingdom of God" does not appear with the frequency it did in Jesus'
preaching and teaching as recorded in the Synoptics. But this does not
mean that "kingdom of God" is a foreign concept to the Epistles. As we
saw above in Acts, there can be infrequent mention but still foundational
importance. Or as we saw in John's Gospel, the reality of the "kingdom of
God" can be upheld with almost totally different language. We will now
survey the kingdom references tallied above and show how they point to
the presence and development of what Jesus referred to when he used the
expression.

Romans

The sole reference to "kingdom of God" in Romans is 14:17: "For the
kingdom of God is not a matter of eating and drinking but of righteousness and peace and joy in the Holy Spirit." The fact that Paul can use the
expression with no introduction or explanation suggests that both for
him and for his readers, the term is already familiar. The gospel message of which Paul is not ashamed (1:16) is a message that brings salvation (13:11) and calls on believers to "put on the Lord Jesus Christ"
(v. 14). Romans 14 gives important counsel for those who have done
this in terms of accepting one another despite differences of conviction
and practice in secondary matters. "Kingdom of God" serves as a cipher
for the salvation believers have received that makes putting on the Lord
Jesus Christ a coherent concept.

Jesus provided at least part of the basis for Paul's statement. He taught
that "whatever goes into a person from outside cannot defile him, since
it enters not his heart but his stomach, and is expelled" (Mark 7:18–19).
Mark adds here, "Thus he declared all foods clean" (v. 19). This is part of
Paul's point in minimizing the gravity of "eating and drinking" in believers'
lives together compared to weightier matters like "righteousness, peace,
and joy in the Holy Spirit." It hardly needs to be pointed out that these
things were all spoken of, offered, and bestowed by God and/or Jesus during his earthly ministry of announcing and commending the "kingdom of

[13]Bertold Klappert, "King, Kingdom," in *NIDNTT*, ed. Colin Brown (Grand Rapids, MI: Zondervan, 1986), 2:388.

God."[14] Paul's statement does not veer from anything found about Jesus and the kingdom in the Gospels; it merely applies dominical example and instruction to the challenging issues that Romans 14 must deal with.

1 Corinthians

In terms of frequency of mention, 1 Corinthians has the most to say about kingdom of any New Testament epistle. First, Paul remarks, "For the kingdom of God does not consist in talk but in power" (4:20). His abrupt and unexplained reference to "the kingdom of God" indicates that here as in his missive to the Roman congregation(s), Paul assumes familiarity with the term on the part of the readers. Also as in Romans, Paul makes a claim that has grounding in the Jesus of the Gospels. He did not simply talk. He showed the authority behind his proclamation with acts like forgiving sins (Matt. 9:6), empowering disciples to exorcise and heal (10:1), and sending out his disciples to make disciples and to baptize because "all authority in heaven and on earth" was given to him (28:18). The ripple effect of the Matthew 28 commissioning is still at work today. The kingdom Jesus proclaimed truly is, as Paul affirms, not just rhetoric (highly prized at Corinth) but God-worked effects both in hearts and in the world of space, time, and matter.

Paul's sense of the powerful reality of the kingdom is in evidence in his next two mentions of it in 1 Corinthians: "Or do you not know that the unrighteous will not inherit the kingdom of God? Do not be deceived: neither the sexually immoral, nor idolaters, nor adulterers, nor men who practice homosexuality, nor thieves, nor the greedy, nor drunkards, nor revilers, nor swindlers will inherit the kingdom of God" (6:9–10). By connecting inheritance with kingdom, Paul indicates that he is using "kingdom" in its eschatological sense—after this life the Corinthians face an eternity based on their involvement in the kingdom (or lack thereof). Entrance into the kingdom in this life assures an inheritance in the age to come. They can forfeit that inheritance by failure to break with behavior that marks them as worldlings and not gospel believers whose lives have been touched by the reality of the Jesus whom they confess. One need look no farther than Jesus' statement in the Sermon on the Mount to find dominical teaching that comports with Paul's ethical stance here:

---

[14]See, e.g., Matt. 3:15; 5:6, 10, 20; 6:1, 33; 21:32; Luke 1:75; John 16:8, 10 (righteousness); Matt. 10:13, 34; Mark 4:39; 5:34; 9:50; Luke 1:79; 2:14, 29; 7:50; 8:48; 10:5, 6; 12:51; 14:32; 19:38, 42; 24:36; John 14:27; 16:33; 20:19, 21, 26 (peace); Matt. 2:10; 13:20, 44; 25:21, 23; 28:8; Mark 4:16; Luke 1:14, 44; 2:10; 6:23; 8:13; 10:17; 15:7, 10; 24:41, 52; John 3:29; 15:11; 16:20, 21, 22, 24; 17:13 (joy).

"Not everyone who says to me, 'Lord, Lord,' will enter the kingdom of heaven, but the one who does the will of my Father who is in heaven" (Matt. 7:21). By flirting with the immoral practices Paul mentions, the Corinthians were flouting the kingdom claims of Jesus himself.

In connection with teaching about the resurrection, Paul asserts that in the wake of Jesus' resurrection, and following the resurrection of "those who belong to Christ" at his second coming (1 Cor. 15:23), the end of this age will follow, when Christ "delivers the kingdom to God the Father after destroying every rule and every authority and power" (v. 24). Here "kingdom" refers to the rule that Christ exercises until such times as all rival powers are destroyed. Then in Paul's own immortal words, "the Son himself will also be subjected to him who put all things in subjection under him, that God may be all in all" (v. 28). "The kingdom" is a primary component in the mystery Paul describes here of subjection (which implies distinction between persons) within the unity of the Trinity.

"Mystery" also helps identify the final kingdom reference in 1 Corinthians: "I tell you this, brothers: flesh and blood cannot inherit the kingdom of God, nor does the perishable inherit the imperishable" (1 Cor. 15:50). Paul's very next words run: "Behold! I tell you a mystery" (v. 51). He is seeking to describe the ineffable. The kingdom in its future fullness and glory defies description even by an apostle who claims to have been caught up into heaven's glory (2 Cor. 12:2).

Galatians, Ephesians, Colossians

In writing to the Galatian congregations, Paul assumes they will know what he means with this kingdom reference: those whose lives are enmeshed in "works of the flesh" (5:19) like "envy, drunkenness, orgies, and things like these . . . will not inherit the kingdom of God" (v. 21). Some years later Paul gives similar counsel in writing to the Ephesians: "For you may be sure of this, that everyone who is sexually immoral or impure, or who is covetous (that is, an idolater), has no inheritance in the kingdom of Christ and God" (Eph. 5:5). Here the conflation of Christ and God as head over the kingdom bears notice. In addition, the ethical expectations of kingdom membership, a staple in Jesus' talk of kingdom, are seen to be in operation in Paul's understanding, too.

Part of Paul's opening remarks to the Colossian readers involves kingdom: "He has delivered us from the domain of darkness and transferred us to the kingdom of his beloved Son" (Col. 1:13). This comes at a critical juncture in the letter, as Paul shifts from his thanksgiving and prayer (vv.

3–12) to a celebrated section on the preeminence of Christ (vv. 15–24). His statement about "the kingdom of his beloved Son" serves as a hinge between these two sections and points to the centrality of Paul's kingdom conviction, not only in his understanding but also in the outlook of the recently planted Gentile churches. As in the Romans and 1 Corinthians references, Paul can assume that the Colossian believers (and those at Laodicea, too: Col. 4:16) understand the kingdom concept. These would be primarily Gentile believers, and Paul had founded neither church. This implies that "the kingdom of God" in its christological import was part and parcel of gospel transmission in the early decades of Christianity's existence. Jesus was no longer on earth to talk about it, but what he had talked about was going viral on earth.

Given the literary placement of Colossians 1:13, it could be argued that the rest of Colossians is a commentary on the meaning of "kingdom" for the Colossian readers. The sovereign of this kingdom is the divine Son who shares in "the fullness of God" (v. 19). The constitution of the kingdom revolves around the Son's reconciling achievement and the shift this effected in the Colossians' lives (vv. 21–22). The disposition of the kingdom has been delegated to apostles like Paul (vv. 24–29), to whom "the stewardship from God . . . was given" so that Paul might "make the word of God fully known" (v. 25). One could continue through the rest of the epistle and interpret Paul's discourse as an application of his view of kingdom. Because "the kingdom of his beloved Son" (v. 13) is essentially about the lordship of that Son, and almost all of Colossians is an application of that lordship, almost all of Colossians is essentially about the kingdom. This explains why at the end of the epistle, when Paul lists "the only men of the circumcision" who are to be found among his "fellow workers" in preaching Christ, he terms them workers "for the kingdom of God" (4:11).

Thessalonians

The Colossian epistle is thought to have been written in the early AD 60s during Paul's imprisonment in Rome. But a full decade before that, as Paul and Silas planted churches on the so-called second missionary journey (see Acts 15:36–18:22), Paul used kingdom language in his dealings with another primarily Gentile church, the one at Thessalonica. In his first epistle to them, he describes his labors among them like this: "We exhorted each one of you and encouraged you and charged you to walk in a manner worthy of God, who calls you into his own kingdom and glory" (1 Thess. 2:12). This only makes sense if from the beginning of his ties with them "the kingdom of God" was part of the gospel message he shared.

The centrality of kingdom comes to the fore perhaps even more clearly in Paul's second Thessalonian letter, written scant weeks or at most only a few months after the first. These new believers continue to undergo persecution. How should they interpret this dire threat to their safety and very existence? Paul interprets the afflictions they are enduring in kingdom categories; their persecution is "evidence of the righteous judgment of God, that you may be considered worthy of the kingdom of God, for which you are also suffering" (2 Thess. 1:5). In life and in death, if it comes to that, the Thessalonians as followers of Jesus are at the same time in Paul's understanding subjects of God's kingdom.

Timothy

Acts represents Paul as summing up his first missionary journey with the words, "Through many tribulations we must enter the kingdom of God" (14:22). One of those who heard Paul's preaching in those days would have been Timothy (16:1). Late in Paul's life, "kingdom" is still one of the convictions that joins him with Timothy in their faith in Christ: "I charge you in the presence of God and of Christ Jesus, who is to judge the living and the dead, and by his appearing and his kingdom: preach the word" (2 Tim. 4:1–2). The only Pauline reference to Jesus as "king" occurs in Paul's other letter to Timothy (1 Tim. 1:17; 6:15). Clearly an underlying assumption about Jesus for Paul and Timothy is that he reigns sovereign over his people and over all the world. That reign, "his kingdom" (2 Tim. 4:1), is at the core of Paul's eternal hope as he faces execution and seeks to rally and assure Timothy: "The Lord will rescue me from every evil deed and bring me safely into his heavenly kingdom. To him be the glory forever and ever. Amen" (v. 18).

Our survey of Paul's epistles confirms that "the kingdom of God" (or of Christ) is a foundational concept, like an invisible software program running at all times in the background as Paul ministers and from time to time composes his letters. This has been confirmed by painstaking examination of the evidence by David Wenham.[15] He shows that "the overall similarity of Jesus' kingdom preaching to Paul's gospel is clear."[16] He lists five significant points of contact: (1) Paul uses "kingdom of God" language as

[15]David Wenham, *Paul: Follower of Jesus or Founder of Christianity?* (Grand Rapids, MI: Eerdmans, 1995), especially 34–103.
[16]Ibid., 70.

Jesus did, as a blanket term to describe the salvation Jesus brought; (2) like Jesus Paul speaks of kingdom as both present and future; (3) many of Paul's kingdom sayings are linked thematically with Jesus' kingdom teachings; (4) some of Paul's kingdom statements suggest direct links with tradition that eventually crystallized in the Gospels; and (5) on the basis of (3) and (4), Wenham calls it "quite likely that Paul has been influenced directly or indirectly by specific sayings within Jesus' kingdom teaching."[17]

More recently, Paul Barnett has devoted a monograph to the Jesus-Paul link, if any.[18] He finds the connection nuanced but pervasive and strong. Specifically, for Barnett "Paul's employment of his key concept 'righteousness of God' was consistent with and in genuine extension of Jesus' key concept 'kingdom of God.'"[19] Both Jesus and Paul taught a salvation that was "grace-based and ritual-free."[20] The difference in terminology cannot be used to deny the numerous ways in which Paul's epistles at point after point are at least indirect and sometimes even direct reflections of Jesus' kingdom-intensive language and representation of the saving work he came to accomplish.

Other Epistles

Other New Testament epistles, too, show that their authors have been influenced by an understanding of the kingdom of God like that found in the Gospels. There can hardly be a more blatant depiction of Jesus in his kingdom identity and implications than that found in Hebrews 1:8: "But of the Son he says, 'Your throne, O God, is forever and ever, the scepter of uprightness is the scepter of your kingdom.'" The Jesus who announced the kingdom in the Gospels is for Hebrews the one who fulfills the lofty prediction of Psalm 45:6. The next verse, like Paul, links this throne and kingdom with righteousness: "You have loved righteousness and hated wickedness; therefore God, your God, has anointed you with the oil of gladness beyond your companions" (Heb. 1:9; cf. Ps. 45:7). In summing up the epistle's expositional sections, Hebrews exhorts, "Therefore let us be grateful for receiving a kingdom that cannot be shaken, and thus let us offer to God acceptable worship, with reverence and awe" (Heb. 12:28). As in the Gospels and in Paul, "kingdom" is a blanket term for the salvation believers have received and eagerly await.

---

[17]Ibid., 75.
[18]P. Barnett, *Paul: Missionary of Jesus* (Grand Rapids, MI: Eerdmans, 2008).
[19]Ibid., 196.
[20]Ibid.

Two final epistolary references show how widespread and intuitively present "the kingdom of God" was among the early Christian communities whose leaders under divine inspiration penned our canonical letters. James wrote, "Listen, my beloved brothers, has not God chosen those who are poor in the world to be rich in faith and heirs of the kingdom, which he has promised to those who love him?" (James 2:5). Themes here that echo Jesus' teaching include not only kingdom but also listening, election, the blessedness of the poor, faith, inheritance, and love for God. Moreover, James speaks of kingdom in the same futuristic way that Jesus sometimes did.

While 1 Peter does not use the term "kingdom," its author accords "dominion" to God and Christ in two separate passages (4:11; 5:10–11). "Dominion" (Greek *kratos*) is virtually synonymous with "kingdom" understood as rule or reign. Believers have an inheritance kept for them as they are guarded by God's power (1:4–5). They are "a chosen race, a royal priesthood, a holy nation, a people for his own possession" (2:9), language that is congruent with the grace bestowed by those entering the kingdom Jesus announced. Peter's readers were chosen that they might "proclaim the excellencies of him who called [them] out of darkness into his marvelous light" (v. 9), words reminiscent of Paul's "He has delivered us from the domain of darkness and transferred us to the kingdom of his beloved Son" (Col. 1:13).

In 2 Peter the writer refers to "kingdom" explicitly: "For in this way there will be richly provided for you an entrance into the eternal kingdom of our Lord and Savior Jesus Christ" (1:11). In addition, Christ's power (vv. 3, 16), status as "Master" (2:1), and the coming "day of God" (3:12) are all concepts that comport with Jesus' kingdom claims.

The New Testament Epistles differ from the Gospels in genre, subject matter, time of writing, audience, purpose, authorship, setting, and much else. One can hardly demand linguistic conformity to Gospel documents in documents that make no claim to be Gospels. Yet explicit kingdom language and echoes are hardly epistolary rarities. It is fair to say that the Epistles faithfully, if sparingly, appropriate the Gospels' variegated presentations of "the kingdom of God," particularly in the way Jesus, the life of faith in him, and the coming age including the day of judgment are represented.

Conclusion

Other chapters in this book highlight contemporary application of what the New Testament says about the kingdom of God. We will therefore not attempt here to synthesize and apply for our own times and settings the findings of this chapter.

In a way, meaningful summary would at best be an exercise in reductionism. The term "kingdom of God/heaven" in the New Testament is used in a variety of ways by different authors in different settings and in various literary genres. Even Jesus, who is remembered for having the most to say about kingdom, was not univocal in his usage. As Gilbert noted long ago, the term "in the usage of Jesus is not easy to be defined" and "appears to be an elastic, poetic symbol rather than the vehicle of a single sharply-bounded conception."[21]

Nevertheless, we may venture to furnish a summary statement, not so much to make readers feel they have the gist of this chapter in a nutshell as to encourage them to read the pertinent sections (already highly abbreviated) for themselves. Pennington's recent comprehensive study of the kingdom in Matthew's Gospel arrived at five conclusions (to which we add a sixth), which happen to square with what this chapter's investigation has substantially confirmed. Pennington's conclusions,[22] given verbatim with only slight variation below, summarize well not only "the heaven and earth theme" in Matthew but also what the whole New Testament has to say about the kingdom of God. New Testament teaching about that kingdom:

1) Emphasizes the universality of God's dominion.
2) Make[s] a biblical-theological connection[23] with the Old Testament.
3) Serves to strengthen the christological claims of the Gospel.[24]
4) Undergird[s] the radical nature of the ethics and teachings of Jesus.
5) Serves to legitimate and encourage Matthew's readers[25] that they are the true people of God.
6) Asserts that God's kingdom is at once past, present, and future—in addition to being eternal and therefore transcending human history without in any way minimizing it.

[21]G. Gilbert, "Kingdom of God (or Heaven)," in *DCG*, ed. James Hastings (Edinburgh: T & T Clark, 1906), 1:933.
[22]J. Pennington, *Heaven and Earth in the Gospel of Matthew* (Grand Rapids, MI: Baker Academic, 2009), 343–48.
[23]We would add "historical"—it is unlikely that New Testament writers understood the Old Testament documents in purely literary or idealist terms.
[24]We would add "and of the whole New Testament."
[25]We would add "and all who heed the kingdom message and summons."

6

THE KINGDOM, MIRACLES, SATAN, AND DEMONS

CLINTON E. ARNOLD

God reigns supreme over all of his creation. Yet something is dreadfully awry. His beautiful handiwork is in need of rescue and *shalom*. People get horribly sick, natural evils abound, some are tormented by alien spiritual presences, and sin is all-pervasive—afflicting everyone indiscriminately, even God's old covenant people. The creation stands in need of divine intervention.

The good news of the kingdom of God has to do with this loving intervention of God to begin the process of redeeming his creation. Jesus' proclamation of the kingdom announces the coming and presence of this hope for divine help. He declares the arrival of the promised era of well-being when the devastating curse of sin and evil would be reversed. Jesus' miracles provide a living and real demonstration that it is truly taking place in him. The forgiveness of sins, the creation of a new people of God, the fulfillment of prophecy, a relationship with the Messiah, and the future hope of complete restoration are all a part of this. Jesus' healings and exorcisms signal the arrival of God's reign. But what is here in part—instances of physical healing and the overcoming of Satan and evil spirits—will only arrive in completeness when Jesus returns again.

The significance of the miracle stories is seen in their sheer number in the Gospels. They approximate one-third of the content of Mark's Gospel and are numerous in Matthew, Luke, and John. If the proclamation of the kingdom of God was the central thrust of the teaching of Jesus in his earthly ministry, the miracles certainly reflect the prominent part of the active work of Jesus before his passion. The Gospels "summarize his whole ministry before the cross in terms of exorcism and healing."[1] Jesus himself summed up his work this way in responding to the threat issued by Herod: "And he said to them, 'Go and tell that fox, "Behold, I cast out demons and perform cures today and tomorrow, and the third day I finish my course"'" (Luke 13:32). The many summary statements of Jesus' ministry suggest that exorcism[2] and healing were a near daily activity of Jesus.

In this essay, we will explore the purpose of Jesus' miracles and the nature of their connection to his teaching about the kingdom as reflected in the Gospels,[3] but also from the vantage point of the full New Testament witness about the meaning of the kingdom of God.

What Are Miracles?

It is necessary first of all to define what we mean by "miracle." The eighteenth-century Scottish philosopher David Hume suggested that "a miracle is a violation of the laws of nature" and that "nothing is esteemed a miracle, if it ever happened in the common course of nature."[4] This statement is perhaps a good starting point since it underlines the surprising and unexpected nature of a miracle, which corresponds with the biblical terms for "wonder" (*thaumasia* and *terata*) sometimes used to refer to such phenomena. The problem with this definition is the inadequacy of the term "violation" when we think of the creator of the universe as the source of power behind the extraordinary event. Thus, N. T. Wright speaks of a miracle as something that is not anticipated in the "natural world," but as a happening giving evidence for a power enabling it to be more truly itself.[5] Thus healing and resurrection, for instance, while unexpected, do represent a change of affairs in the direction of the way things ought to be.

---

[1]Mark Saucy, *The Kingdom of God in the Teaching of Jesus* (Dallas: Word, 1997), 326.

[2]Chrys C. Caragounis ("Kingdom of God, Son of Man and Jesus' Self-Understanding, Part II," *TB* 40, no. 2 [November 1989]: 230) objects that it is improper to use the terms "exorcist" or "exorcism" with reference to Jesus since this term is not used by the New Testament writers to describe his confrontation with demons in the various accounts. I have chosen, however, to use the terms throughout this essay since they are deeply embedded in popular usage, which tends to understand them in the simple sense of casting out spirits and does not necessarily associate them with magical means.

[3]In this essay, I will assume the integrity and accuracy of the Gospel accounts eschewing the hopeless skepticism of Norman Perrin who once remarked, "We cannot, today, reconstruct a single authentic healing or exorcism narrative from the tradition we have" (*Rediscovering the Teaching of Jesus* [New York: Harper & Row, 1967], 137). An excellent defense of the historicity of the miracle accounts in the Gospels has now been provided by Graham H. Twelftree, *Jesus the Miracle Worker: A Historical and Theological Study* (Downers Grove, IL: InterVarsity, 1999).

[4]David Hume, *An Enquiry Concerning Human Understanding* (Chicago: Open Court, 1907), 120.

[5]N. T. Wright, *Jesus and the Victory of God* (Minneapolis: Fortress, 1996), 188.

Augustine defined a miracle as "whatever appears that is difficult or unusual above the hope and power of them who wonder."[6] His focus on those who behold the miracle is important because it enables him to point people to how "unmarvelous" it is when one considers God. In his sermon on the miracle of the five loaves and two fish (John 6:9), Augustine remarks that it is "a great miracle; but we shall not wonder much at what was done, if we give heed to Him that did it. He multiplied the five loaves in the hands of them that brake them, who multiplieth the seeds that grow in the earth, so that a few grains are sown, and whole barns are filled. But, because he doth this every year, no one marvels."[7]

The most common word for miracles in the New Testament is *dynameis*, "mighty works" or "displays of power." The explicit subject behind all of these incredible acts is God. He is the source of power behind the act that causes those who behold it to marvel simply because it defies their everyday experience. But as we will see in the course of our discussion, there is nothing that God does that violates who he is or what he has established. What makes the miraculous exceed our expectations and causes us to marvel has more to do with what has happened to set our expectations at a certain mundane level. Life the way we live it and life the way God created it to be are two different things, as we shall see. The reason for this disparity is the entrance and presence of sin in the world.

As we look at the various miracle stories narrated in the Gospels and Acts, there appear to be three different categories that emerge: exorcisms, healings, and nature miracles. Yet a hard and fast line between these three cannot be established because they overlap significantly. For instance, a healing might be effected through an exorcism. Jesus stilled a storm by rebuking it, much as he would a "demon." The focus of this discussion will be primarily on miracles of exorcism and healing.

It is not part of the scope of this essay to compare the New Testament miracles with miracle reports from the first-century Mediterranean world. Were we to do so, however, we would find that they are distinct from any known pattern or form. The closest parallels might be in the story of Apollonius of Tyana, the rituals of power performed by various shamanistic figures (exemplified by the texts known as the Greek Magical Papyri), and a few Jewish wonder-workers known from rabbinic texts.

---

[6]Augustine, *On the Profit of Believing* 34, NPNF 103, 364, as cited in Colin Brown, *Miracles and the Critical Mind* (Grand Rapids, MI: Eerdmans, 1984), 7, 95, 291.
[7]Augustine, "On the Words of the Gospel, John vi. 9, 1," in *Sermons on Selected Lessons of the New Testament, Nicene and Post-Nicene Fathers* 106; Sermon LXXX, 498.

Wright has correctly observed that there are some similarities, but Jesus' miracles are fundamentally distinct.[8]

The point of departure is not only the technique, but principally the source of power. As Twelftree observes, "The miracles of Jesus carry in them the signature or the fingerprints of the One who performed them. That is, the emphasis on the One who is the source of the miracle."[9]

What Was the Purpose of Jesus' Miracles?

If the miracles of Jesus were such a prominent part of his three-year ministry, it is important for us to ask why this was so and how they were related to his teaching about the kingdom of God. When we do so, we will find that there was an inextricable connection.

To Attest to His Identity

Many of the miracle stories point to the identity of Jesus as someone more than a mere man and who exceeds even prophets like Elijah or Elisha. In a number of the exorcism accounts, the demons accurately shout out the identity of Jesus as "the Holy One of God" (Mark 1:24), "the Son of God" (3:11; Matt. 8:29), and the "Son of the Most High God" (Mark 5:7). In the story of the healing of the paralytic, Jesus declares that the man's sins are forgiven, but the observing scribes rightly entertain the question, "Who can forgive sins but God alone?" (2:7). When Jesus raises Lazarus from the dead, he tells the sister of the man, "Did I not tell you that if you believed you would see the glory of God?" (John 11:40).

Although many more examples could be given, these are adequate to show that one of the purposes of Jesus' miracles was to show that God himself was powerfully at work in and through Jesus. Twelftree rightly concludes, "The miracles of Jesus reveal his identity as God himself at work: indeed, God is encountered in the miracles."[10]

To Elicit Faith

Another purpose of the miracle stories in the Gospels was to commend the importance of faith. Jesus called attention to the faith of those who brought the paralytic man to him by digging through the roof of the house (Mark 2:5). He tells the woman who had suffered with an internal hemorrhage for twelve years that "your faith has made you well" (5:34). Similarly,

---

[8]Wright, *Jesus and the Victory of God*, 191.
[9]Twelftree, *Jesus the Miracle Worker*, 349.
[10]Ibid., 343.

he credits Bartimaeus's faith as a factor in why his sight was restored (10:52). When Jesus heals the horribly demonized boy, he attributes his disciples' inability to cast out the spirit to their "little faith" (Matt. 17:20) and bemoans the fact that they are so deeply influenced by this "faithless" generation (v. 17). He then suggests that they could do much greater works of demonic deliverance with the right kind of faith: "Truly, I say to you, if you have faith like a grain of mustard seed, you will say to this mountain, 'Move from here to there,' and it will move, and nothing will be impossible for you" (v. 20).

To Signify and Demonstrate the Arrival of the Kingdom of God

The main purpose behind the many miracles Jesus performed throughout his three-year public ministry, however, was to signify and demonstrate the arrival of the kingdom of God. Jesus makes this purpose explicit in a very important statement:

> But if it is by the Spirit of God [Luke: "finger of God"] that I cast out demons, then the kingdom of God has come upon you. (Matt. 12:28; Luke 11:20)

This statement shows the clear connection between Jesus' exorcisms and the kingdom of God. One writer put it this way, "The Kingdom of God is present where the dominion of the adversary has been overthrown."[11]

There are two very important points to glean from Jesus' saying: First, note the significant role of the Holy Spirit in Jesus' performance of these miracles. The Gospel writers (and particularly Luke) emphasize the empowerment by the Holy Spirit for much of Jesus' ministry. After the Holy Spirit descends upon Jesus in his baptism (Luke 3:22), he is "full of the Holy Spirit" (4:1) and is led by the Spirit into the wilderness where he successfully resists the various temptations by which the Devil entices him to sin (vv. 1–13). As Jesus announces the beginning of his public ministry while he speaks at the synagogue at Nazareth, he reads a passage from Isaiah 61 to explain his new covenant–inaugurating and Spirit-empowered ministry: "The Spirit of the Lord is upon me, because he has anointed me to proclaim good news to the poor. He has sent me to proclaim liberty to the captives and recovering of sight to the blind, to set at liberty those who are oppressed, to proclaim the year of the Lord's

---

[11]Ethelbert Stauffer, *Theology of the New Testament*, 5th ed. (New York: Macmillan, 1955), 124.

favor" (Isa. 61:1–2; Luke 4:18–19). In the context of Luke's Gospel, this announcement becomes the interpretive grid by which we understand the Lord's miracles. The new covenant gift of the Spirit has come in the person of the Messiah and, by the power of that Spirit, Jesus performs mighty works.[12]

Luke's reference to the "finger of God" is an allusion to Exodus 8:19, where Pharaoh's magicians attributed the miracles Moses performed to "the finger of God," a metaphorical expression for God's power. Luke views this as coextensive with the empowering work of the Holy Spirit—something that Matthew's version of the saying makes more explicit. Luke's allusion to the exodus, however, highlights the theme of conflict. It may also point to a "new exodus" theme with its attendant miracles.[13] God is now powerfully at work to redeem for himself a new people.

Second, Jesus wants to point all who marvel at his exorcisms to what they really signify: *that the kingdom of God has arrived with him.* As many scholars have observed, the expression translated here as "has come upon" (*ephthasen epi*) should be understood as indicating that it has "arrived" and is not pointing to a strictly future coming or even a potential coming.[14] The kingdom is here because the king is here. Jesus came to begin his kingly rule as Messiah and Son of God, but the nature of that rule would be different from what the Jewish people commonly expected. His exertion of kingly power would be directed at the spiritual enemies. As Craig Evans observes, "The exorcisms demonstrate the reality of the presence of the kingdom (or rule) of God . . . . Casting out demons is seen as proof that the kingdom of God has come."[15] This is nothing other than the beginning of the fulfillment of what every Jew had longed for. Mark Saucy thus rightly concludes that the miracles "proclaim the eschatological reign of God anticipated in the Old Testament prophetic hope."[16]

Most scholars would agree that the kingdom of God was the central

---

[12]See the discussion in Max Turner, *Power from on High: The Spirit in Israel's Restoration and Witness in Luke-Acts*, JPTSS 9 (Sheffield, UK: Sheffield Academic Press, 1996), 255–61. He concludes, "Luke saw Jesus' redemptive miracles and exorcisms very much as part of the Isaianic commission of 4.18–19, and so as attributable to the Spirit upon him" (261).

[13]Ibid., 260.

[14]Donald A. Hagner, *Matthew 1–13*, WBC (Dallas: Word, 1993), 343, notes that the verb "necessitates the conclusion that the kingdom of God has in some sense actually become present," yet properly avers, "admittedly this has happened without the fullest effects that one must associate with the kingdom; we thus have fulfillment but fulfillment short of consummation."

[15]Craig A. Evans, "Exorcisms and the Kingdom: Inaugurating the Kingdom of God and Defeating the Kingdom of Satan," in *Key Events in the Life of the Historical Jesus: A Collaborative Exploration of Context and Coherence*, ed. Darrell L. Bock and Robert L. Webb, WUNT 247 (Tübingen: Mohr Siebeck, 2009), 151. See also John P. Meier, *A Marginal Jew: Rethinking the Historical Jesus*, vol. 2: *Mentor, Message, and Miracles* (New York: Doubleday, 1994), 422.

[16]Saucy, *Kingdom of God*, 322.

and all-important message in the teaching of Jesus during his three-year public ministry. Jesus' miracles, which comprise a substantial portion of his deeds recorded by the Gospel writers, are closely connected to his teaching in that they demonstrate the arrival of the kingdom he proclaimed. They declare the intervention of God's kingly rule in a world marred by sin, disease, and the oppressive mayhem of the Evil One. This kingdom is now present with Jesus. As Wright comments, "He claimed that the kingdom had arrived where he was, and with his activity."[17]

This passage is one of the clearest indicators in the Gospels that when Jesus spoke of the "kingdom" (*basileia*), he was not thinking strictly of a political entity but was using the term in the more expanded sense of a "kingly rule."[18] In and through Jesus, God was beginning to assert his divine dominion over his wayward creation. The miracles provide us with a brilliant illustration of what the full manifestation of the kingdom would be like.[19] But they are more than examples, "the miracles are themselves the eschatological kingdom of God in operation."[20]

But once again, as this passage asserts, the miracles are also evidence of God's Spirit powerfully at work in and through the life of Jesus. This work of the Spirit heralds the arrival of the new covenant age and stands in continuity with the scriptural testimony of God working powerfully to bring redemption to his people.

The Conflict between Kingdoms

A careful reading of the Gospels shows that Jesus proclaims and demonstrates the arrival of the kingdom of God in a context of strenuous opposition. This intense resistance comes principally from Satan—a powerful supernatural figure who commands a host of evil spirits all ranged against God and his redemptive purposes. George Ladd accurately summed up this theme when he said, "The theology of the kingdom of God is essentially one of conflict and conquest over the kingdom of Satan."[21]

God's Universal Reign

It would be wrong to assert that the Gospels teach that God once reigned but has been dethroned by Satan sometime before the coming of Jesus. The Bible is univocal in its testimony that God is sovereign and reigns

---

[17]Wright, *Jesus and the Victory of God*, 472.
[18]See George E. Ladd, *A Theology of the New Testament*, rev. ed. (Grand Rapids, MI: Eerdmans, 1993), 58.
[19]Saucy, *Kingdom of God*, 322.
[20]Twelftree, *Miracles*, 347.
[21]Ladd, *Theology of the New Testament*, 48.

supreme at all times. There has never been a time that God's power or sovereignty has been compromised.

Psalm 10:16 declares, "The LORD is king forever and ever." Similarly, Psalm 29:10 asserts, "The LORD sits enthroned over the flood; the LORD sits enthroned as king forever." The plight of God's people during their period of Egyptian slavery did not pose a threat to his sovereign control. God knew their situation and had planned their deliverance. After Pharaoh's army perished in the sea, Israel exclaimed, "The LORD will reign forever and ever" (Ex. 15:18). Even under the horrors of captivity and exile, God remains king. Speaking through the prophet Jeremiah, the Lord assured his people by asserting, "the LORD is the true God; he is the living God and the everlasting King" (Jer. 10:10).[22]

The numerous scriptural assertions of God's ruling sovereignty allow for opposition and suffering. These experiences do not provide a counterargument against God's universal reign. The presence of evil, however, demonstrates that God will need to assert his reign against those who would seek to oppose him and his people. Jesus' proclamation of the kingdom and his demonstration of its power do just that.

The Real Enemy Is Not Rome

Most of the Jewish people living at the time of Jesus were longing for God to raise up his "horn of salvation" in the house of David to come and powerfully liberate them from the oppression and captivity under Roman rule (Luke 1:69). A well-known text from a first-century document called *The Psalms of Solomon* captures this sentiment well:

> See, Lord, and raise up for them their king, the son of David,
> to rule over your servant Israel in the time known to you, O God.
> Undergird him with strength to destroy the unrighteous rulers,
> to purge Jerusalem from Gentiles who trample her to destruction;
> in wisdom and in righteousness to drive out the sinners from the
>   inheritance;
> to smash the arrogance of sinners like a potter's jar. (*Pss. Sol.* 17:21–25)

The apocalyptic worldview of much of Judaism at this time anticipated God decisively intervening in human history and bringing the oppressive course of the Gentile kingdoms to a sudden and catastrophic

---

[22]On the universal kingship of God, see the texts and discussion in Evans, "Exorcisms and the Kingdom," 152–57.

end. The second-temple apocalyptic literature gives ample and dramatic testimony of this conviction. The principal fountainhead of apocalyptic, however, is the book of Daniel. At the same time, as John Goldingay asserts, "The theme that is central to Daniel as it is to no other book in the OT is the kingdom of God."[23] Nebuchadnezzar's dream of the enormous human image representing four successive kingdoms exerted a powerful impact on the subsequent history of Judaism (Daniel 2). The hope for the Jewish people was rooted in the "stone cut out by no human hand" (v. 34) that struck and pulverized the image and then became "a great mountain and filled the whole earth" (v. 35). Daniel explicitly says that "the God of heaven will set up a kingdom that shall never be destroyed" (v. 44; see also Daniel 7). For most Jews, then, the kingdom hope was closely tied to a powerful military and political victory over the kingdoms of the earth. But this was not Jesus' way, at least not yet.

But the book of Daniel also gives us our first glimpse into the connection between the kingdom and powerful spiritual opposition. During an extended period of intercession for the people of Israel, an angel visited Daniel and revealed to him that there had been conflict in heaven: "The prince of the kingdom of Persia withstood me twenty-one days, but Michael, one of the chief princes, came to help me . . . " (10:1–21, esp. v. 13). This "prince" was a demonic spirit with some connection to the Persian Empire. The angel then informs Daniel, "Now I will return to fight against the prince of Persia; and when I go out, behold, the prince of Greece will come" (v. 20). This passage provides us with one of the few revealed insights we have in the OT about the nature of spiritual struggle at this high level—the level of nations and empires. It unveils the fact that there are powerful supernatural opponents that have an impact on the course of human affairs. It is quite possible that behind these affairs stand "the angels of the nations" tradition from the OT and Judaism (see esp. Deut. 32:8; Psalm 82) in which all the nations of the world are assigned to "the sons of God/angels of God."[24] These angels were part of the rebellion and now lead the nations astray (Ps. 82:6–8).

In Mark's record of the beginning of Jesus' ministry, the very first episode after his baptism and temptation involves conflict with the demonic. In this situation, a demonized man confronts Jesus as he speaks in the synagogue at Capernaum (Mark 1:21–28). Jesus immediately goes on the

---

[23]John E. Goldingay, *Daniel*, WBC (Dallas: Word, 1989), 330.
[24]See Loren T. Stuckenbruck, "Angels of the Nations," *DNTB*, 29–31.

attack by enjoining the demon to silence and then commanding him to depart from the man (v. 25). This was the first of many such encounters Jesus would have with demonic spirits. Just a few verses later, Mark provides one of his summary statements of Jesus' ministry in which he claims that Jesus "healed many who were sick with various diseases, and cast out many demons" (v. 34). A typical day in the life of Jesus in his three-year ministry could have included exorcism. It is quite possible that in the course of these three years Jesus brought deliverance to hundreds of individuals.[25]

In his next major encounter with a demon-afflicted man, Jesus is on the east bank of the Sea of Galilee and is sought out by a man from Gerasa who is being tormented by a legion of demons. In the time of Augustus, a Roman legion would have numbered about six thousand soldiers.[26] The man was so powerful that he could even break chains (Mark 5:4). Mark emphasizes that "no one had the strength to subdue" him. That is, no one could until he met Jesus. After a period in which the spirits attempt to negotiate with Jesus, the Lord demands that they come out of the man, and this horribly tormented individual is completely healed.

Some interpreters have looked at this account and have sought to reinterpret the language as a series of metaphors for Roman imperial power. This is an interpretive call at least partly suggested by the term "legion." Warren Carter, for instance, understands this passage as something of a political parable aimed at subverting Roman rule and envisioning its violent overthrow. He interprets the word "legion" as a reference to Rome and its military power. Carter says that, "Mark's Jesus identifies Rome and the military power of its legions as demonic (Mark 5:1–20). He anticipates God's powerful destruction of Rome by casting the demons called legion into the sea" (vv. 9–13).[27] The problem with this view is that it completely misses the fact that Mark is establishing the cosmic supremacy of the Lord Jesus Christ over demons. Jesus shows himself more powerful than even the most formidable collection of supernatural forces. N. T. Wright aptly notes, "But Rome is not the enemy; it is the Satan and his hordes, who are deceiving Israel into

---

[25]This was cogently argued in a paper presented by Thomas J. Sappington, "Reexamining Common Assumptions Regarding Demonic Influence and the Ministry of Deliverance in the Synoptic Gospels," delivered at the annual meeting of the Evangelical Theological Society, Thursday, November 18, 2010, in Atlanta, Georgia.
[26]See "λεγιών/*legion* in BDAG, 588.
[27]Warren Carter, *The Roman Empire and the New Testament: An Essential Guide* (Nashville: Abingdon, 2006), 121.

thinking that Rome is the real enemy, so that she (Israel) will not notice the reality."[28]

Evil goes far beyond political or human enemies. Evil is present within each individual *and* it is associated with Satan and his demons. The Gospels describe Jesus' battles with these more ultimate enemies.

The Ultimate Enemies: Sin and Satan

For many years, Israel had myopically focused on the militaries and political powers ranged against her as the enemies she truly needed to fear. Little did she realize that the true enemy was within. As Wright notes, *"That which was wrong with the rest of the world was wrong with Israel, too.* 'Evil' could not be located conveniently beyond Israel's borders, in the pagan hordes. It had taken up residence within the chosen people. The battle against evil—the correct analysis of the problem, and the correct answer to it—was therefore of a different order from that imagined by his [Jesus'] contemporaries."[29] It is for this reason that up to one-third of each of the Gospel accounts is taken up with the story of his passion, and in the intervening material Jesus makes numerous predictions of his passion.

Jesus came not to vanquish the power of Rome or any other political enemy in a show of superior and overwhelming power. He went to the cross in abject humility to overcome the greatest problem of all—the specter of sin residing in the hearts of every individual and in the community as a whole. This is why he announced that "the Son of Man came not to be served but to serve, and to give his life as a ransom for many" (Mark 10:45). He made the reason for his approaching death even more clear during the Last Supper when he gave the cup and said, "This is my blood of the covenant, which is poured out for many for the forgiveness of sins" (Matt. 26:28).

Yet the Gospels also reveal that Jesus came to fight another battle of superhuman proportions. This battle involved Satan and a vast army of evil spirits in league with him to oppose God and his redemptive purposes. This warfare was waged in Jesus' resistance of Satan in his temptations, his many exorcisms of evil spirits, the equipping of his disciples for the mission they would engage in, and, above all, in his cross and resurrection. The importance of recognizing the role of Satan and demons in this regard is greatly underscored by Ladd:

---

[28]Wright, *Jesus and the Victory of God,* 196; see also, 294, 451, and 455.
[29]Ibid., 447.

Heart of Jesus mission

The demonic is absolutely essential in understanding Jesus' interpretation of the picture of sin and of humanity's need for the Kingdom of God. People are in bondage to a personal power stronger than themselves. At the very heart of our Lord's mission is the need of rescuing people from bondage to the satanic kingdom and of bringing them into the sphere of God's Kingdom. Anything less than this involves an essential reinterpretation of some of the basic facts of the Gospel.[30]

As we begin to develop this dimension of Jesus' work, it is crucial that we do not separate Jesus' battle against the demonic too far from his battle against the power of sin. The two are closely related. It was precisely in and through the cross that Jesus won a major victory over Satan. By virtue of his death on the cross, Jesus took away from Satan the power to justly accuse the people of God in the divine court. The name "Satan" is the transliteration of a Hebrew term (*Sätän*), which not only means "adversary, opponent" but also "accuser" (especially in a context of jurisprudence).[31] This idea can also be seen in the Greek name given to this figure, "devil" (*diabolos*), which in its basic meaning refers to "one who engages in slander."[32] The Evil One's work in this regard can be seen in the visionary scene described by the prophet Zechariah of the divine court: "Then he showed me Joshua the high priest standing before the angel of the LORD, and Satan standing at his right hand to accuse him" (Zech. 3:1). In that episode, Satan lost his ability to effectively accuse Joshua because of the provision made by God: "Behold, I have taken your iniquity away from you, and I will clothe you with pure vestments" (v. 4). The cross of Christ accomplishes this once and for all in a way that is effective for everyone who puts his or her faith in Christ. Satan can no longer make an accusation that sticks because of the forgiveness of sin achieved by Christ's blood and the gift of righteousness he bestows on us through his sinless life.

The cross therefore represents the decisive and important battle against Satan (see Col. 2:15). Because of the work of Christ, there is nothing that Satan can do to sever believers from their relationship to their loving Lord. The writer of Hebrews says that the purpose of his death was to "destroy the one who has the power of death, that is, the devil" (Heb. 2:14). The resurrection of Jesus guarantees this victory. Jesus has vanquished the sting of death and thereby provides us with the great hope of life beyond the grave that lasts forever.

---

[30]Ladd, *New Testament Theology,* 50.
[31]See "שָׂטָן"/"śāṭān" in HALOT, 2:1317.
[32]See "διάβολος/*diabolos*" BDAG, 226.

But Jesus' conflict with Satan was even more extensive than what took place on the cross. He struggled with Satan in his temptation and in numerous direct confrontations with evil spirits. Ladd observes that "The chief purpose of Satan in the Gospels is to oppose the redemptive purpose of God."[33] The temptation of Jesus by Satan demonstrates the Evil One's efforts to derail God's redemptive plan by enticing the Son of God to sin. It also illustrates Satan's ongoing desire to rob God of the glory due to his name by seeking to deflect worship onto himself ("all these I will give you, if you will fall down and worship me," Matt. 4:9). Yet there is a further purpose that underlines this account, and that is to set an example to future generations of believers on how to resist the impulses of Satan by the power of the Holy Spirit.

The exorcism accounts provide us with extraordinary insight into the hideous ways that Satan endeavors to create misery and suffering in the lives of people. Jesus' confrontation of these evil spirits shows his mercy and compassion, but these deliverances also signal the presence of the power of the kingdom of God in the person of Christ. Jesus clearly has the power to bring deliverance and healing because the Holy Spirit is present with him. His exorcisms also provide an example to the church on how they can carry on Jesus' work until he returns.

Resisting and Overcoming Satan as Kingdom Work

The purpose of the Gospel writers in narrating the exorcism accounts in the Synoptic Gospels was not only to magnify the person of Jesus; they were written for the instruction of the church. These stories served as important examples to the followers of Jesus as they took up Jesus' mantle to be the channel of his presence in the world. This was one of the major conclusions of Graham Twelftree's important monograph *Jesus the Miracle Worker*. In his discussion of Mark's Gospel, Twelftree notes, "Insofar as the disciples are called to emulate the ministry of Jesus—the miracle stories also provide models for ministry."[34] He reaches similar conclusions about the purpose of these accounts in each of the other two Synoptic Gospels and concludes his monograph with the bold assertion:

> What is now seen as Christianity, at least in Western traditional churches, as primarily words and propositions requiring assent and further propagation will have to be replaced by a Christianity that involves

---

[33]Ladd, *New Testament Theology*, 47.
[34]Twelftree, *Jesus the Miracle Worker*, 336.

and is dominated by understanding God's numinous power to be borne
uniquely in Jesus and also in his followers in the working of miracles.[35]

Although his conclusion is overstated, it is not without merit. It
would be entirely inappropriate for churches today to move to a form of
Christianity "dominated by" the miraculous. If the pendulum has swung
too far one way in the past, it is not helpful for it to swing too far the other
way in the present. Balance between knowing and doing is essential. The
gospel is and always will consist of a right confession of faith, not only
or primarily of deeds of power. The Synoptic Gospels themselves teach
us this much by their emphasis on providing an account of the identity
of Jesus and underlining the significance of his passion and resurrection. The rest of the New Testament also stresses the importance of right
belief. (See Acts 2:42 and the early Christian devotion to "the apostles'
teaching"; 1 Cor. 15:3–4 and the importance of the common confession
of faith; 2 Tim. 1:13–14 and sound teaching as "the deposit" Timothy is
charged to keep.)

Yet Twelftree is likely correct in pointing out the paradigmatic function of the Gospels for the church in how to continue the ministry of Jesus
by following the example of the master.

The Power of the Kingdom Is Present

Despite Satan's suffering a massive and decisive defeat by Jesus' death on
the cross and his resurrection, he has not died and gone away. He is still
active, powerful, and doing all that he can to oppose the redemptive work
of God in the world. We see this amply illustrated in the book of Acts when
Satan (and/or his demons) makes repeated attempts to stop the spread of
the gospel by the apostles throughout the Mediterranean world: there are
still people tormented by evil spirits who need help and healing (Acts
5:16; 8:7; 19:12), Satan works to prevent people from hearing the gospel
(13:10), and he continues to effectively tempt believers to sin (5:3). The
New Testament Epistles also emphasize the ongoing opposition by Satan
and evil spirits to the growth and development of the church. In fact, Paul
stressed this by stating that the struggle for believers is not "against flesh
and blood, but against the rulers, against the authorities, against the cosmic powers over this present darkness, against the spiritual forces of evil
in the heavenly places" (Eph. 6:12). Moreover, the apostle Peter empha-

---

[35]Ibid., 359.

sizes the seriousness of this threat when he says, "your adversary the devil prowls around like a roaring lion, seeking someone to devour" (1 Pet. 5:8).

As we noted earlier, Jesus' display of the power of the Spirit in exorcism was a sign that the kingdom of God had arrived. The presence and power of the Spirit is one of the principal blessings of the inaugurated kingdom.

When Jesus gave his "Great Commission" in Matthew's Gospel, he prefaced the imperative of "make disciples" with "all authority in heaven and on earth has been given to me" (28:18). He possessed divine authority before this time (11:27), but he mentions it here because he is passing on this authority to the disciples as they engage in the mission. This authority entails representing Jesus in the world, not only in carrying the message of redemption and making disciples, but also in carrying on the works of Jesus as they fulfilled this task of building the church. This authority is passed on to all believers.

Paul speaks of this shared power and authority in different terms when he writes to the Colossians. He tells them that in Christ "the whole fullness of deity dwells bodily, and you have been filled in him, who is the head of all rule and authority" (2:9–10). The essence of what Paul is teaching them is that they share in the power and authority of Christ over the realm of the demonic (viz. "all rule and authority"). For the Colossians, this meant that they should resist the impulse to rely on other forms of ritual power taught to them by false teachers.

Luke's narration of the coming of the Spirit in the book of Acts and the subsequent success of the followers of Jesus in making disciples in Jerusalem, Samaria, Syria, Cyprus, Roman Asia, and throughout the Mediterranean world illustrate this point. These missionaries were able to stand up against a wide variety of assaults brought against them by evil spirits and to bring healing to those who were oppressed.

Resisting Temptation

The temptation narrative thus becomes an example of how to successfully resist solicitations to evil brought to us by Satan or demonic spirits (Mark 1:12–23; Matt. 4:1–11; Luke 4:1–13). Luke stresses that Jesus was "full of the Holy Spirit" as he began his period of time in the desert (4:1; see also Matt. 4:1 where "Jesus was led up by the Spirit"). This narrative introduction suggests that the Spirit's presence and power were significant for Jesus in resisting the Devil. Jesus also countered the three temptations by citing relevant portions of Scripture to the Devil. The way this is told implies that Jesus had an intimate familiarity with the Scripture and knew precisely what portion of God's Word was relevant to each situation of temptation.

Jesus therefore modeled the use of the Spirit and the Word as the principal means of resisting demonic temptation. In the apostle Paul's familiar delineation of divine armor for spiritual warfare, he, too, stresses this indispensable combination: "and take . . . the sword of the Spirit, which is the word of God" (Eph. 6:17).

Delivering the Oppressed

It is quite likely that the writers of the Synoptic Gospels intended Jesus' exorcisms to serve as examples for God's people as they continued Jesus' ministry in the world. Jesus prepared the Twelve for this kind of ministry when he called them and "gave them authority over unclean spirits, to cast them out, and to heal every disease and affliction" (Matt. 10:1; see also Mark 3:14–15; Luke 9:1–2). This mission was a foundational experience for the Twelve in preparing them for their task after the day of Pentecost. As such, it was preparatory to the later mission of the church and therefore is instructive for our mission. I. Howard Marshall notes, "The basic principles in them [the three Synoptic accounts] were regarded as of lasting value for the church."[36]

This authority over the demonic was not limited to the Twelve but was extended to the seventy-two whom Jesus sent out (Luke 10:1–20). When they returned from their mission, they exclaimed, "Lord, even the demons are subject to us in your name!" (v. 17). This passage prefigures the mission of the church.[37] Its relevance to the church is even more pronounced since those sent out go beyond the twelve apostles.

The prophetic description of the mission of the Messiah declared by Isaiah that Jesus applies to himself (61:1–2) has now been passed on to the church. The Spirit of the Lord has come upon the new covenant people of God; they have been anointed to proclaim the good news; and they are called "to proclaim liberty to the captives and recovering of sight to the blind, to set at liberty those who are oppressed" (Luke 4:18).

We see this pattern of mission and service unfold in the book of Acts. The Spirit comes in power on the day of Pentecost (2:1–12), the good news is proclaimed in Jerusalem and throughout the Mediterranean

---

[36]I. Howard Marshall, *Luke*, NIGTC (Grand Rapids, MI: Eerdmans, 1978), 351.
[37]Ibid., 413. See also Robert Stein, *Luke*, NAC (Nashville: Broadman, 1992), 310.

world, people are healed, and those who are oppressed by demonic spirits are delivered. This is seen particularly in the lives of the two most prominent characters whom Luke develops in Acts—Peter and Paul.

Note that Acts records Paul engaging in a ministry of deliverance even during the period that he was writing his letters. Throughout his three-year ministry at Ephesus (c. AD 52–55), Luke tells us that "God was doing extraordinary miracles by the hands of Paul" (Acts 19:11). This included healing and exorcism. This passage demonstrates that Paul was engaging in this kind of ministry after he had written Galatians and 1 and 2 Thessalonians, while he was writing 1 Corinthians, and just shortly before he wrote 2 Corinthians and Romans.

While it is true that Paul never mentions exorcism in his letters, he does provide an extensive and important theological basis for carrying out the mission of building the church in light of ongoing demonic opposition.[38] Paul's teaching on the demonic includes: (1) a strong emphasis on the supremacy of Christ over all demons and the power of the Devil, (2) an equally strong emphasis on the participation of believers with Christ and their sharing in his power and authority over this domain, and (3) a call to stand firm, resist the enemy, and engage in the mission in dependence on Christ's power.[39] The entirety of his teaching is based on the assumption that Satan and demons are real. Paul never suggests that they should be understood as metaphors of human or structural evil.

It is clear that the early church of the first few centuries interpreted the Scripture as affirming the ongoing validity of deliverance and exorcism. A review of the literature of the pre-Nicene church reveals that the most common time deliverances were done was during the period of the catechumenate.[40] This was the time of discipleship and training after a person made a confession of faith in Christ and before he or she formally joined the church. During this two-to-three-year period, believers were immersed in the Scripture, taught the central doctrines of the faith, received help in spiritual and moral formation (often in mentoring relationships), and underwent deliverance ministry.[41] This was the logical time for the early church to deal with evil spiritual attachments—since

---

[38]See my *Powers of Darkness: Principalities and Powers in Paul's Letters* (Downers Grove, IL: InterVarsity, 1992).

[39]See also now the important work by Kabiro wa Gatumu, *The Pauline Concept of Supernatural Powers: A Reading from the African Worldview* (Eugene, OR: Wipf & Stock, 2008).

[40]See my "Early Church Catechesis and New Christians' Classes in Contemporary Evangelicalism," *JETS* 47 (March 2004): 39–54.

[41]"Ibid.," 51–54.

the vast majority of these people were in the process of renouncing their allegiances to various pagan deities and magical practices to embrace the living and true God.

Overcoming Opposition to the Mission

The sending out of the Twelve and the seventy-two, the testimony of the book of Acts, and the examples of Paul and Peter are all in the context of mission. God has called his people to go and make disciples everywhere throughout the world. And this call is still valid.

James Kallas has observed that, "The command to go out and preach the kingdom of God is never, not once, separated from the command to heal and cast out demons."[42] One can expect that confrontation with the demonic may happen more often in the context of mission.

When the seventy-two returned from their mission full of joy and reported to Jesus their success in casting out demons, he observed, "I saw Satan fall like lightning from heaven" (Luke 10:18). Quite apart from the issue of when "the fall" of Satan occurred, it is important to note that Satan stormed "like lightning." Lightning is frequently found in the OT as an image of warfare, e.g., "he sent out his arrows and scattered them; he flashed forth lightnings and routed them" (Ps. 18:14). Any Greek reader of the Gospel would have been familiar with the numerous stories of Zeus angrily rocketing through the heavens like lightning to oppose the other Olympians or to rout a human army. What this means is that the mission that Jesus has called the church to engage in will not be a smooth and easy task. There will be powerful supernatural opposition. Satan will storm in anger against those who come to proclaim the good news in places it has not been heard. But they have been endowed with God's empowering presence—the new covenant gift of the Holy Spirit, the power of God's reign. Because of this, "the gates of hell shall not prevail against it" (Matt. 16:18).

Jesus revealed some of the spiritual dynamics behind this redemptive mission in a brief parable he told shortly after a group of scribal teachers outrageously accused him of being possessed by the prince of demons. Jesus said, "No one can enter a strong man's house and plunder his goods, unless he first binds the strong man. Then indeed he may plunder his house" (Mark 3:27; Matt. 12:29; Luke 11:22). The "strong man" in this parable represents Satan, and the goods of his house are the people he

---

[42]James Kallas, *The Significance of the Synoptic Miracles* (London: SPCK, 1961), 80.

holds in bondage. The binding of this strong man took place in the event of Jesus' death and resurrection (cf. Col. 2:15). Although Satan has been "bound," it is only with respect to those who are in Christ and appropriate his power and authority. Satan is still active and ominously opposes the redemptive work of God through his people. But as people turn to Christ and enter the kingdom of God, Satan loses his possessions.

God's Sovereignty and Spiritual Conflict

It is important to observe that Jesus did not promise victory in every conflict with the Evil One. Nor does the unfolding history of the church in the chapters of Acts assure us of this.

On numerous occasions the apostle Paul found himself beaten with rods, stoned, shipwrecked, facing travel dangers and threats from robbers, and often in situations of privation and suffering (2 Cor. 11:23–26). In some of these occasions he could sense the unmistakable fingerprints of the Evil One.

When he planted the church at Thessalonica, Paul was able to stay in the city no more than only two or three months before he was forced by the city officials to leave after a mob scene (see Acts 17:1–9). In writing to the Thessalonian believers a few weeks later, he says that he tried to return to them on numerous occasions, "but Satan hindered us" (1 Thess. 2:18). Of all people, it would seem that Paul would know how to pray effectively and to exercise the kingdom power and authority to countermand the work of Satan. But on this occasion Satan appeared to be victorious. Nevertheless, this was only a momentary "victory" and did not take into account the providential work of the sovereign God to work all things out for his purposes. As it turned out, the Thessalonian church was flourishing, and Paul's absence from Thessalonica enabled him to plant the church in Corinth.

Remember that God can and does use Satan's strategies and attacks to further his own purposes. Paul found this out when he was under attack by an "angel of Satan" (*angelos satana*) who afflicted him with what Paul called "a thorn in the flesh," likely some kind of physical ailment (2 Cor. 12:7). Paul appealed to God and specifically asked him to eliminate this attack, but God did not intervene. Rather, Paul says that God used this demonically energized affliction to "keep him from becoming conceited."

Peter learned a similar principle when the Lord announced to him shortly before the passion that Satan had demanded "that he might sift you like wheat" (Luke 22:31). Rather than turning to Peter and assuring him that he had provided a hedge of protection around him and that Satan would not be able to touch him, the Lord simply said, "but I have prayed for you that your faith may not fail" (v. 32).

It is important for believers today to recognize that suffering and difficulties are a normal part of life. Opposition, even demonically induced opposition, can be expected as one engages in the work of the kingdom. Nevertheless, God calls his people to continue to rely on him and his power to do the work of the mission and to bring healing and deliverance to the oppressed.

Healing as a Manifestation of the Kingdom

Healing is also a part of kingdom ministry. The healing miracles that Jesus performed not only helped to establish his messianic identity, but they serve as instructive models for the church as Jesus uses his people to mediate his dominion in the world.

The Messianic Era as an Age of Healing

The OT prophets anticipated the age to come as a time of healing for the people of God. There was an expectation that healing would characterize the kingdom. Isaiah beautifully expresses this hope when he declares: "Then the eyes of the blind shall be opened, and the ears of the deaf unstopped; then shall the lame man leap like a deer, and the tongue of the mute sing for joy" (35:5–6). Jesus clearly saw this passage coming to fulfillment in his ministry when he answered the inquiry of John the Baptist by making allusion to this promise (see Matt. 11:4–6; Luke 7:22–23).[43]

Isaiah's prophecy of the Spirit-anointed Messiah who would "bind up the brokenhearted" and "proclaim liberty to the captives" as he inaugurates "the year of the Lord's favor" (61:1–2) also points to the expectation of healing in the kingdom. At the outset of his public ministry, Jesus cited this passage as the banner for what he had come to do, and it serves as the programmatic introduction to Luke's account of Jesus' ministry (see Luke 4:17–21). As Twelftree observes, Jesus' healing ministry "would have been understood to reflect the messianic hopes of the Old Testament."[44] Kallas notes, "The kingdom was to touch every facet of man's existence. It was to cleanse the world as well as man. To touch man's body as well as his heart."[45]

---

[43]See Wright, *Jesus and the Victory of God*, 428.
[44]Twelftree, *Jesus the Miracle Worker*, 347.
[45]Kallas, *Synoptic Miracles*, 81.

Healing must also be seen as a manifestation of the gift of *shalom*, which was a vital part of the messianic age.[46] The "Wonderful Counselor" and "Prince of Peace" of Isaiah 9 will inaugurate a reign regarding which it can be said, "of *shalom* there will be no end" (v. 7). This will be an era in which the prince of *shalom* takes away from his people all that is bad and all that causes pain. But this *shalom* entails far more than the absence of conflict. As John Goldingay notes, "it suggests a community enjoying fullness of life, prosperity, contentment, harmony, and happiness."[47]

Part of this is accomplished by the subduing of the prince of darkness and his minions—the spiritual forces that create havoc and inflict pain. In reflecting on the healings of Jesus, Evans asserts, "Healing in general is part of the demonstration of the powerful presence of God and his rule, not only because it was part of the eschatological promise of Isaiah (cf. Isa. 26:19; 35:5–6; 61:1–2 in Matt. 11:5 = Luke 7:22; 4:16–30; and in 4Q521), but because there is evidence that some of the healings were linked in various ways to exorcism, or at least to the demonic world."[48] This link is well illustrated by the scene where Jesus encounters Peter's mother-in-law lying in bed with a high fever (Luke 4:38). Rather than praying for her, Luke indicates that Jesus "rebuked the fever" (Luke 4:39) "as though a sentient being was responsible for the fever."[49] Similarly, when Jesus met a woman who had a serious back problem and was bent over for eighteen years, he discerned that there was a "disabling spirit" (*pneuma astheneias*) that was the cause of the problem (13:11–12). He healed her by freeing her from the spirit.

As Wright observes, "The works of power were a vital ingredient in the inauguration of the kingdom."[50] Yet healing entails more than just healing from disease. Goldingay notes that "Healing is a wide-ranging image for God putting things right that were wrong."[51] The greatest healing of all takes place when a person who was at one time at enmity with God is reconciled to him on the basis of the work of Christ. There can be no greater healing experience than of having one's sins forgiven by God and gaining a clear conscience before him. At a time when so many illnesses have a mind-body connection and can be attributable to a psychosomatic

---

[46]Wright, *Jesus and the Victory of God*, 192.
[47]John E. Goldingay, *Israel's Faith*, vol. 2 of *Old Testament Theology* (Downers Grove, IL: InterVarsity, 2006), 79.
[48]Evans, "Exorcisms and the Kingdom," 174.
[49]Ibid.
[50]Wright, *Jesus and the Victory of God*, 193.
[51]Goldingay, *Israel's Faith*, 377.

condition (such as the stresses of life), the healing power of the gospel cannot be underestimated.

Healing in the Church

The most frequent pattern that we find in the New Testament for healing is in connection with the spread of the gospel. Paul alludes to this when he writes to the Thessalonians and says, "Our gospel came to you not only in word, but also in power and in the Holy Spirit and with full conviction" (1 Thess. 1:5). It is likely that the coming "in power" refers to exorcisms and healings that accompanied the proclamation of the gospel.[52] This was customary in the apostle Paul's proclamation of the gospel, as he tells the Romans: "by the power of signs and wonders, by the power of the Spirit of God—so that from Jerusalem and all the way around to Illyricum I have fulfilled the ministry of the gospel of Christ" (Rom. 15:19). The writer of Hebrews observes a similar phenomenon when in describing the spread of the gospel he says, "God also bore witness by signs and wonders and various miracles" (Heb. 2:4).

This is the pattern that we find in the book of Acts. The early Christians not only pray for boldness in proclaiming the gospel amidst danger and opposition, but they also ask the Lord to "stretch out your hand to heal, and signs and wonders are performed through the name of your holy servant Jesus" (4:30). The result was that the apostles performed many miracles in Jerusalem (5:12), as also did Stephen (6:8); Philip did many miracles in Samaria (8:6, 13), as did Paul and Barnabas (15:12). Paul explained that God enabled them to do these signs and wonders as an authenticating testimony to the gospel that they proclaimed.

It seems clear, then, that one of the principal reasons for the miracles performed by the early missionaries was to demonstrate the divine origin of the gospel that people were hearing for the very first time. All of the miracle stories in Acts are part of the missionary spread of the gospel and do not relate to the day-to-day life of the church. They "serve primarily to give divine attestation to the messenger and his message."[53] These miracles, signs, and wonders, however, were still a sure sign of the arrival of the kingdom of God and display of the power of the kingdom through the Holy Spirit.

---

[52]See Gary S. Shogren, *1 & 2 Thessalonians*, ZEC (Grand Rapids, MI: Zondervan, forthcoming), on 1 Thess. 1:5. So also, Gene L. Green, *The Letters to the Thessalonians*, PNTC (Grand Rapids, MI: Eerdmans, 2002), 95–96.
[53]Peter H. Davids, "Healing, Illness," *DLNTD*, 437.

There is very little in the Epistles about the healing ministry of the church. Hebrews 12:13 holds out the prospect of healing for the weak and sick so they can complete the race, that is, so they can continue on the path of spiritual maturity (not losing their morale). Peter O'Brien notes, "The prospect of healing for the weak is an encouragement for all."[54]

The primary teaching about healing in the church is isolated to one very important passage that provides believers with instruction on what to do if someone is sick: James 5:14–16. This passage instructs the sick person in the community to call for the elders of the church. These leaders are to "pray over him, anointing him with oil in the name of the Lord" (v. 14). Although much could be said about this passage, it is important to observe that a spiritual intervention may be called for when someone is ill. The passage also holds out the prospect that God may intervene and heal the afflicted person. The exercise of faith is essential both on the part of the one who is sick (expressed in part by calling for the elders) and by the elders who come and pray. Elijah is held as an example of praying in faith—not because he was an extraordinary prophet, but because he was a human "with a nature like ours" (v. 17). The anointing oil should not be viewed here as a metaphor for medicine but as a symbol for setting the person apart for the Lord (as in the OT anointing of priests and kings) and possibly also for the presence of the Holy Spirit. The background for this instruction is the practice of the Twelve who, when Jesus sent them out, "anointed with oil many who were sick and healed them" (Mark 6:13). The final portion of the passage suggests that in James's particular example there may be (note the conditional clause) a connection between illness and sin since it calls for believers to confess their sins to one another so they may be healed (James 5:16; cf. Mark 2:5; John 5:14).[55]

Eschatology, God's Sovereignty, Suffering, and the Kingdom

The overall eschatological framework of the New Testament needs to serve as an important backdrop to our discussion about healing. The full realization of the kingdom of God has not yet taken place. Consequently, not all are healed, people still die (most everyone!), and sickness and suf-

---

[54]Peter T. O'Brien, *The Letter to the Hebrews*, PNTC (Grand Rapids, MI: Eerdmans, 2010), 472.

[55]The practice of healing continued in the ministry of the church for the first few centuries. Because of this trajectory based on scriptural teaching and the example of Jesus, a recent important monograph on the topic reached this conclusion: "As seems to have been the case in the Early Church, the ministry of healing by prayer, laying on of hands and anointing should be viewed as a normal part of the life of every local church today." See Andrew Daunton-Fear, *Healing in the Early Church: The Church's Ministry of Healing and Exorcism from the First to the Fifth Century* (Eugene, OR: Wipf & Stock, 2009), 165.

fering are still rampant among believers. This has been true of the past two thousand years of church history.

Yet the kingdom of God has arrived in the person of Jesus who now indwells the body of Christ through his Spirit. This serves as our basis for the expectation that God may choose to intervene and heal on occasion. Indisputably, God dramatically intervened on numerous occasions in the initial spread of the gospel throughout the Mediterranean world and beyond. This might suggest that we could expect more healings to take place today as the gospel spreads into places where it has not been heard as a way of authenticating the message.

Nevertheless, a passage such as James 5 leads us to believe that God may still intervene and heal in the ongoing course of church ministry. Church leaders have a responsibility to pray for healing over those who call them and ask for healing prayer. The passage clearly envisions instances of healing taking place.

Yet the reality of life and the experience of countless Christians who have gone before us attest to the fact that sudden, dramatic physical healing is far more the exception than the norm. As the writer of Hebrews asserts, "it is appointed for man to die once" (9:27). Since this death will come as a result of some form of physical malady (heart failure, cancer, organ failure, etc.) or "natural" evil (car crash, serious fall, etc.), it is clear that no one in this age will experience ongoing healings that will prevent their ultimate demise.

The important question we then need to ask is, "Whom will God choose to heal?" The answer to this is that we do not know unless God reveals that answer to us (perhaps to prompt us and guide us into how to pray more specifically and directly). We are essentially thrust, once again, onto God's sovereignty. He is our wise and loving Father.

The privilege that children have, however, in relationship to their father is the opportunity to ask for favors. Jesus told his disciples, "Whatever you ask the Father in my name, he may give it to you" (John 15:16). God invites his children to ask, and this is the essence of prayer. The apostle John declared, "This is the confidence that we have toward him, that if we ask anything according to his will he hears us" (1 John 5:14).

From this, we can infer that when leaders of a church gather for healing prayer over an individual, they should approach God as their Father whom they humbly entreat for his healing intervention in someone's life. They do this fully expecting that he might dramatically intervene and heal the sick person but ultimately deferring to his sovereign will.

This kind of deferral to God's sovereignty regarding the miraculous is well illustrated in the book of Acts after the imprisonment of Peter and James (12:1). The king had James put to death by the sword, yet Peter is miraculously led safely out of the prison by an angel and lives many more years in productive ministry. Many people had been praying for Peter's release, but it would be inappropriate for us to conclude that they had not prayed adequately for James or that for some reason they did not have enough faith that God would release him. We can only defer to God's sovereignty in the matter.

What we can be assured of—although this is one of the more unpleasant features of the Christian life—is that suffering should be expected by believers until the kingdom of God comes in its fullness. The apostle Paul made it his goal to know Christ and to "share his sufferings, becoming like him in his death" (Phil. 3:10). He encourages believers to "rejoice in our sufferings" (Rom. 5:3), not only because suffering refines our character, but it produces hope (v. 4). The hope that he refers to is in the promise of a future with Christ that will be totally devoid of suffering. He later says to the Romans that, "we suffer with him in order that we may also be glorified with him" (8:17), but that glorification is something we will experience only when the kingdom has been fully realized (see v. 18).[56]

Complete Healing and Final Defeat of Satan in the Eschaton

Believers still await the "not yet" of their kingdom existence. The eternal and absolute reign of the Lord Jesus Christ is still on the horizon. This is "the blessed hope" that every Christian longs for. This final stage of the kingdom will take place in conjunction with the bodily return of Christ to the earth (the *parousia*; 1 Thess. 2:19; 3:13; 4:15; 5:23). In his Olivet Discourse, Jesus announced that all "will see the Son of Man coming in clouds with great power and glory" (Mark 13:26; Matt. 24:30; Luke 24:27). This will be a time of rescue for all of God's people from the constraints of living in this world in the present evil age where sin, sickness, and evil abound. At that time believers will be "glorified" (Rom. 8:30). Their bodies will be transformed into "heavenly bodies" that possess a certain kind of glory (1 Cor. 15:40), are imperishable (*aphtharsia*; v. 42), and are "spiritual" (*pneumatikos*; v. 44). This transformation entails a complete healing for every Christian, but it goes far beyond any kind of healing in their

---

[56]See Christopher W. Morgan and Robert A. Peterson, eds., *Suffering and the Goodness of God*, Theology in Community 1 (Wheaton, IL: Crossway, 2008).

former existence because their bodies will no longer be susceptible to disease or decay.

Similarly, believers still await the final subjugation of Satan and his demons. They have been defeated by Jesus through his passion and his resurrection, yet they are still active and hostile to God and his people. But their day is coming. The apostle Paul envisioned a sequence of events at the end that includes (1) the resurrection of the dead (along with the rapture of all who are still alive; 1 Thess. 4:13) followed by (2) the final subjugation of all of Christ's supernatural enemies. Paul explains, "Then comes the end, when he delivers the kingdom to God the Father after destroying every rule and every authority and power" (1 Cor. 15:24). In Ephesians he speaks of this as bringing all of rebellious creation under the sovereign headship of Christ (Eph. 1:10). At this time, "every knee should bow, in heaven and on earth and under the earth, and every tongue confess that Jesus Christ is Lord, to the glory of God the Father" (Phil. 2:10–11). Jesus said that the Devil and his angels will be consigned to the torment of an eternal fire that is prepared for them (Matt. 25:41). The Revelation of John speaks of this as a time when the Devil and his powers will be thrown into a pool of fire, where they will be tormented throughout eternity (20:10, 14).[57]

When these events occur, there will no longer be any need for exorcism or healing. Satan will have been banished once and for all. All of God's people will not only be completely healed but will be incapable of any kind of sickness or suffering. From the perspective of the present time, this will be an age of the constant miraculous, where the miraculous becomes the new normal.

When the miraculous becomes the New Norm. Rev. 20:10; 14

---

[57]See Christopher W. Morgan and Robert A. Peterson, eds., *Hell under Fire* (Grand Rapids, MI: Zondervan, 2004).

7

THE KINGDOM AND THE CHURCH

GREGG R. ALLISON

The kingdom of God is a predominant theme of Scripture,[1] and for this reason alone its relationship to the church is important and must be addressed. Add to this the fact that throughout its history, the church has entertained vastly different notions of its relationship to the kingdom of God, with the result that different ecclesiologies have arisen.[2] At the same time, no monolithic notion of the kingdom of God has existed or exists, further complicating the issue. Indeed, at least five elements coalesce in my attempt to describe the relationship between the church and the kingdom of God. Before discussing that multifaceted relationship, I will first articulate my understanding of the church, followed by a presentation of my understanding of the kingdom of God. Having noted five biblical themes regarding the kingdom, I will next explain the complex relationship between the church and the kingdom according to those five themes,

---

[1]Some scholars would even say it is the unifying theme for all Scripture; e.g., John Bright, *The Kingdom of God: The Biblical Concept and Its Meaning for the Church* (Nashville: Abingdon, 1953), with criticism noted in Brevard S. Childs, *Biblical Theology of the Old and New Testaments: Theological Reflection on the Christian Bible* (Minneapolis: Augsburg Fortress, 1993; Graeme Goldsworthy, *The Goldsworthy Trilogy (Gospel and Kingdom, Gospel and Wisdom, The Gospel in Revelation)* (Carlisle: Paternoster, 2000).

[2]Due to his misunderstanding of the parable of the wheat and the weeds (Matt. 13:24–30, 34–43), Augustine equated the church with the kingdom of God (e.g., *City of God*, 20.9; *The Letters of Petilian, the Donatist*, 3.4–5). This mistaken identification became the basis for his conviction that the church is and is to be a mixed society of Christians (the wheat) and non-Christians (the weeds). Following Augustine's lead, the Roman Catholic Church considered the church to be the kingdom of God and began to think of it as similar to earthly kingdoms. As the church became more and more a political power, the church-state model began to monopolize medieval ecclesiology. This development paved the way for military endeavors such as the Crusades; religious persecution of non-Christians and heretics by the Inquisition; political machinations such as investiture (i.e., the pope possessed authority to crown the emperor with the symbols of civil authority) and other church interference in secular matters fueled by papal claims of superiority over the state. For example, Boniface VIII's startling claim: "And we learn from the words of the Gospel that in this church and in her power are two swords, the spiritual and the temporal. For when the apostles said, 'Behold, here'—that is, in the church, because it was

specifically: (1) the church and the kingdom as God's universal rule and eternal dominion, (2) the church and the kingdom as Israel, (3) the church and the kingdom as belonging to the Son of Man/Davidic King, (4) the church and the kingdom as an inaugurated reality, and (5) the church and the kingdom as an eschatological reality. Finally, I will offer a few words of encouragement and exhortation regarding how the church should live in light of its complex relationship to the kingdom of God.

The Identity of the Church[3]

The church is the people of God who have been saved through repentance and faith in the gospel of Jesus Christ (e.g., Acts 2:22–41) and incorporated into his body through baptism with the Holy Spirit (Luke 3:15–17; 1 Cor. 12:12–13). As this statement emphasizes, the church is the people of God or, in the words of the Apostles' Creed, "the communion of saints." In contrast with some common notions today,[4] the church is not a building (the red-brick, colonial-style building with white pillars and a steeple just a few blocks down from where we live), a denominational tag (e.g., the Presbyterian Church, USA), a national or state church (e.g., the Lutheran Church of Sweden), avatars worshiping together in the virtual world of Second Life, or the Catholic Church (with its claim that "the one Church of Christ . . . subsists in the Catholic Church").[5] Rather, the church is people; specifically, the church is the new-covenant people of God.[6] Though the people of God have existed from the beginning of the human

---

the apostles who spoke—'are two swords,' the Lord did not reply, 'It is too much,' but 'It is enough.' Truly he who denies that the temporal sword is in the power of Peter misunderstands the words of the Lord, 'Put up your sword into the sheath.' Both are in the power of the church, the spiritual sword and the material. But the latter is to be used *for* the church, the former *by* it; the former by the priest, the latter by kings and captains but at the will and the permission of the priest. The one sword, then, should be under the other, and temporal authority subject to spiritual. For when the apostle says, 'There is no power but from God, and the powers that exist are ordained by God' (Rom. 13:1), they would not be so ordained were not one sword made subject to the other. . . . Furthermore we declare, state, define, and pronounce that it is altogether necessary to salvation for every human creature to be subject to the Roman pontiff." Boniface VIII, *Unam Sanctam* (1302), *Corpus Iuris Canonici* (Friedberg) 2.1245, in *Documents of the Christian Church*, 3rd ed., ed. Henry Bettenson and Chris Maunder (Oxford: University Press, 1998), 126–27.

[3]Because I am developing much of the following section on the identity of the church in a forthcoming book for the Foundations of Evangelical Theology series (ed. John Feinberg, Crossway), I will provide only minimal warrant here. Suffice it to say that extensive biblical and theological warrant is possible and will be fully developed in the forthcoming volume.

[4]By this statement I am not saying that the use of the word *church* in regard to the following entities is completely illegitimate; rather, all I mean to indicate is that I will not use the word *church* to refer to them in this discussion.

[5]Second Vatican Council, Dogmatic Constitution *Lumen Gentium*, 8.2, cited in William Cardinal Levada, Congregation for the Doctrine of the Faith, "Responses to Some Questions Regarding Certain Aspects of the Doctrine on the Church" (June 29, 2007).

[6]God's relationship with his people is always mediated through a covenant, whether that be the Adamic, Noahic, Abrahamic, Mosaic (old), Davidic, or new covenant. That the latter is the covenant in which the church exists is clear from passages such as Luke 22:20; 1 Cor. 11:25; 2 Cor. 3; and Heb. 8.

race (one thinks especially of the people of Israel who lived under the old covenant), the church (adhering to the new covenant) did not exist prior to the first coming of Jesus Christ.[7] He is the Redeemer who accomplished salvation through his atoning death and resurrection for the people of God who compose the church. It is through the gospel, and a response to it of repentance from sin and faith in Christ, that Christians have been saved (and by this term I mean all aspects of the mighty work of God that are commonly regarded as encompassing salvation, including election, effective calling, regeneration, justification, adoption, sanctification, perseverance, and glorification). An additional aspect of the salvific work of God—one that is often overlooked but relates directly to the identity of the members of the church—is the incorporation of Christians into the body of Christ as he baptizes them with the Holy Spirit. Accordingly, all who are "in Christ" are de facto "in the church" and compose its members.

The church consists of two interrelated elements, commonly referred to as the "universal" church and "local" churches. The universal church is the company of all Christians stretching from its inception (accomplished by the death, resurrection, and ascension of Jesus Christ, and created by the descent of the Holy Spirit at Pentecost) to its terminal point, Christ's second coming at the end of this present age (or, specifically, the rapture of the church prior to his return).[8] It incorporates both the deceased believers who are currently in the presence of Christ in heaven (Heb. 12:23) and the living believers scattered throughout the world.[9] Whereas the former aspect is gathered together as the "heavenly" church, the latter aspect does not assemble in only one particular place, does not possess a single specific structure or organization, does not have one particular set of human leaders, and does not have a specific space-time address (e.g., the Church of God in Corinth; Sojourn Community Church). These intangibles do not render the universal church any less real, however, as the next point demonstrates.

---

[7]Thus, we can speak of the one people of God consisting of different and distinguishable expressions, e.g., the old-covenant people of Israel, and the new-covenant people of the church.

[8]In using the word *terminal*, I am not indicating that the people who now compose the church will cease to exist at the second coming of Christ, only that the current earthly manifestation of the church in its "already/not yet" reality will come to a conclusion. Moreover, in affirming the rapture of the church, I am not committing myself necessarily to any of the specific end-times views, as amillennialists, post-millennialists, historic premillennialists, and dispensational premillennialists all agree (based on 1 Thess. 4:13–18) that at the second coming, the dead in Christ and believers alive at the moment "will be caught up [rapture] together . . . to meet the Lord in the air."

[9]According to Hodge, "The 'church' is the company of the redeemed here and in heaven, which constitutes one body." Charles Hodge, *A Commentary on the Epistle to the Ephesians* (1856; repr. Charleston, SC: BiblioBazaar, 2008), 136.

1. Doxological
2. Logocentric
3. Pneumadynamic
4. Covenantal

5. Confessional
6. Missional
7. Spatio-temporal-eschatological

182   Gregg R. Allison

7 Attributes of the Local Church

This universal church (at least its living members) is manifested (by Christ, its head, and the Spirit) and manifests itself (through Christians associating themselves with one another; Heb. 10:24–25) in local churches,[10] characterized by seven attributes.[11] Local churches are: (1) doxological, or oriented to the glory of God (Eph. 3:20–21); (2) logocentric, or centered on the incarnate Word of God, Jesus Christ (Matt. 16:18–19; Eph. 1:22; 2:20), and the inspired Word of God, Scripture (e.g., Acts 2:42; 6:2); (3) pneumadynamic, or created, gathered, gifted, and empowered by the Holy Spirit (Acts 2:1–5; 20:28; Eph. 4:3; 1 Cor. 12:7, 11); (4) covenantal, or gathered as members in new-covenant relationship with God and in covenantal relationship with each other (e.g., Eph. 4:25–32); (5) confessional, or united by both personal confession of faith in Christ (Rom. 10:8–13) and common confession of the Christian faith (e.g., 1 Tim. 3:15–16); (6) missional, or identified as the body of divinely called and divinely sent ministers to proclaim the gospel and advance the kingdom of God (John 20:19–23); and (7) spatio-temporal-eschatological, or assembled as a historical reality (located in space and time; e.g., 1 Cor. 1:2; Rev. 2:5) and possessing a certain hope and clear destiny while they live the strangeness of ecclesial existence in the here-and-now (1 Pet. 2:11; Eph. 4:13–16).

16 Local Church - Pastors/Elders

Local churches are led by qualified and publicly recognized men who are called pastors or elders (as used in the New Testament, two other terms—"bishops" and "overseers"—are other interchangeable terms) who have the responsibilities of teaching sound doctrine (1 Tim. 3:2; 5:17), governing (under the headship of Christ; Eph. 1:22; 1 Tim. 3:4–5), praying (including for the sick; James 5:13–16), and shepherding (leading through exemplary lifestyles; 1 Pet. 5:1–3). These assemblies are also served by deacons, qualified and publicly recognized persons who serve Jesus Christ in the many church ministries (1 Tim. 3:8–13; Rom. 16:1–2). Because of divine grace and provision, local churches possess both purity and unity; because of sin, however, they must also pursue greater purity and maintain unity through both divine aid and Spirit-empowered human

17 Officers - ...

---

[10]This affirmation does not mean that all redeemed people join themselves to a local congregation. For various reasons—e.g., disobedience, laziness, sickness, incarceration, lack of accessibility, persecution—some do not participate in a local church, and Christians who have come under church discipline are excommunicated, or expelled, from their church. Neither does the affirmation mean that local churches are composed solely of redeemed people. Non-Christians who are being moved by God toward salvation but who are not yet converted may participate in a church community, while others, believing themselves to be genuine Christians, may be members of a local church.

[11]Because the universal church becomes manifested in local churches that possess these seven characteristics, it should come as no surprise that it is characterized by many of these same attributes.

effort (Eph. 4:1–6, 13–16). When their members persist in sin, churches exercise discipline for the purposes of restoring erring members and rectifying entrenched sinful situations, containing such sin-saturated realities, and preserving the honor of Christ and their own reputation (Matt. 20:15–20; 1 Corinthians 5; 2 Thess. 3:6–15). Churches also develop strong connections with other local churches for the purposes of cooperative high-impact ministry, the sharing of resources, mutual accountability, and the like (e.g., Acts 15; 2 Corinthians 8–9).

In terms of their ministry and mission, local churches regularly gather to worship the triune God, proclaim his Word through the preaching of Scripture, celebrate the ordinances of baptism and the Lord's Supper, engage non-Christians with the gospel, exercise spiritual gifts for the building up their members, disciple those members through education and sharing in community life, care for people through prayer and giving, stand for and against the world by helping the poor and marginalized through holistic ministries, and denounce the evils wrought by sin.

The Identity of the Kingdom of God

As any kingdom is ruled by a king, in the matter before us, "God is the King of all the earth" (Ps. 47:7), the "Most High" who "rules the kingdom of men and gives it to whom he will" (Dan. 4:25; cf. Ps. 22:28). His sovereignty is such that "the king's heart is a stream of water in the hand of the Lord; he turns it wherever he will" (Prov. 21:1), so that it may be said that "he removes kings and sets up kings" (Dan. 2:21). This divine reign is not confined to earth and its citizens: God is also ruler of the angelic domain: "All the inhabitants of the earth are accounted as nothing, and he [the Most High] does according to his will among the host of heaven and among the inhabitants of the earth; and none can stay his hand or say to him 'What have you done?'" (Dan. 4:35; cf. Ps. 135:6). As such, universality and eternity apply to God's sovereign rulership: "his kingdom rules over all" (Ps. 103:19) and is "an everlasting kingdom" (145:13). This aspect of the kingdom focuses on God's reign or rule over all the created order—he is the King who exercises absolute sovereignty over his kingdom, which consists of everything he has brought into and keeps in existence.

Of particular interest to us is the kingdom of humanity created and ruled over by him. In one sense, God is the sovereign Lord of all the peoples of the world (Acts 17:25–26). Indeed, he has created all human beings in his image and given to them the responsibility and ability (though diminished because of the fall) to be "fruitful and multiply and fill the earth and subdue it and have dominion over the fish of the sea and over the birds of the heavens and over every living thing that moves on the earth" (Gen. 1:28). Consequently, all people exist as vice-regents of and under the sovereign King.

At the same time, out of all the nations of the world, this sovereign King chose Israel to be the kingdom of his covenant people; thus, it was said of the Israelites, "The LORD their God is with them, and the shout of a king is among them" (Num. 23:21). This kingdom of Israel was first a theocracy ruled by God himself, then later led by human kings, first as a united kingdom (under Saul, David, and Solomon) and then as the divided kingdoms of Israel and Judah.[12] Why were these people recipients of God's particular attention? The reason certainly did not lie with the natural great-ness of these—rather than of other—people, as the Lord informs them: "It was not because you were more in number than any other people that the LORD set his love on you and chose you, for you were the fewest of all peoples" (Deut. 7:7). Rather, divine election was the reason—the sovereign Lord chose Israel to be his particular people as an expression of his uncon-ditional grace and kindness. As a result, God spoke of the people of Israel as "my treasured possession among all peoples, for all the earth is mine, and you shall be to me a kingdom of priests and a holy nation" (Ex. 19:5–6). Ultimately, the sovereign plan was that the election of Israel would not only bring salvation to this people but eventually result in the blessing of the entire world (Gen. 12:1–3; Isa. 45:21–22).

While this theocratic/monarchical kingdom experienced its many ebbs and flows, the Old Testament prophets wrote about the anticipation of a glorious future. In part, this hope had specific reference to Israel, in terms of a restoration of its people to the land of promise and abundant blessing (e.g., Ezekiel 36–37). Still, this future, glorious kingdom of God was associated with a coming Davidic king (2 Samuel 7; Ps. 89:27; Mark 11:10) and "one like a son of man" who would have a worldwide impact: "And to him was given dominion and glory and a kingdom, that all peo-ples, nations, and languages should serve him; his dominion is an ever-lasting dominion, which shall not pass away, and his kingdom one that shall not be destroyed" (Dan. 7:14). Indeed, this Son of Man/Davidic King would have the responsibility of bringing light to "the people who walked in darkness" (Isa. 9:2–7), to "stand as a signal for the peoples—of him shall

---

[12]"Resistance to the institution of the monarchy in Israel . . . was based on the conviction that God should be the sole ruler of his people (Judg. 8:23)." Charles H. H. Scobie, *The Ways of Our God: An Approach to Biblical Theology* (Grand Rapids, MI: Eerdmans, 2003), 106.

the nations inquire, and his resting place shall be glorious" (11:10)—to be "as a covenant for the people, a light for the nations" (42:6). By means of this coming King, the kingdom of God would be extended to all the peoples of the world, in fulfillment of the original vision. Ultimately, all the kingdoms of this world would be destroyed, "And the kingdom and the dominion and the greatness of the kingdoms under the whole heaven shall be given to the people of the saints of the Most High; his kingdom shall be an everlasting kingdom, and all dominions shall serve and obey him" (Dan. 7:27). The Old Testament prophetic hope included a particular emphasis on the people of Israel, yet extended beyond to encompass a vision for an eternal kingdom to be established for the King and all of his subjects.

Jesus of Nazareth inaugurated the fulfillment of this Old Testament vision, being identified as both the son/descendant of David (Matt. 1:1; Luke 1:32; Rom. 1:3) and the Son of Man (Luke 19:10; Matt. 26:64). In particular, "the Son of Man came not to be served but to serve, and to give his life as a ransom for many" (Mark 10:45), which is Jesus' own self-identification with the Son of Man figure of the Old Testament and his advancement of that image to include the accomplishment of salvation. Indeed, a conjunction between the gospel and the kingdom was central to the mission of Jesus who, at the outset of his ministry, "came into Galilee, proclaiming the gospel of God, and saying, 'The time is fulfilled, and the kingdom of God is at hand; repent and believe in the gospel'" (1:14–15). This ministry of proclaiming the gospel of the kingdom was accompanied by Jesus' "healing every disease and every affliction among the people" (Matt. 4:23; 9:35). Because at least some of these physical ailments were the result of demonic activity, Jesus also engaged in exorcisms. When he healed "a demon-oppressed man who was blind and mute," Jesus used that occasion to draw attention to the power of the Holy Spirit at work through him: "But if it is by the Spirit of God that I cast out demons, then the kingdom of God has come upon you" (12:22, 28). Thus, the miraculous signs and Spirit-empowered exorcisms underscored Jesus' inauguration of the kingdom of God. While he healed a great number of people, and many more people sought him out for his curative touch and even tried to detain him from leaving them, Jesus did not allow himself to be sidetracked by less important ventures: "'I must preach the good news of the kingdom of God to the other towns as well; for I was sent for this purpose.' And he was preaching in the synagogues of Judea" (Luke 4:42–44).

The preaching of the gospel of the kingdom of God was at the core of the earthly mission of Jesus.

Thus far, our discussion has focused on the present reality of the kingdom in the ministry of Jesus. He again underscored this "already" aspect in an encounter with the religious leaders of his day: "Being asked by the Pharisees when the kingdom of God would come, he [Jesus] answered them, 'The kingdom of God is not coming in ways that can be observed, nor will they say, 'Look, here it is!' or 'There!' for behold, the kingdom of God is in the midst of you'" (17:20–21). But there was another side of this kingdom reality.

An eschatological aspect balances this realized aspect of the kingdom, making the kingdom inaugurated but incomplete, here but not here, "already" but "not yet." Indeed, according to Jesus, the kingdom he ushers in begins small, "like a grain of mustard seed that a man took and sowed in his field. It is the smallest of all seeds, but when it has grown it is larger than all the garden plants and becomes a tree, so that the birds of the air come and make nests in its branches" (Matt. 13:31–32; cf. 33–34).[13] As it expands, however, the kingdom is countered by another domain. As for the kingdom, parabolically, the sower sows good seed on good soil that sprouts and produces good grain. In other words, the "children of the kingdom" hear the word of the kingdom, understand it, and bear fruit; they are the result of Jesus' work in the world. As for the counter domain, parabolically, the sower sows good seed on bad soil that fails to develop fully. Alternatively, an enemy sows weeds among the wheat such that in the midst of the good grain, weeds appear also. In other words, the "sons of the evil one" hear the word of the kingdom but either fail to understand it or, though understanding it, do not persist so as to bear fruit. Alternatively, they are the weeds among the wheat; they are the result of Satan's work in the world. Accordingly, the world, which is ultimately God's kingdom, is populated by two diverse groups of citizens, two opposing domains: the "children of the kingdom" and the "sons of the evil one." This world/kingdom will encompass these two opposing citizenries until the end. Parabolically, at harvest time the reapers will first gather the weeds and tie them in bundles to be burned, then gather the wheat into the sower's barn. In other words, at the close of the age, Jesus "will send his angels, and they will gather out of his kingdom all causes of sin

---

[13]This and other similar parables do not seem to emphasize the speed of the growth of the kingdom but the amazing contrast between the size of the kingdom at its inauguration and at its consummation.

and all law-breakers, and throw them into the fiery furnace. In that place there will be weeping and gnashing of teeth. Then the righteous will shine like the sun in the kingdom of their Father" (Matt. 13:1–9, 18–23, 24–30, 36–43). To them, Jesus the King will say, "Come, you who are blessed by my Father, inherit the kingdom prepared for you from the foundation of the world" (25:34). As history progresses, God's kingdom-as-the-world moves patiently yet resolutely toward the actualization of this eschatological vision of the demise of all opposition and the exaltation of its rightful citizens.

In summary, the kingdom of God includes: (1) the universal rule and complete reign of the sovereign King over everything he has created and sustains in existence; (2) the people of Israel, graciously chosen from among all the peoples of the world to be God's covenant kingdom people; (3) an anticipated future vision associated with a Davidic King and the Son of Man; (4) an inaugurated reality, fulfilled "already" in Jesus Christ who preached the gospel of the kingdom of God, which message gives rise to and results in children of the kingdom and citizens of opposition; and (5) a hope for the "not yet" aspects of the kingdom reality in Jesus to be completed soon. Accordingly, the church relates to the kingdom of God according to these five themes, all of which will be explored in the following discussion.

The Church and the Kingdom as God's Universal Rule and Eternal Dominion

Because of its multifaceted nature, the kingdom of God enjoys a complex relationship to the church. In one sense, the church owes its existence to the kingdom, which is intended as God's universal rule and eternal dominion. The sovereign king reigning over everything purposed, brought forth, and established the church as part of his reign (Eph. 1:11). The church, then, is one reality that exists and develops under the exhaustive sovereignty of God over all things. It takes its place with the angelic hosts, the subkingdoms appointed by God (Rom. 13:1–7), all humanity, and the entirety of the created order as constitutive elements of the kingdom rule of God. Ladd explains this reality of the church as the community of the kingdom of God:

> The Kingdom is primarily the dynamic reign or kingly rule of God, and, derivatively, the sphere in which the rule is experienced. In biblical idiom, the Kingdom is not identified with its subjects. They are the

people of God's rule who enter it, live under it, and are governed by it. The church is the community of the Kingdom but never the Kingdom itself. Jesus' disciples belong to the Kingdom as the Kingdom belongs to them; but they are not the Kingdom. The Kingdom is the rule of God; the church is a society of men.[14]

Without equating or fusing the two realities, we may affirm that the church is the community of citizens of the kingdom of God.[15]

This identity is most thoroughly affirmed by Jesus in what certainly is the *locus classicus* in historical and contemporary discussions of the church:

> Simon Peter replied, "You are the Christ, the Son of the living God." And Jesus answered him, "Blessed are you, Simon Bar-Jonah! For flesh and blood has not revealed this to you, but my Father who is in heaven. And I tell you, you are Peter, and on this rock I will build my church, and the gates of hell shall not prevail against it. I will give you the keys of the kingdom of heaven, and whatever you bind on earth shall be bound in heaven, and whatever you loose on earth shall be loosed in heaven." (Matt. 16:16–19)

In speaking with his disciples, Jesus indicates that he is about to establish a new entity, different from yet with some similarities to the *qahal* featured in Israel in earlier days. In the Old Testament, *qahal* referred to the congregation of Israel assembled together under Yahweh (Num. 16:3) to hear and respond to (Neh. 13:1–3) his authoritative and revealed word (Deut. 31:30).[16] Jesus will institute a new assembly of his people gathered under him—μου τὴν ἐκκλησίαν (*mou tēn ekklēsian*), "my church," he calls it—involving the Twelve and built on Peter and his authoritative word—the confession of faith of the identity of Jesus of Nazareth as "Christ, the Son of the living God," that was revealed to him by the Father (Matt. 16:16–17).[17]

---

[14]George Eldon Ladd, *A Theology of the New Testament* (Grand Rapids, MI: Eerdmans, 1974), 111.

[15]As Moltmann explains the kingdom and its relationship to the church: "The church in the power of the Spirit is not yet the kingdom of God, but it is its anticipation in history. Christianity is not yet the new creation, but it is the working of the Spirit of the new creation. Christianity is not yet the new mankind but it is its vanguard, in resistance to deadly introversion and in self-giving and representation for man's future. . . . In this sense the church of Jesus Christ is *the people of the kingdom of God.*" Jürgen Moltmann, *The Church in the Power of the Spirit: A Contribution to Messianic Ecclesiology*, trans. Margaret Kohl (New York: Harper & Row, 1977), 196.

[16]We see this response specifically in the people assenting to the covenant with Yahweh (Deut. 5:27) or their renewing of the covenant (Josh. 8:30–35).

[17]As Herman Bavinck explained with regard to Jesus' reference to the "church" in Matt. 16:18 and 18:17, "He is therefore still employing it in a very general sense. He does not say whether that *lh'q'* [*qahal*], ekklhsia, will be local or spread itself out over the whole earth. The later distinction between the local church and the universal church cannot yet be found here. Instead, Jesus here states very generally that he will build his ekklhsia" Herman Bavinck, *Holy Spirit, Church, and New Creation*, vol. 4 of *Reformed Dogmatics*, ed. John Bolt, trans. John

Specifically, the church is the instrument through which entrance into the kingdom is granted, as the church has been entrusted with and employs "the keys of the kingdom of heaven" (v. 19). These keys have to do with the gospel and people's response to it. Those who repent of sin and embrace Jesus Christ by faith are "loosed" from their sin, death and condemnation, domination by the world, and enslavement to the Evil One. Oppositely, those who refuse to heed the good news are "bound" in that persistent hellish nightmare.

Accordingly, those who have been loosed from sin are incorporated into the church as citizens of the kingdom of God. "The implication is inescapable that, in the establishment of the church, there was to be a manifestation of the kingdom or rule of God."[18] Though the King and his reign/subjects will be fiercely challenged—by the kingdom-opposing world, Satan, the sons of the Evil One (Matt. 12:22–37; 13:3–7, 18–22)— all such attempts to depose him and destroy his church will ultimately fail; "the gates of hell" or death will not prevail against the church. Though indestructible, the church as the display of the kingdom progresses through trial and temptation, suffering and persecution, as it is built by Christ himself.

For such a task of exercising the keys of the kingdom and offering entrance into the kingdom, Jesus himself prepared his disciples. Such activity was inaugurated while Jesus was still with them: "And he called the twelve together and gave them power and authority over all demons and to cure diseases, and he sent them out to proclaim the kingdom of God and to heal" (Luke 9:1–2). After Jesus' resurrection and ascension, and the outpouring of the Holy Spirit on the day of Pentecost, the apostles were empowered and emboldened to continue this proclamation of the gospel of the kingdom. They were joined by others: Philip "preached good news about the kingdom of God and the name of Jesus Christ" (Acts 8:12), resulting in the conversion of a large number of Samaritans. A late addition to the apostolic group—the apostle Paul—engaged in several missionary journeys, bringing the good news to the Gentiles as well as to the Jews. Appropriately, Luke "closes" his book of Acts with Paul's "proclaiming the kingdom of God and teaching about the Lord Jesus Christ with all boldness and without hindrance" (28:3–31; cf. 14:21–23; 19:8; 20:25).

Vriend (Grand Rapids, MI: Baker Academic, 2008), 279. While concurring with Bavinck, I would add that Jesus' reference to the "church" in Matt. 16:18 certainly includes its concretization in specific local churches. This idea comes out even more strongly in 18:17, in which Jesus prescribes the steps of discipline that are to be carried out in a specific church racked by the problem of sin among its members.

[18]Ned B. Stonehouse, *The Witness of Matthew and Mark to Christ* (Grand Rapids, MI: Eerdmans, 1944), 235.

This preaching of the gospel of the kingdom demands to be appropriated, and this reception takes place through a combination of divine and human actions. On the one hand, Jesus instructed Nicodemus, "Truly, truly, I say to you, unless one is born of water and the Spirit, he cannot enter the kingdom of God" (John 3:5). This regenerative action is completely the work of God apart from any human cooperation. As the Holy Spirit brings about the new birth, or the impartation of new spiritual life, regenerated people become citizens of the kingdom of God. On the other hand, Jesus called people to repentance and faith (Mark 1:15), warning that "whoever does not receive the kingdom of God like a child shall not enter it" (Luke 18:17). Indeed, acquisition of the kingdom, which "is like treasure hidden in a field, which a man found and covered up," demands that "he goes and sells all that he has and buys that field" (Matt. 13:44; cf. 45–46). Through both divine and human actions, the kingdom of God opens for sinful human beings to enter.

The church is the key instrument in announcing the good news, and through its communication of the gospel new citizens enter the kingdom of God. Thus, the church, as the community of the kingdom, provides entrance into the kingdom through its untiring preaching of the gospel, and its newly born citizens live as kingdom people under the sovereignty of the king. Indeed, the church gives thanks to and honors its king. Specifically, as "heirs of the kingdom, which he [God] has promised to those who love him" (James 2:5), Christians give thanks to the Father, knowing "he has delivered us from the domain of darkness and transferred us to the kingdom of his beloved Son, in whom we have redemption, the forgiveness of sins" (Col. 1:13–14).

The Church and the Kingdom as Israel

A second important theme of the kingdom in Scripture is the Jewish people or the nation of Israel as the kingdom of God. This emphasis raises the question of the relationship between the church and Israel. For most of the church's history, the relationship was regarded as one of continuity and substitution. In terms of continuity, the people of Israel under the old covenant and Christians of the new covenant are both part of the people of God, joined together under the one covenant of grace. According to this continuity position, "the term 'the church' is used to apply to all those whom Christ died to redeem, all those who are saved by the death of Christ. But that must include all true believers for all time, both believers in the New Testament age and believers in the Old Testament age as well."[19] Specifically, Berkhof identifies the church in the patriarchal period with "the pious households, where the fathers served as priests. . . . At the time of the flood the Church was saved in the family of Noah, and continued particularly in the line of Shem." Then, "the families of the patriarch were the real repositories of the true faith," constituting the church. In the period of Moses, Berkhof maintains:

> After the exodus the people of Israel were not only organized into a nation, but were also constituted the Church of God. They were enriched with institutions in which not only family devotion or tribal faith but the religion of the nation could find expression. The Church did not yet obtain an independent organization, but had its institutional existence in the national life of Israel.

As for what the death, resurrection, and ascension of Christ brings, Berkhof offers: "The New Testament Church is essentially one with the Church of the old dispensation. As far as their essential nature is concerned, they both consist of true believers, and of true believers only. And in their external organization both represent a mixture of good and evil."[20] There is essential continuity between the church and Israel.

In terms of substitution, the church has replaced Israel such that the Jews as a national people hold no special place in the salvific work of God now or in the future. Because of their rejection of Jesus as the long-awaited Messiah, the Jews have forfeited the promises of blessing that are replete throughout the Old Testament. Other proponents of the continuity view insist that those promises are now being spiritually fulfilled in the church. In either case, there is no residual hope for a national restoration of the Jews to the Promised Land or a fresh outpouring of salvation upon the people of Israel in the future. Some who hold this view maintain that while Scripture makes no promises of salvation to *national* Israel, it does make them to *ethnic* Israel (cf. Rom. 11:25–32) and that these will be fulfilled in the church age and/or at the second coming.[21]

A key passage in support of the continuity view, along with others to which its proponents appeal, is Galatians 6:16: "And as for all who walk

[19]Wayne Grudem, *Systematic Theology: An Introduction to Biblical Doctrine* (Grand Rapids, MI: Zondervan, 2000), 853.
[20]Louis Berkhof, *Systematic Theology*, 4th rev. and enlarged ed. (Grand Rapids, MI: Eerdmans, 1982), 570–71. Berkhof notes that his view is in keeping with the historic Reformed position, citing the Belgic Confession (art. 27) and the Heidelberg Catechism (21) as illustrations.
[21]E.g., Anthony A. Hoekema, *The Bible and the Future* (Grand Rapids, MI: Eerdmans, 1979), 139–47. See also Grudem, *Systematic Theology*, 861; cf. 1009, 1104.

by this rule, peace and mercy be upon them, and upon the Israel of God." The rule to which Paul refers is that articulated in the preceding verse: the key is not circumcision nor uncircumcision, but "a new creation" (v. 15) through the cross of Jesus Christ. For all who keep in step with this rule, the apostle prays divine peace and mercy.

For our discussion, the important question focuses on the referent of the expression "the Israel of God." Scholars are divided on the answer. Some consider the referent to be Jewish believers in Jesus the Messiah; accordingly, Paul prays a special blessing on this particular Jewish-Christian part of the church. This interpretation is highly unlikely, however, for it would cut across the grain of the entire letter and its theme of Jews and Gentiles together in Christ (e.g., Gal. 3:26–29). Moreover, it would contradict Paul's belittling of circumcision and uncircumcision (e.g., 5:6), the very point that has led him to frame the rule of Galatians 6:15. "Having just made an all-inclusive statement in verse 15, is it not inconceivable that Paul suddenly would distinguish between two kinds of Christians, one Gentile, the other Jewish?"[22]

Other scholars, including the editors of this volume, understand the referent to be the church—mostly Gentiles, with a remnant of Jews—that now constitutes "the new people of God—the new and true Israel."[23] They hold the referent of the expression "all who walk by this rule" and the referent of the expression "the Israel of God" to be equivalent. Furthermore, these interpreters point to Paul's description of all Christ's followers—including those from a Gentile background—as "Abraham's offspring, heirs according to the promise" (Gal. 3:29; cf. 3:9, 14). Thus they contend that the apostle prays for peace and mercy to be upon the church, which is the "Israel of God":

> Such an interpretation fits with the remainder of the letter, for believers in Christ are the true sons of Abraham. But if they are Abraham's children and belong to his family, then they belong to the Israel of God. It would be highly confusing to the Galatians, after arguing for the equality of Jew and Gentile in Christ (3:28) and after emphasizing that believers are Abraham's children, for Paul to argue in the conclusion that only Jews who believe in Jesus belong to the Israel of God. By doing so a wedge would be introduced between Jews and Gentiles at the end of the

---

[22]Marten H. Woudstra, "Israel and the Church: A Case for Continuity," in *Continuity and Discontinuity: Perspectives on the Relationship Between the Old and New Testaments*, ed. John S. Feinberg (Westchester, IL: Crossway, 1988), 235.
[23]Tom Schreiner, personal correspondence with the author.

letter, suggesting that they are not part of the true Israel. Such a wedge would play into the hands of the opponents who would argue that to be part of the true Israel one must be circumcised. Instead, Paul confirms one of the major themes of the letter. All believers in Christ are part of the true Israel, part of God's Israel.[24]

This interpretation, which is a plausible understanding, equates the church with the new Israel. If this identification is true, it is a direct affirmation of the continuity between the church and Israel.

A third interpretation, which disagrees with the first two "continuity" understandings, takes the referent to be ethnic Israel. In this case, as he nears the end of his letter to the Galatians, Paul is aware that he has been highly critical of his own people the Jews—"the Israel of God." He has magnified his ministry to the Gentiles (2:7–9), recounted his rebuke of Peter and other Jewish believers for their hypocrisy (1:13–16; 2:11–14), clarified the role of the Mosaic law (3:15–25), underscored the barrenness of the Jews according to the flesh (4:21–31), noted Jewish persecution of the church (4:29), and exposed the unimportance of circumcision (5:2–12; 6:11–15). Such strong criticism, he feared, could be misunderstood to be a scathing indictment of the Jewish people—not at all what Paul intended to communicate. Appropriately, he prays for divine blessing both for the church—"all who walk by this rule"—as well as for "the Israel of God." This plausible interpretation supports the discontinuity position emphasizing the distinction between the church and Israel.

Support for this interpretation includes New Testament and Pauline usage of the term "Israel." In almost all cases, the term refers to ethnic Israel; indeed, if it were the case that "the Israel of God" refers to the church, it would be the only instance in all of Scripture.[25] Also, as highly unlikely as it is that Paul would single out Jewish believers in the church for special blessing (an objection to the first interpretation), it is equally unlikely that he would call the church with its large Gentile majority "the Israel of God." His point has been to deflate the importance of Jewish identity, so why would he suddenly refer to the church with an expression with such little weight? If this interpretation is correct, then Galatians 6:16 is not a passage in support of the identity between the church and Israel. The case for continuity between the church and Israel in the people

---

[24]Tom Schreiner, personal correspondence with the author. Cf. Andreas Köstenberger, "The Identity of the Ἰσραηλ του θεου (Israel of God) in Galatians 6:16," *Faith and Mission* 19, no. 1 (Fall 2001), 3–24.

[25]Robert L. Saucy, "Israel and the Church: A Case for Discontinuity," in Feinberg, *Continuity and Discontinuity*, 246.

of God and the replacement of the latter by the former, though the traditional perspective of the church, may not rely on this verse, though of
course it appeals to others.

Beginning in the nineteenth century, this prevailing, historic view was
challenged by the doctrine of the church articulated by dispensational theology. Two contributors to this development were J. N. Darby and Lewis
Sperry Chafer. Darby insisted on a complete discontinuity between the
remnant of the Jewish people and the church—each has its own history,
destiny, and hope. Concerning the church, Darby believed that it was a
mystery that was not revealed until the apostle Paul wrote his letters[26] and
concluded that the doctrine of the church "was thus wholly unknown to
the saints of the Old Testament."[27] More specifically, the entire doctrine of
the church was communicated by the apostle Paul—it is found nowhere
else, even in the New Testament.[28]

According to Lewis Sperry Chafer, some of the key differences
between the Jewish people and the church include the permanent
indwelling of Christians by the Holy Spirit, the baptism of the Holy Spirit
for Christians, earthly promises to Israel versus heavenly promises to the
church, law as the rule of life for the Jews versus grace for Christians,
and incorporation into the body of Christ for Christians.[29] Furthermore,
Chafer argued that the church began at Pentecost and did not exist for the
old-covenant people of God because its existence was dependent on the
death, resurrection, and ascension of Jesus Christ and the descent of the
Holy Spirit to regenerate, baptize, and seal people as part of the church.[30]
This church, being dominated by grace and having no connection what-
soever to law, finds its instructions for doctrine, worship, ministry, ordinances, and government solely in (parts of) the New Testament, not at all
in the Old Testament.[31] Indeed, for Chafer, the church is an "intercalation"
or parenthesis interjected into the plan of God for his people, the Jews:
"The present age of the church is an intercalation into the revealed calen-
dar or program of God as that program was foreseen by the prophets of
old."[32] Once this interruption in the divine plan comes to completion—at

---

[26]J. N. Darby, "The Rapture of the Saints," in *The Collected Writings of J. N. Darby*, ed. William Kelly, 14 vols. (repr. Sunbury, PA: Believers Bookshelf, 1972), 11:149.
[27]Ibid. Darby listed Rom. 16:25–26; Eph. 3:4–5, 9; and Col. 1:24 in support.
[28]Ibid., 150–51.
[29]Lewis Sperry Chafer, *Systematic Theology*, vol. 4: *Ecclesiology—Eschatology* (Dallas: Dallas Seminary Press, 1948), 34.
[30]Ibid., 45–46.
[31]Ibid., 16, 19, 28, 29.
[32]Ibid., 41.

the rapture of the church just prior to the seven years of the great tribulation leading up to the second coming of Christ—God will once again turn
to his people the Jews and renew his saving work toward them.

Since the formulation of this classical dispensational ecclesiology, a
new expression of this theology has challenged some of its key tenets.
This so-called progressive dispensationalism[33] denies that the church is a
parenthesis in the divine program but has always been an essential feature
of God's plan to extend his salvation to all people, both Jews and Gentiles.
Moreover, progressive dispensationalism does not distinguish between
the church and Israel in terms of spiritual and heavenly blessings for the
former and physical and earthly blessings for the latter. Rather, both in
their own ways participate in the kingdom of God and its multifold blessings. Furthermore, the strict dichotomy between the law for Israel and
grace for the church is rejected as utterly untenable.

Still, for progressive dispensationalism, discontinuity between the
church and Israel can be clearly seen in certain experiences of salvation—
the baptism of the Holy Spirit who permanently indwells Christians and
endows them with spiritual gifts, for example.[34] At the same time, this
discontinuity is not absolute, as seen in the following: The church is the
beneficiary of both the new covenant, which was prophesied for Israel
and Judah (Jer. 31:31–34, cited in Heb. 8:6–13), and the promise of the
outpouring of the Holy Spirit for Judah (Joel 2:28–29, cited in Acts 2:17–
21). In addition, certain terms used for the Jewish people—the "offspring"
or "sons" of Abraham (Rom. 4:16; Gal. 3:7, 29), "a chosen race, a royal
priesthood, a holy nation, a people for his own possession" (1 Pet. 2:9), for
example—are applied to the church. And ultimately, the church and Israel
are part of the one people of God, as vividly portrayed by Paul's metaphor
of the olive tree (Rom. 11:13–24).[35] But the dissimilarities are significant
enough so as to maintain the distinction between the church and Israel.
Progressive dispensationalism also holds to a future fulfillment of Old
Testament prophecies directed at national Israel, including the salvation
of many Jewish people and restoration to the land of Israel.

---

[33]Craig A. Blaising and Darrell L. Bock, Dispensationalism, Israel and the Church: The Search for Definition
(Grand Rapids, MI: Zondervan, 1992); idem., Progressive Dispensationalism (Wheaton, IL: BridgePoint,
1993); Robert L. Saucy, The Case for Progressive Dispensationalism: The Interface Between Dispensational
and Non-Dispensational Theology (Grand Rapids, MI: Zondervan, 1993).

[34]The editors hold to more continuity in salvation than is reflected in these statements.

[35]In this Pauline image, the natural branches represent the Jewish people and the wild olive shoots now grafted
into the tree represent the Gentiles who have embraced Jesus Christ so as to become the church. Both discontinuity—the natural branches have been broken off but will be grafted in again, while the wild olive shoots are
currently grafted into the root—and continuity—the two types of branches are part of the one cultivated olive
tree—are emphasized in this image. But plainly the emphasis is on continuity.

What is the import of this discussion for the relationship of the church and the kingdom of God? Jesus' striking words, offered at the conclusion of his parable of the tenants (Matt. 21:33–41), shape my perspective. Severely rebuking the Jewish leaders of his day,

> Jesus said to them, "Have you never read in the Scriptures:
>
> 'The stone that the builders rejected
>   has become the cornerstone;
> this was the Lord's doing,
>   and it is marvelous in our eyes'?
>
> Therefore I tell you, the kingdom of God will be taken away
>   from you and given to a people producing its fruits."
>   (Matt. 21:42–43)

Jesus indicated a change in the administration of the kingdom of God. Foretelling the ultimate rejection of himself as the promised Davidic King/Son of Man by his own people, and highlighting that rejection as the reason for the change, Jesus promised that he would wrench the administration of the kingdom of God from its current—and divinely appointed—Jewish administrators and hand it over to "a people" (ἔθνος, *ethnos*, the common Greek word for Gentiles) who would live by kingdom values and engage in kingdom works. This "people" would not be the Gentiles per se, but the church that would be composed mostly of Gentiles and a remnant of Jews. Keeping in mind what I wrote previously, this conferring of the kingdom to the church results in their association, with the church as the community and administrator of the kingdom of God.

The Church and the Kingdom as Belonging to the Son of Man/Davidic King

A third major theme, noteworthy especially among Old Testament prophets, was an anticipation of a future, glorious kingdom of God belonging to a coming Son of Man/Davidic King. As seen immediately above, the Jewish rejection of Jesus as the fulfillment of this prophetic hope for Israel resulted in the initial fulfillment of the same prophetic hope expanded to include "the people who walked in darkness" (Isa. 9:2–7), as the Son of Man/Davidic King would be "a light for the nations" (42:6). Specifically, at the Jerusalem Council—which was convened to investigate a claim by unendorsed Judaizers that Gentiles embracing Jesus must also be "circumcised according to the custom of Moses" and "keep the law of Moses" in order to be saved (Acts 15:1, 5)—James explains that the nascent movement of Gentiles' turning to Jesus and entering the church is the beginning fulfillment of Amos's prophetic vision (vv. 16–17, citing Amos 9:11, 12):

> After this I will return,
> and I will rebuild the tent of David that has fallen;
> I will rebuild its ruins,
>   and I will restore it,
> that the remnant of mankind may seek the Lord,
>   and all the Gentiles who are called by my name,
>   says the Lord, who makes these things known from of old.

Thus the early church associated the inclusion of the Gentiles in the divine plan of redemption through the church with a restored house of David.

Similarly, Paul noted "that Christ became a servant to the circumcised to show God's truthfulness, in order to confirm the promises given to the patriarchs, and in order that the Gentiles might glorify God for his mercy" (Rom. 15:8). After listing several Old Testament passages that confirm this divine intention to include the Gentiles in redemption (vv. 9–11, citing 2 Sam. 22:50; Deut. 32:43; and Ps. 117:1), the apostle cites the prophet Isaiah: "the root of Jesse will come, even he who arises to rule the Gentiles; in him will the Gentiles hope" (Rom. 15:12, citing Isa. 11:10). Again, language about Davidic kingship—"the root of Jesse" (cf. "the stump of Jesse;" Isa. 11:1)—is related to the inclusion of the Gentiles in the divine plan of redemption through the church.

Following the apostle Paul's teaching, this increasingly Gentile church professed "Jesus is Lord" not only as recognition of the identity of their sovereign King, but as subversion of all other claimants to ultimate allegiance. The acknowledgment of King Jesus entailed the renunciation of all other so-called kings, whether earthly Caesars ruling from Rome or rulers and authorities and powers and dominions threatening human beings from the heavenly places. Such subversion was demanded because through the death, resurrection, and ascension of Jesus, God had "disarmed the rulers and authorities and put them to open shame, but triumphing over them in him" (Col. 2:15) and established Jesus "far above all rule and authority and power and dominion, and above every name that is named, not only in this age but also in the one to come" (Eph. 1:21). The christological hymn in Paul's letter to the Philippians pays tribute to the ultimate demise of all other kings, rulers, authorities, and powers—be they earthly or heavenly—as they acknowledge the true Lord: "Therefore God has highly exalted him and bestowed on him the name that is above every name, so that at the name of Jesus every knee should bow, in heaven and on earth and under the earth, and every tongue confess that Jesus Christ is Lord, to the glory of God the Father" (Phil. 2:9–11).[36]

The Church and the Kingdom as an Inaugurated Reality

Accordingly, and as a fourth theme, the church relates to the kingdom of God as an inaugurated reality. As noted above, the church corresponds to one of the two citizenries that encompass God's kingdom-as-the-world, the "children of the kingdom."

Specifically, this relationship means that the church is missional, or identified as the body of divinely called and divinely sent ministers to proclaim the gospel and advance the kingdom of God. Such is the crux of Jesus' affirmation: "As the Father has sent me, even so I am sending you. . . . If you forgive the sins of any, they are forgiven them; if you withhold forgiveness from any, it is withheld" (John 20:21, 23). That is, the missio Dei—the mission of God—with which the Son was commissioned by the Father and which was accomplished by the Son through his sacrificial death for all humanity. This then becomes the same mission with which the Son commissions his disciples—the church announces the salvation accomplished by the Son. Hence, the missional church obeys Jesus' commission: "All authority in heaven and on earth has been given to me. Go therefore and make disciples of all nations, baptizing them in the name of the Father and of the Son and of the Holy Spirit, teaching them to observe all that I have commanded you. And behold, I am with you always, to the end of the age" (Matt. 28:18–20). And the missional church is well prepared for the missio Dei: "But you will receive power when the Holy Spirit has come upon you, and you will be my witnesses in Jerusalem and in all Judea and Samaria, and to the end of the earth" (Acts 1:8).

Accordingly, the missional church is expansive (extending from its beginning in Jerusalem to church planting endeavors around the globe

---

[36]In exalting Christ, Paul's language is clearly taken from Isa. 45:23, whose context is an affirmation that God alone is God and there is no other (Isa. 45:14, 18, 21, 22). N. T. Wright develops this aspect of the confession "Jesus is Lord" from Phil. 2:5–11: "Paul is not simply articulating a breathtaking vision of who Jesus is, and indeed of who God is. He is also, quite directly and explicitly, subverting the claims of the other great would-be lord of his day, namely Caesar." N. T. Wright, *What Saint Paul Really Said: Was Paul of Tarsus the Real Founder of Christianity?* (Grand Rapids, MI: Eerdmans, 1997), 56–57. The Roman Empire's persecution of the early church was often motivated by its understanding that Christians were atheists, that is, they refused to acknowledge that "Caesar is Lord." Certainly, this refusal grew out of the subversion inherent in their confession that "Jesus is Lord."

today), contextually sensitive (compare three Lukan narratives—Acts 2:14–41; 14:8–18; and 17:16–34—to gain a strong sense of this emphasis), and (potentially) catholic, which is the goal of the missional church in terms of its extension—complete universality.[37] As Moltmann notes, this universality flows from the lordship of Christ: "The *catholicity* of the church is not initially her spatial extent or the fact that she is in principle open to the world; it is the limitless lordship of Christ, to whom 'all authority is given in heaven and on earth.' Where, and so far as, Christ rules, there, consequently, the church is to be found. She acquires her openness to the world in the breadth of his rule."[38] Indeed, the missional church presses on into all lands, anticipating the realization of this heavenly worship song directed to the glory of the bloodied Lamb of God: "Worthy are you to take the scroll and to open its seals, for you were slain, and by your blood you ransomed people for God from every tribe and language and people and nation, and you have made them a kingdom and priests to our God, and they shall reign on the earth" (Rev. 5:9–10). These "children of the kingdom" are the fruit of the missional church living the reality of the inaugurated kingdom of God.

Moreover, the church lives this inaugurated reality by pressing on toward kingdom maturity. As it is characterized by certain qualities, the church works hard to develop them more fully, supplementing "faith with virtue, and virtue with knowledge, and knowledge with self-control, and self-control with steadfastness, and steadfastness with godliness, and godliness with brotherly affection, and brotherly affection with love. For if these qualities are yours and are increasing, they keep you from being ineffective or unfruitful in the knowledge of our Lord Jesus Christ. . . . For in this way there will be richly provided for you an entrance into the eternal kingdom of our Lord and Savior Jesus Christ" (2 Pet. 1:5–8, 11). Being in the world and thus in close quarters with "the sons of the evil one" who are enemies of Christ afflicting his followers, the church experiences suffering as it waits for the realization of the kingdom (2 Thess. 1:5). Indeed, the church acknowledges that, in reference to Christ, it "should not only believe in him but also suffer for his sake" (Phil. 1:29). As Paul announced, "through many tribulations we must enter the kingdom of God" (Acts 14:22). Accordingly, the church is in this world and for this world, but it is not of this world,

---

[37]According to the Second Helvetic Confession (17): "We, therefore, call this Church catholic because it is universal, scattered through all parts of the world, and extended unto all times, and is not limited to any times or places."

[38]Moltmann, *The Church in the Power of the Spirit*, 338.

reflecting Jesus' reply to Pilate: "My kingdom is not of this world. If my kingdom were of this world, my servants would have been fighting, that I might not be delivered over to the Jews. But my kingdom is not from the world" (John 18:36). So the church as the community of the kingdom renounces the wisdom of the world (1 Cor. 1:18–2:5) and fleshly warfare (2 Cor. 10:1–6) while it trusts in the power of God and obeys his kingdom's values.

Additionally, the church lives the reality of the inaugurated kingdom by seeking to advance that kingdom wherever the church's members—the citizens of the kingdom—live, work, and play: in neighborhoods, workplaces, governmental agencies, financial establishments, sports programs, and other institutions and structures. Specifically, the church takes seriously the so-called "cultural mandate" (Gen. 1:28), or the commission enjoined upon all human beings to engage in civilization-building as vice-regents of the King. Accordingly, the church prepares redeemed "civilian citizens" to participate well in human endeavors such as politics, business, the arts, medicine and health care, athletics, science and technology, farming, and economics.[39]

Furthermore, because this world is fallen and thus sin-stained and susceptible to disasters of all kinds (human evil, systemic evil, natural evil, Satanic and demonic evil), civilization-building encounters severe obstacles and is in need of other structures that intervene to minimize or relieve misery, poverty, marginalization, injustice, crime, financial failure, and the like. The church, a place of mercy and justice, challenges its members to bear the responsibility to build the "city of man" and overcome its dark side. As they endeavor to provide such tangible aid for others, they realize that their brothers and sisters according to creation are being helped—and this is pleasing to the Lord who has created all human beings equally in his image.[40] In these and many other ways, the church is *for* the world and *against* (the sinful corruption of) the world.[41]

[39]For an excellent presentation of what the political focus entails, see Wayne Grudem, *Politics—According to the Bible: A Comprehensive Resource for Understanding Modern Political Issues in Light of Scripture* (Grand Rapids, MI: Zondervan, 2010).
[40]Tragically, this notion of the brotherhood (and sisterhood) of all humanity was co-opted by Protestant liberalism and twisted in a warped direction to affirm the unbiblical positions of sin as mere deprivation, salvation as education or re-socialization or political liberation, and universalism (i.e., because God is the Father of all people [in the creation sense], he will also be the Savior of all people [in the soteriological sense]). This liberal development of the concept has frightened away many evangelicals from embracing it, but the evangelical church does not need to be afraid to affirm that God is the Father of all people in the sense that he has created each and every person (Acts 17:26). This affirmation is very different from the affirmation of universalism that God will be the Savior of each and every person. Furthermore, this brotherhood and sisterhood of all humanity—this unity of the human race—has important ramifications for how human beings treat other human beings.
[41]The germination of this idea comes from a discussion of Karl Barth, who emphasized the solidarity of Christians with God in Christ as they stand at his side: "They have not placed themselves at His side. They do not stand there on their own merits. They do so only in the power of the call of His free grace as it has come to

Concretely, the church expresses this commitment through its particular concern to care for the poor and marginalized, an engagement viewed as flowing from its embrace of the good news of Jesus Christ. Indeed, in the midst of clarifying the gospel of grace and protecting it from harmful accretions, Paul voices the sole instruction urged upon him by the apostles: "Only, they asked us to remember the poor, the very thing I was eager to do" (Gal. 2:10). As the Gospel Coalition appropriately affirms:

God is concerned not only for the salvation of souls but also for the relief of poverty, hunger, and injustice. The gospel opens our eyes to the fact that all our wealth (even wealth for which we worked hard) is ultimately an unmerited gift from God. Therefore the person who does not generously give away his or her wealth to others is not merely lacking in compassion, but is unjust. Christ wins our salvation through losing, achieves power through weakness and service, and comes to wealth through giving all away. Those who receive his salvation are not the strong and accomplished but those who admit they are weak and lost. We cannot look at the poor and the oppressed and callously call them to pull themselves out of their own difficulty. Jesus did not treat us that way. The gospel replaces superiority toward the poor with mercy and compassion. Christian churches must work for justice and peace in their neighborhoods through service even as they call individuals to conversion and the new birth. We must work for the eternal and common good and show our neighbors we love them sacrificially whether they believe as we do or not. Indifference to the poor and disadvantaged means there has not been a true grasp of our salvation by sheer grace.[42]

Accordingly, salvation by grace, a gospel focus, and promotion of sac-

---

them and been received by them. But they do stand there: in the world yet over against it; like, yet unlike it; with it, yet in solidarity with God against it." Karl Barth, *The Doctrine of Reconciliation*, part 3, second half, vol. 4 of *Church Dogmatics* (Edinburgh: T & T Clark, 1962), 557. P. T. Forsyth adds: "We must make it clear that Christianity faces the world with terms, and does not simply suffuse it with a glow; that it crucifies the world, and does not merely consecrate it; that it recreates and does not just soothe or cheer it; that it is life from the dead, and not simply bracing for the weak or comfort for the sad." P. T. Forsyth, *The Church, the Gospel and Society* (London: Independent Press, 1962), 18.

[42]Gospel Coalition, "Theological Vision for Ministry," v. 5. http://www.thegospelcoalition.org. Within a similar framework, Christopher Wright advocates "a cross-centered theology of mission": "The cross is the unavoidable center of our mission. All Christian mission flows from the cross—as its source, its power, and as that which defines its scope. It is vital that we see the cross as central and integral to every aspect of holistic, biblical mission, that is, of all we do in the name of the crucified and risen Jesus." Whether the church is engaged in preaching the gospel, feeding the hungry, working to right an injustice, or teaching English as a second language to immigrants, its theological warrant for its mission is the cross. Wright continues: "Bluntly, we need a holistic gospel because the world is in a holistic mess. And by God's incredible grace we have a gospel big enough to redeem all that sin and evil has touched. And every dimension of that good news is good news utterly and only because of the blood of Christ on the cross." Christopher J. H. Wright, *The Mission of God: Unlocking the Bible's Grand Narrative* (Downers Grove, IL: IVP Academic, 2006), 314–315. Cf. Timothy J. Keller, *Ministries of Mercy: The Call of the Jericho Road* (Grand Rapids, MI: Zondervan, 1989), 106–119, 211–16.

rificial concern for the poor and disenfranchised are all bound together as the church lives out the reality of the inaugurated kingdom of God, looking for and hastening the return of its King.

The Church and the Kingdom as an Eschatological Reality

While the church participates in and relishes the inaugurated reality of the kingdom of God, it hopes for the "not yet" aspects of the kingdom—indeed, the consummation of the kingdom in its fullness—to transpire soon. It longs for the fulfillment of Jesus' promise, uttered at his trial before the high priest: "But I tell you, from now on you will see the Son of Man seated at the right hand of Power and coming on the clouds of heaven" (Matt. 26:64). From a premillennial perspective, the triumphant return of the King either (1) will be preceded by the rapture of the church seven years in advance so as to provide escape from the divine wrath poured out on the earth during the great tribulation (dispensational premillennialism), or (2) will take place concurrently with the rapture of the church (historic premillennialism).[43] In either case, the second coming will feature "the Word of God"—also named "King of kings and Lord of lords"—slaying all the enemies aligned against him (Rev. 19:11–21) and the resurrection of believers (Rom. 8:11; 1 Cor. 15:42–49; Phil. 3:20–21).[44] The returning King and Lord will next establish his millennial kingdom on earth, during which the saints "will reign with him for a thousand years" (Rev. 20:1–6). According to some premillennialists, the millennium will feature the fulfillment of the Old Testament prophecies of a national restoration of the Jewish people to the land of Israel; thus, the millennial kingdom will be strongly Jewish in flavor. At the conclusion of the millennium, Satan and his minions will engage in one last desperate battle against the Lord but will ultimately be defeated (vv. 7–10). The great white throne judgment follows (vv. 11–15), in which King Jesus exercises the authority delegated to him by the Father to judge (John 5:22, 26–27; Acts 10:42; 17:30–31; 2 Tim. 4:1). "Then comes the end, when he delivers the kingdom to God the Father after destroying every rule and every authority and power. For he must reign until he has put all his ene-

---

[43]Two other eschatological perspectives—amillennialism and postmillennialism—are noteworthy as evangelical positions on the end times. The first identifies the millennium with the present church age and holds out future hope for the return of Christ—along with the contemporaneous events of resurrection and judgment—to be followed immediately by the new heaven and new earth. The second holds that, through the preaching of the gospel and the Christianization of the world, this present church age will gradually yield to a golden age of peace and prosperity, to be followed by the return of Christ, resurrection, judgment, and the new heaven and new earth.

[44]For believers who are alive when Christ returns, their resurrection bodies will be slipped over their current earthly bodies (2 Cor. 5:4), an instantaneous transformation (1 Cor. 15:51–52) needed because "flesh and blood cannot inherit the kingdom of God, nor does the perishable inherit the imperishable" (1 Cor. 15:50).

mies under his feet. . . . When all things are subjected to him, then the Son himself will also be subjected to him who put all things in subjection under him, that God may be all in all" (1 Cor. 15:24–28). This last reality is the new heaven and new earth (Revelation 21–22).

Accordingly, the church's hope is to participate in an eschatological kingdom featuring the following: the return of the King; the warrior "King of kings and Lord of lords"; the King's reigning with his subjects over a millennial kingdom; the King as Judge; and the King's yielding his kingdom to God the Father, "that God may be all in all." Clearly, the church is not the ultimate reality in the redemptive plan of God, but as it lives the inaugurated reality of the kingdom of God, it fixes its hope on the eschatological kingdom to come.

To summarize, a complex relationship exists between the church and the kingdom according to five themes. First, the church relates to the kingdom as God's universal rule and eternal dominion such that, in one sense, the church owes its existence to the kingdom and, in another sense, the church is the instrument through which entrance into the kingdom is granted. The second relationship between the church and the kingdom as Israel has been viewed in several different ways, with my own perspective being that the administration of the kingdom has been wrenched away from the Jewish people and granted instead to the church, yet with pride of place being restored to the Jewish people in the millennial kingdom. A third relationship is that between the church and the kingdom as belonging to the Son of Man/Davidic King. As Jesus fulfilled the Old Testament prophetic hope for a Son of Man/Davidic King to be a light for all peoples, the church confesses that "Jesus is Lord," acknowledging his absolute kingship while subverting all other claimants to such allegiance, whether those are earthly kings or heavenly dominions. Fourth, the church relates to the kingdom as an inaugurated reality, specifically living as a missional church that presses on toward kingdom maturity through suffering for Christ. A final relationship is between the church and the kingdom as an eschatological reality, which features the church intensely longing for this angelic announcement: "The kingdom of the world has become the kingdom of our Lord and of his Christ, and he shall reign forever and ever" (Rev. 11:15).

How the Church Should Live in Light of Its Complex Relationship to the Kingdom

If I may be permitted a few points of encouragement and exhortation from the above discussion, I call the church to engage in the following action points: First, members of the church are urged to "not pass judgment on one another any longer, but rather decide never to put a stumbling block or hindrance in the way of a brother." The reason for this prohibition flows from our topic: "For the kingdom of God is not a matter of eating and drinking but of righteousness and peace and joy in the Holy Spirit" (Rom. 14:13, 17). Empowered by the Spirit, who fosters an atmosphere conducive to love and unity, church members renounce petty preferences, yield their rights to one another, and "pursue what makes for peace and for mutual upbuilding" (v. 19).

Second, church members are called to be worthy ambassadors for Christ, as Paul instructed:

> All this is from God, who through Christ reconciled us to himself and gave us the ministry of reconciliation; that is, in Christ God was reconciling the world to himself, not counting their trespasses against them, and entrusting to us the message of reconciliation. Therefore, we are ambassadors for Christ, God making his appeal through us. We implore you on behalf of Christ, be reconciled to God. For our sake he made him to be sin who knew no sin, so that in him we might become the righteousness of God. (2 Cor. 5:18–21)

The church's ministry of reconciliation is primarily about the message (λόγος; logos; word) of reconciliation, the gospel of the substitutionary, sacrificial death of Jesus on behalf of the world and his resurrection from the dead (1 Cor. 15:1–4). As his ambassadors, the church must understand its missional identity and thus prioritize its gospel ministry.

Third, the church engages in this ministry of reconciliation, while living circumspectly with self-discipline, because of the following reality: "Or do you not know that the unrighteous will not inherit the kingdom of God? Do not be deceived: neither the sexually immoral, nor idolaters, nor adulterers, nor men who practice homosexuality, nor thieves, nor the greedy, nor drunkards, nor revilers, nor swindlers will inherit the kingdom of God. And such were some of you. But you were washed, you were sanctified, you were justified in the name of the Lord Jesus Christ and by the Spirit of our God" (1 Cor. 6:9–11). Living in the midst of an increasingly tolerant society, whose tolerance of kingdom-shutting sin tragically spreads, the church must be in the world and for the world, but never of the world in the sense of compromising with its sin.

Fourth, as it lives in light of the kingdom as an eschatological reality, and thus cognizant of the impending destruction of this present earth—"the removal of things that are shaken"—the church must heed the encouragement of the writer to the Hebrews: "Therefore let us be grateful for receiving a kingdom that cannot be shaken, and thus let us offer to God acceptable worship, with reverence and awe, for our God is a consuming fire" (Heb. 12:27–29). Indeed, this God whom the church worships through its Savior, Jesus Christ, is worthy of the church's praise and devotion: "To the King of ages, immortal, invisible, the only God, be honor and glory forever and ever. Amen" (1 Tim. 1:17).

8

THE KINGDOM AND ESCHATOLOGY

GERALD BRAY

When [the disciples] had come together they asked [Jesus], 'Lord, will you at this time restore the kingdom to Israel?' He said to them, 'It is not for you to know times or seasons that the Father has fixed by his own authority'" (Acts 1:6–7).

The End of the Beginning?

This incident, which occurred immediately before Jesus' ascension, marks a turning point in the history of biblical theology. Until then, it had been possible to read the history of Israel in terms of the formation, dissolution, and promised future re-creation of an earthly kingdom centered on Jerusalem and ruled over by a descendant of the house of David (Jer. 33:17). Jesus of Nazareth was a credible candidate for that throne, having been generally acknowledged as the "son of David" during his earthly ministry and regarded by many as the promised Messiah (Matt. 9:27; 12:23; 21:9, 15).

The events of Palm Sunday were still fresh in the disciples' minds and seemed to portend the creation of a movement for the fulfillment of the promise. The popular reaction to Jesus' entry into Jerusalem made it clear enough what was expected of him, and his subsequent arrest, trial, and crucifixion are a reminder of how nervous the authorities were of losing control. From their point of view, the events of that week were a deliberate mockery of the claims made for Jesus' kingship, a technique often used by governments when dealing with rebels. In their eyes, if the absurdity of a man's pretensions can be demonstrated, the temptation to follow him will vanish and the problem will be solved. At first, everything seemed to go according to plan. Jesus' disciples ran away and the few people left to bury him were women and old men who were most unlikely to start an insurrection. But then came the resurrection and the forty days during which Jesus taught his disciples the meaning of the events that had just occurred (Luke 24:44–48). This was not what anyone had expected, and it is easy to see why it would have inspired Jesus' followers with new hope. Not only was he back among them, but he was back as Superman, able to appear and disappear at will and promising them that in a few days' time they would receive power from on high as the Holy Spirit descended on them (v. 49; Acts 1:4–5). With a superhuman leader and a band of followers filled with the power of God, what could now stand in the way of the restoration of the kingdom?

Jesus' reply put an end to those hopes by adjourning them immediately. This is the real meaning of the statement that only the Father knows the times and seasons fixed by his authority. The Father revealed himself in and through the Son to whom he had committed all things, so if the Son did not know something, it was because there was nothing for him to know. The kingdom was not going to be restored to Israel in the way the disciples understood it, either then or later. The Christian church was not going to be a revolutionary messianic movement for the recovery of Israelite independence, but something else altogether.

What that something would be is defined by the ascension. This event has never received the attention it deserves. Few people notice it, but as the last thing that occurs in the Gospels and the first in the Acts of the Apostles, it is the link between the earthly and heavenly ministries of Christ. In his ascension, Jesus took his resurrected human body with the scars of his sacrifice, made once for all on the cross, back up to heaven. He took our captivity to sin captive, sat down at the right hand of his Father, and gave us gifts, of which the first and most important is the gift of his Holy Spirit (Eph. 4:7–8; John 15:26). But because he did not die for sins as abstract things, the effects of the ascension cannot be understood as a simple over-the-counter transaction: "sin committed, price for it paid, forgiveness obtained." Jesus came to die, not just for sins but for sinners—for people, not for things. This is why the apostle Paul could tell the Ephesians that by virtue of the ascension, we too are "seated . . . with him in the heavenly places in Christ Jesus" (Eph. 2:6). Where he is in his glory, there his servants are also, because we are united with him in his body and all that it suffered on our behalf.

The transition from time to eternity gives the temporal work of Jesus a new meaning, and that is what Jesus was trying to communicate to his disciples. In time and space there is a past and a future, but in eternity there is only the present. What was "present" for the disciples as they watched Jesus ascend into heaven is long past for us, and what is here today will be gone tomorrow. Time marches on, pushing everything into the past, and gallops with ever-increasing speed into an unknown future that we regard with a mixture of hope and dread.

It is the intersection between these two worlds, time and eternity, that is the province of eschatology. The word derives from the Greek *eschaton* meaning "last" or "final," which is used in the New Testament to refer specifically to the end of time. It may be in what we would call the future, as seems to be the case in Jude 18 where the apostles are recorded as having said that: "In the *last* time there will be scoffers," the implication being that they had not yet appeared. Elsewhere, it refers to what we would think of as the present, most notably in Hebrews 1:2: "in these *last* days [God] has spoken to us by his Son"; and even to the past, as in 1 Peter 1:20: "He [Jesus] was foreknown before the foundation of the world but was made manifest in the *last* times for the sake of you." As far as time is concerned, the *eschaton* can be surprisingly hard to pin down! In another sense though, it is not difficult to reconcile all three of the above, because it is clear that the phrase "last time(s)" refers to the period from the incarnation of Christ to his second coming, i.e., the age in which we are still living. It is we who have heard and received him, and we who meet the scoffers. Whether it is expressed as past, present, or future, there is something about the *eschaton* that is real in our current experience and that we expect to be permanent—the scoffers will not go away, any more than the Word of God will be withdrawn.

Both Peter and the writer to the Hebrews define the earthly work of Jesus as eschatological. At one level, this is understandable because it was the fulfillment of Old Testament prophecy. It represented the culmination of a centuries-old promise, though it was not of the kind that people generally expected. From their point of view the return of the kingdom was put on hold in a way that effectively shelved it, but in the eyes of God the Father and of Jesus himself, that was not what had happened. On the contrary, the kingdom had come and the promises had been fulfilled, albeit in a different way. Jesus was crowned with thorns at Calvary. His throne was the cross. His kingdom was (and is) the sum total of all those who come to the cross to be healed and restored by the blood that he shed there in payment for their sins. This was foreshadowed in the Old Testament, where sacrificial atonement for sin is a major theme, but it was never associated with the monarchy. Israel did not have priest-kings, which is why Jesus was described as "a priest forever after the order of Melchizedek," the non-Israelite ruler to whom Abraham himself offered a tithe (Heb. 7:1–3, 17). Melchizedek had no ancestors or descendants, which is a way of saying that his priesthood was not bound by time and space. Essentially, he was an eschatological figure, just as Jesus himself was.

Does the Old Testament contain a vision of kingly rule that could be called eschatological? The question is pertinent because the reference in Hebrews to Melchizedek is a quotation from Psalm 110:4, which shows that the early Christians interpreted it in that way. It can also be argued that the many allusions in the psalms and prophets to the Lord reigning in Zion over an earth in which the lion lies down with the lamb and Israel is reconciled to its historic enemies also reflect an eschatological way of thinking, since there was no prospect of those things happening in any foreseeable future. The difference between Old Testament eschatology (or at least, the way it was interpreted by most people at the time) and that of the early church was that the Jews thought that it would come to pass in a temporal future. How far the ancient kingdom of David could be restored remained uncertain and depended on the interplay of the great powers of the time, but the Jews had come remarkably close to re-establishing a genuine national independence in the century or two before Jesus was born, and the memory of that was still alive in Jesus' day.

The incarnation of the Son of God and his subsequent ministry on earth altered that perspective radically. Jesus of Nazareth was the king of the Jews, but he was also the high priest who paid the price for the sins of the people by sacrificing himself on a cross. It was this that made Christianity something more than a Jewish sect, because the king of the Jews was also the Lamb who was slain before the foundation of the world (Rev. 13:8). The reign of Christ on earth was not the result of human conquest but of a divine self-revelation that went against all the normal canons of kingship. The king did not come to "live forever" as the salutation to the Persian monarchs went (Neh. 2:3), but to die and to rise again to a new and different kind of life. The coming of Jesus changed the discussion about the nature of the kingdom of God. No longer would it be some kind of earthly fulfillment in the future but a heavenly reality in the eschatological present, something that in spiritual terms we can (and must) participate in here and now if we are to be saved.

The death and resurrection of Jesus, followed by his ascension, refocused his followers' vision. No longer would they look ahead to some future time; instead, they would focus on a heavenly reality that was always present with them. But of course, such a change of vision raised a number of questions to which there was no ready answer. Why should there be a future if the end has already come? Why did Jesus not simply wind up human history then and there? All we are told is that God rejected Israel for a time so that the non-Jewish (Gentile) nations would have an opportunity to be gathered into the fold (Rom. 11:25–27; see also Mark 13:10). How long that might take nobody could say, but the commission to take the gospel to the Gentiles was given by Jesus himself just before his ascension, and it has been a recurring theme in later Christian history (Matt. 28:19–20; Acts 1:8). Already in the late second century, Tertullian believed that the gospel had been preached to the ends of the earth, which meant that the end was near, and a similar impulse inspired Christian missionary work both in the sixteenth and in the nineteenth centuries.

"Win the world for Christ in this generation" was the slogan of the first ecumenical missionary conference, held at Edinburgh in 1910, and the motive was clear: once the world was won, the kingdom of God would come on earth. We still sing the hymn written by Henry Ernest Nichol (1862–1928) in 1896:

We've a story to tell to the nations
That shall turn their hearts to the right,
A story of truth and sweetness,
A story of peace and light.

For the darkness shall turn to the dawning
And the dawning to noonday bright,
And Christ's great kingdom shall come on earth,
The kingdom of love and light.

The message here is that the kingdom of God is already within our grasp, if only we can complete the work of evangelization. Since that hymn was written, the gospel has indeed been spread to the far corners of the earth, but whether it has triumphed in a way that will usher in the kingdom is less clear. In the lands of traditional Christendom a spirit of secularization has taken hold, to the extent that most of them no longer recognize the message of Christ and some are (or have been) openly hostile to it. More people died for their faith in the twentieth century, not in unevangelized lands but in the heart of Europe, than in the rest of Christian history put together. Is this how the kingdom of God is meant to come? Perhaps it is, but it was certainly not the vision that inspired Mr. Nichol and his contemporaries!

The triumphalist eschatology represented by his hymn is dubious at best, and a good case can be made for saying that it is not biblical at all. It certainly does not chime in with what Jesus told his disciples shortly before his death: "In the world you will have tribulation. But take heart; I have overcome the world" (John 16:33). The New Testament picture seems to be not that the world will be won for Christ but that it will be cast down and overturned by the victory of the Lamb who was slain over all the forces of rebellion that are ranged against him. "For we do not wrestle against flesh and blood, but against the rulers, against the authorities, against the cosmic powers over this present darkness, against the spiritual forces of evil in the heavenly places" (Eph. 6:12). The spiritual forces of evil are not here on earth, but in the heavenly places, says the apostle Paul, and it is with spiritual weapons that we must combat them. When Jesus ascended into heaven he returned to that world and brought the earthly revelation of God's purposes to an end. But that end was the beginning of something else, the revelation of the kingdom of God as it truly is, in all its eschatological dimensions and eternal glory.

Present or Future?

It is clear from the above that Jesus talked in terms of a fulfillment of his ministry that would come in the future, and that would in effect be the end of time as we know it. It is also clear that he would come on the clouds of heaven to take up the kingdom that the Father had prepared for him. His disciples naturally thought that they would have a special place in that kingdom, but Jesus disabused them of that notion (Matt. 20:21–23). In the kingdom of heaven, the last would be first and the first last, a warning to us that no amount of faith or Christian service in this life can guarantee us special honor in God's presence (20:26–27). It is commonly believed that the first generation of Christians thought that the return of Jesus was imminent and that barring unfaithfulness or laxity on their part, they would live to see it (1 Cor. 15:6). This is a very difficult subject, because while it was certainly true that Christ could have returned during their lifetimes and that they were expected to be prepared for him to come at any moment, they were not told to abandon what they were doing and gather in a specific place to await his return. Life went on, and the instructions the apostles gave to the churches presupposed that they were to continue as they had been doing and not try to "jump the gun" as we might say today.

In the nineteenth century many scholars associated with the so-called Tübingen school of church history came to believe that the expectation of Jesus' imminent return, or *parousia* ("presence") as it was called in Greek, died out. In the process, the church changed from being a charismatic community led by the Spirit to a social institution governed by rules determined by a priestly hierarchy. As that happened, hope of the *parousia* and the general understanding of the coming kingdom of God changed to fit the new situation.

The origins of this change can be found in the New Testament. From the very beginning, the church consisted of spiritually minded people (*pneumatikoi*) and others, who were labeled *psychikoi*, a word that is notoriously difficult to translate nowadays (1 Cor. 2:14). The *psychikoi* were the unspiritual ones, but they were given that name because they were accused of obeying the dictates of their "souls" rather than the Spirit of God. Some of the *pneumatikoi* claimed to possess a secret knowledge (*gnôsis*) that set them apart from lesser believers, but this aberration was soon condemned, not least because some of these Gnostics apparently believed that their superiority entitled them to lead immoral lives. True spirituality would manifest itself in behavior, not knowledge, and as time went on that behavior was thought to be a harbinger of the kingdom that would come in its fullness when Christ returned.

This was the logic that underlay a good deal of medieval monasticism and that occasionally resurfaces today in various forms of extreme sectarianism. The principle is that the *pneumatikoi* must withdraw from the world as much as they can in order to live the eschatological life here and now. The most obvious (though by no means only) sign of that life is celibacy. The New Testament speaks of this as a virtue that Christians should strive for in order to serve God more wholeheartedly, but marriage is never forbidden and is even recommended for those unable to keep themselves sexually pure in the single life (1 Cor. 7:6–9). Nevertheless, the eschatological fact is that there is no marriage in heaven, and if the life of heaven is to be lived on earth, it follows that celibacy must be part of it (Matt. 22:30). To this must be added intentional poverty, since the goods of this world cannot be taken to heaven, and obedience, because in the kingdom of God all will hear his voice and obey it without question.

At the time of the Reformation, this form of piety was rejected but the underlying principle was not. What had previously been the preserve of the few who were able to endure it now became (in a modified form) the calling of the many. Monasticism gave way to Puritanism, and there were many pious souls who thought that Calvin's Geneva or the New England colonies were a foretaste of the kingdom of heaven. None of these people abandoned the *parousia* hope, and the return of Christ remained an essential article of Christian belief, but those who tried to hasten the day of his coming were social revolutionaries who had to be repudiated. The *eschaton* had been domesticated, and God's people were expected to work out their future bliss in their present lives of sexual continence, frugality, and obedience.

This tradition came into its own in the nineteenth century as the supernatural receded from the realm of practical politics and more secular concerns began to dominate the social and religious agenda. In Germany, scholars of the stature of Albrecht Ritschl (1822–1889) and Adolf Harnack (1851–1930) developed what we now call "realized eschatology," meaning that the language of Jesus had to be interpreted exclusively in terms of what we can do now to further the kingdom of God on earth. Before long, this produced the Social Gospel movement, whose most famous representative was the American pastor of German origin, Walter Rauschenbusch (1861–1918). But even as these men were developing their theory, a reaction was also occurring. Ritschl's own son-in-law, Johannes Weiss (1863–1914), was diametrically opposed to it, and in his landmark work *Die Predigt Jesu vom Reiche Gottes*, which appeared in 1892, he tore it to shreds.[1] Weiss insisted that Jesus preached an apocalyptic and eschatological kingdom of God that was in stark contrast to its enemy, the kingdom of Satan. Far from being built gradually by human labor, it would burst on the scene as an act of God and overturn the present world order. Weiss's views were picked up by Albert Schweitzer, who interpreted Jesus' teaching and ministry in totally eschatological terms. Schweitzer went so far as to say that Jesus was so convinced that the end was near that he rushed headlong to his death, thinking that by his supreme sacrifice he would force God to act and usher in the kingdom. His tragic failure was rescued by his disciples, who moderated his teaching and made it the basis of a new world religion.[2]

---

[1] Interestingly enough, the book was not translated into English until 1971, when it appeared as *Jesus' Proclamation of the Kingdom of God*.
[2] This thesis is developed at length in Schweitzer's book *Von Reimarus zu Wrede*, which was published in 1906. It created such a sensation that an English translation, *The Quest for the Historical Jesus*, appeared as early as 1910.

Needless to say, Weiss and Schweitzer were seen to have gone too far in correcting the secular views of Ritschl and his followers, and before long various compromise positions came into being. One of these is associated with the name of Rudolf Bultmann (1884–1976), who agreed with Weiss and Schweitzer that Jesus' teaching was eschatological but who divorced this from any historical future. In Bultmann's eyes, the *eschaton* was a supernatural reality that bursts into human consciousness from time to time, demanding an existential decision similar to what we might call conversion. The kingdom of God is within us, transforming our outlook on life and giving us new spiritual energy to live in the right way, but with no reference to a future fulfillment.

Another influential reaction was that of Charles Harold Dodd (1884–1973), who believed that the kingdom of God had come in the birth of Jesus with whom it was completely identified. The fact that he cast out demons demonstrated that it was a present reality, and from there it was a short step to claiming that it was essentially timeless as well. In the incarnation, the absolute and wholly other has entered into time and space and become a human reality.[3] Dodd's views have been very influential, but they have not succeeded in eliminating the futuristic dimension of the eschatological kingdom of God. A very thorough examination and rebuttal of Dodd's position from a conservative point of view was put forward by Herman Ridderbos (1909–2007) in his classic work *The Coming of the Kingdom*, which makes a strong case for the traditional view that the *eschaton* must be seen as a future event, however much it is spiritually present with us now.[4] Typical of the mediating position between present and future eschatology is the work of Werner Georg Kümmel (1905–1995), who admitted the futuristic leanings of Jesus but agreed with Dodd that they were already being worked out in his life and ministry. Somewhat more conservative than this but basically similar was the work of George Eldon Ladd (1911–1982). Today it would be fair to say that most scholars in the field adopt a both/and approach to this question. They believe that the kingdom of God is essentially realized in the teaching of Jesus but that there is also a future dimension whose exact parameters remain to be defined.

The basic problem with realized eschatology is that it is reductionist. The classical forms of it that we find in medieval monasticism and in

---

[3]C. H. Dodd, *The Parables of the Kingdom* (London: Nisbet, 1935), 81.
[4]H. Ridderbos, *The Coming of the Kingdom* (Philadelphia: Presbyterian and Reformed, 1962), 444–527.

post-Reformation Puritanism tried to fence off a part of the world and make the *eschaton* a living reality for the spiritually minded, but attractive as that vision was to many, it ended by creating a counterculture that took Christ out of the world as much as it preached his rule over it. Most people simply did not make the grade and were left in the position of *psychikoi*, second-class Christians without the zeal needed to achieve the highest possible performance. In theological terms, the end result was the exact opposite of the kingdom, which is built on grace, not on works, and therefore cannot be reduced to a scheme devised by human beings and tailored to their abilities, however extraordinary they might be.

In its more modern forms, realized eschatology suffers from essentially the same defect. The kingdom of God becomes a moral code that may be life-transforming, particularly in the case of people who have lived notoriously sinful lives, but it is all too likely to be assimilated to middle-class niceness. Albert Schweitzer accused the scholars of his time of having turned Jesus into a nineteenth-century German university professor, and something not unlike that can be said of more recent attempts to apply the teaching of Jesus today. The great benefit of true eschatology is that it preserves the kingdom of God from such easy domestication. Weiss's belief that it is entirely of grace may not necessitate a dramatic eruption into time and space from a world beyond, but that vision is certainly more theologically consistent with what the New Testament teaches than the opinions of those who differed from him. We must affirm the biblical teaching that the kingdom of God is present in our midst, but we must never allow that conviction to dull our sense that it is also above and beyond us and that we have not yet begun to know it as it really is.

The Future in the Context of Eternity
When Jesus ascended to heaven he left his disciples behind. That in itself should remind us that a realized eschatology cannot be the whole story. However much we may be in touch with him in heaven, we are obliged to go on living in the time and space universe that he entered but has now transcended once more. What are we doing here? Is the presence of the Holy Spirit in our hearts all we shall ever know of the kingdom of God? Is there something more to come in this life, and if so, what is it? Or are we just marking time until the inevitable end, when this life will be swept away and the hitherto unknown kingdom of God will descend as a stranger from heaven?

Questions like these have been asked by Christians for centuries, and the answer usually given is that although the kingdom of God has not yet come in its fullness, it is already present among us in the church. There are different ways of looking at this, but the general drift is the same. Catholics put great emphasis on outward rites and ceremonies—to be baptized is to be made part of the body of Christ and therefore to become a citizen of the kingdom of God. Protestants (and Orthodox) do not like to tie things down so precisely and stress that membership in the kingdom is a spiritual phenomenon, present in baptism and illustrated by it, but more than the outward rite and not necessarily tied to it. After all, the thief on the cross who asked Jesus to remember him when he came into his kingdom was told that he would be in Paradise that same day, and there is no sign that he was ever baptized (Luke 23:42–43)!

But how closely connected is the church to the kingdom? We know that the church grows and changes over time; is that true of the kingdom as well? Or is the kingdom a spiritual reality at the core of the church's being that does not change in itself but is forever shaking the church up and refashioning it, so that it will be a more faithful reflection of God's rule than it has been up to now? Are Christians today better off or closer to God than the disciples of Jesus were, which is what a growth and development model of the church would seem to suggest? Or are we further away, as many who take literally the question of Jesus about whether the Son of Man will find faith on the earth when he returns are inclined to believe (Luke 18:8)? Does it make any difference at what point in human history we are alive, seeing that those who enter at the eleventh hour are promised the same reward as those who have been in the vineyard all along (Matt. 20:6–9)?

The apocalyptic vision of Christ on the throne that John gives us at the beginning of the book of Revelation may help us to answer these questions. The vision is granted to John on a desert island, but it is sent to the seven churches of Asia—seven being the number of perfection, representing the totality of the church in every time and place. Each of these churches belongs to the man seated on the throne, and he speaks with equal authority to all of them—hear what the Spirit says to the churches (Rev. 2:7, 11, 17, 29; 3:6, 13, 22)!

But what a mixed bag those churches are. Smyrna and Philadelphia are plodding along reasonably well, but even they face tribulation and attack from the enemies of the gospel. Ephesus, Pergamum, and Thyatira are good in parts but need greater discipline and vigilance, while Sardis and Laodicea seem to be in the last stages of decay and run the risk of being rejected altogether. If these churches belong to the kingdom of God, then at the very least that kingdom is a work in progress that in some cases has not got very far. But whether they are good or bad, the seven churches are no more than spectators in the great drama of the Lamb's triumph over his enemies. They are recipients of the revelation of the eschatological triumph of the kingdom of God, not participants in it.

What is true of the vision of John in Revelation is equally true of the Gospel witness to the earthly career of Jesus. When Pontius Pilate accused him of fomenting revolt against the authority of Rome, Jesus replied that his kingdom was not of this world (John 18:36–37). He forbade his disciples to fight for it on his behalf, even though they were willing to do so (Matt. 26:51–53; Luke 22:49–51; John 18:10–11). In Matthew's account of Jesus' arrest in the garden of Gethsemane, Jesus was forthright about the spiritual nature of what was happening to him. He reminded his bellicose disciples that although he could appeal to the Father and get more than twelve legions of angels to rescue him, that was not the right way forward, because the Scriptures had to be fulfilled (Matt. 26:53–54). However willing and able the church might be to defend him, it has no mandate to act against his revealed will. The kingdom will come at the time appointed for it, and not a moment earlier.

This lesson is very hard for the church to learn. In the Middle Ages it identified itself so closely with the kingdom of God that it claimed sovereignty over the secular rulers of Europe. In the late eleventh century, the popes were even able to raise whole armies and send them on crusade to liberate Jerusalem from its Muslim overlords. But after a few initial successes, the Crusades turned into a long-drawn-out failure, the church was increasingly corrupted by its involvement in worldly affairs, and eventually the authority of its leaders was fatally weakened. When Joachim da Fiore (d. 1202) invented modern millenarianism, he was able to cast the Holy Roman emperor as the Antichrist and predict that a good pope would come to reform the church and conquer the world. But a century later it was the pope himself who had come to be seen as the Antichrist, a popular image that stuck in the minds of religious dissidents and resurfaced at the time of the Reformation. Today we find it hard to imagine how the Reformers could wax so vehement in their denunciations of the papacy, but they saw very clearly how its claims to worldly dominion were both false and dangerous and how they had corrupted the church.

Unfortunately, the Reformers' attempts to reform the institution failed, and the church split into half a dozen different pieces, which in the passage of time have multiplied into many hundreds. The nations that the church had controlled were forced to reconstruct their social unity on a different basis, and the claims of the different churches were increasingly ignored because of their inherently divisive character. Today the church has become a series of voluntary associations that anyone can join or leave, usually without penalty. Far from being a manifestation of the kingdom of God, the modern church has retreated into private life where it does whatever it can to protect its members from the onslaughts of the aggressive secularism that is increasingly dominant in secular society.

The lesson we must draw from this sad history is that the church cannot claim to be an incarnation of the kingdom of God. At best it is a theater of war in which spiritual issues are proclaimed and confronted, with varying degrees of success. As was the case in the Roman province of Asia, some individual churches are more faithful than others and better equipped for the struggle, but even the best of them cannot claim to have won the victory and established the kingdom of God on earth. The difference between the church and the world is that the church is privileged to know the mind of God and has the promise that, despite its defects and failures, it will be redeemed in the end. The eschatological nature of God's kingdom ensures that there can be no progress from a lower to a higher manifestation of it in this life. "Jesus Christ is the same yesterday and today and forever" (Heb. 13:8). If he does not change then we can be sure that his kingdom does not change either, because the two are inseparable. This is the framework within which the events described in the book of Revelation have to be interpreted and the way in which the church must understand its own relationship to the eschatological kingdom of God.

As far as our future on earth is concerned, it is probably true to say that more energy has gone into plotting the course of the end times than into any other aspect of Christian theology. Other doctrines tend to be the preserve of theologians, but Armageddon and everything associated with it has captured the popular imagination in a way that few other things have. Down through the ages people have identified the circumstances of their own time with the coming end. The persecutions of the early church were thought to be the great tribulations prophesied by John, the fall of Rome was interpreted as the beginning of the great woes preceding the final judgment, the rise of Islam was regarded as the appearance of the Antichrist or the beast, the bubonic plague was identified with one of the four horsemen of the apocalypse, and so on. Modern predictive prophecy began with the French Revolution, which was interpreted as the triumph of all that is anti-God in what had been the temple of the Lord. Needless to say, the horrors of the twentieth century have provided a rich vein of plagues and disasters, convincing many that the end cannot be far off, and there has been a marked rise in the number of dates proposed for the end of the world. So far at least, none of these predictions have turned out to be true, but this does not deter the activists, who are constantly on the lookout for new identifications around which conspiracy theories can be concocted and the imminence of the end predicted.

Faced with these tendencies, the Christian believer is in something of a dilemma. On the one hand, it is hard to give credence to any particular theory because the one-hundred-percent failure rate to date strongly suggests that it is unlikely to be true. At the same time, there are huge and potentially catastrophic problems in the world, and Christians cannot escape from them. Persecution is a reality for many, and it may be spreading. There is certainly no sign that wars, famines, and plagues are decreasing, and all the evidence suggests that they are more threatening than ever. Consider that as recently as 1945 it was extremely unlikely that innocent civilians living far from a battlefield would be at risk of losing their lives, but now that we are subjected to urban terrorism, nobody is safe. Biological warfare, the contamination of food and water supplies, and death by the thousands have become realistic possibilities in a way that was not true in earlier times. What happens on the other side of the world can have immediate and dramatic effects on us because globalization has made the entire planet both accessible and vulnerable. Given this situation, it is hardly surprising that apocalyptic fears are on the rise. Does this not say something about the approaching end of time? Is the coming of the kingdom of God not more likely now than it has ever been before?

In one sense, it is hard to deny the logic of arguments like these. If the kingdom of God is going to come at some point in the future, then every day must be bringing us one step closer to that goal. If that is true, we must be nearer to it now than Jesus' disciples were, and the fact that it is now objectively possible for the human race to destroy itself in an instant is bound to lend credence to the theory that the end will come with a bang. It might even be said that a slow descent into chaos is unlikely, because if that were to become a threat, those with their fingers on the nuclear triggers might decide to risk everything in the hope of preventing it, and mass destruction would ensue. Panic and disaster on a worldwide scale are no longer fantasies but probabilities, if ever these forces were to be unleashed, and the slow but seemingly unstoppable spread of atomic power to unstable and irresponsible regimes around the world makes it increasingly likely that this will happen sooner or later. Before 1914 people believed that the spread of science and prosperity had reached the point where world war was unthinkable, but as we know, the unthinkable happened and wreaked havoc on a scale that up to then had been unimaginable. A century later, we have advanced a long way in terms of both science and prosperity, but who would dare to claim that history will not repeat itself, with even more serious consequences?

In secular terms, mass destruction in the foreseeable future is only too likely, but Christians cannot assume that it will be the prelude to the coming of the kingdom of God. It is of course possible that God will use those events to bring the world to an end, and it is certain that he will be glorified in them whatever happens, but we cannot identify nuclear self-destruction with the inauguration of the future reign of Christ. The problem with this kind of analysis is that those who spend their time developing doomsday scenarios out of current events are locating an eternal, spiritual reality somewhere in time and space. From the perspective of Christian theology, it matters little whether we are talking about Jerusalem in AD 70, Rome in AD 410, New York in 2001, or Shanghai at some as yet unknown date. The politics of Palestine in the time of Jesus were highly volatile, and the chances of violence were great. We know that only a generation later Jerusalem would be razed to the ground and its temple destroyed, events that were either imminent or already past when the Gospels were committed to writing. But in spite of all the warning signs, Jesus refused to be drawn on this point, and when the Pharisees asked him at what point the kingdom of God would come, he told them that it was unpredictable (Luke 17:20–21). What looked like harbingers of the end were nothing of the kind; the end would come when nobody was looking for it. Furthermore, Jesus warned his disciples not to listen to those who tried to fix a date for his return, a warning that has all too often been ignored by some of his overzealous followers (Matt. 24:26–28; Luke 17:22–23).

The message of the book of Revelation is that events on earth are only a picture of the war that has been going on in heaven since the revolt of Satan and will continue until he is finally crushed. This war spills over into our world because we have been beguiled by Satan and trapped into becoming subjects of his kingdom, which is a counterfeit of the kingdom of God. But the battle is not concentrated here and will not be decided by earthly means. Satan succeeded in getting the human race on his side by

promising Adam and Eve that if they obeyed him they would become like
God, knowing good and evil. That is what happened, but the price they
paid for it was subjection to an alien power that still claims the allegiance
of their descendants (Gen. 3:22). To this end, wars and rumors of wars
continue and will go on till the end of time (Matt. 24:6). At a superficial
level there is change in the sense that the names of the principal human
actors and the means they use to secure their ends vary from one age to
the next, but the basic struggle remains the same.

In this spiritual warfare, the greatest danger to Christians comes
not from the open enemies of the kingdom of God but from those who
want to create a caricature of it and put us in charge as puppet kings. We
boast of having independent authority, but in reality we are subject to
the machinations of Satan. In years gone by, human societies sought to
co-opt God and his revelation for their own ends, but now they prefer to
ignore it and set themselves up in its place. In the secular universe there
is no God. This does not mean that there is no freedom of worship, but
rather that, as in ancient Athens, anything can have a divine label stuck on
it and an altar raised to its glory, even if it is completely unknown (Acts
17:23). Today, secular belief in progress, in the triumph of reason and science, and in the goodwill and ultimate perfectibility of humankind is as
strong as it ever was, despite all the evidence to the contrary. Those who
point out that it is all a lie are regarded as eccentrics at best and antisocial
troublemakers at worst; either way, they are relegated to the sidelines and
effectively silenced by the media. Modern secular worship is protected by
law in a spirit of "tolerance," the pseudo-virtue that has replaced devotion
to the Truth.

In this mental universe, the biggest problem with Jesus Christ is not
his claim to divinity but the exclusivity that that claim entails. If only he
had said: "I am one of the ways, an insight into truth, and an outlook onto
life. Please come to the Father by me because I can get you there faster
and with less pain than any of the competition" (see John 14:6 for what
he really said). The world would have no problem with that, but it would
be a denial of everything the life and work of Jesus means. Where that
approach has taken hold, the Lie is in control and the kingdom of God is
nowhere to be seen. "You did not choose me, but I chose you" said Jesus,
the king who brooks no rivals (15:16). When the kingdom comes it will
do so on God's terms, not ours, and no power on earth will be able to
claim any special favors from him. The king will not come to set the seal

on human achievements but to judge them, and it is on the basis of that judgment that he will build his kingdom.

The Judgment of This World

In the book of Revelation John was caught up into heaven where he witnessed the king on his throne pronouncing the judgment that would establish the foundations of his kingdom (Rev. 4:1–3). The right to execute judgment is fundamental to any meaningful rule, and perhaps it is this aspect of the kingdom of God that modern theologians have found the most difficult to accept. The eschatological vision of the kingdom insists that the judgment will be future (in our terms) and definitive. The alternative, put forward by many theologians in the twentieth century, is to say that the judgment occurred on the cross, when Jesus suffered and died for the sins of the world. It was at that moment that the forces ranged against God in the world were brought low and defeated. Three days later the divine victory was confirmed in the resurrection, and there has been no looking back since.

There is a sense, of course, in which that is true, and its truth is confirmed by the book of Revelation itself. When John went up to heaven he saw the scroll of judgment in God's hand, but it had been sealed and there was no one worthy to break the seals and open it (Rev. 5:4). When John realized this he started to weep but was stopped by one of the elders around the throne, who told him that the lion of the tribe of Judah, the root of David, had conquered and had been found worthy to open the seals. What John was told is one thing, but what he then saw is another, for it was not a lion but the Lamb who was slain that came into view. Those around the throne greeted the Lamb in the following words: "by your blood you ransomed people for God from every tribe and language and people and nation, and you have made them a kingdom and priests to our God, and they shall reign on the earth" (vv. 9–10).

The historical sacrifice of Jesus on the cross has been taken up into God, and therefore into the timeless eternity of the *eschaton*. It is not a past event but a present reality that forms the basis on which the judgment is made and the foundation on which the kingdom is built. Those who have washed their robes in the blood of the Lamb are the ones who are worthy to share in the kingdom because they have trusted in Christ for their salvation (Rev. 7:14). The means of entering the kingdom have been established, but the ingathering of the nations goes on, as Jesus himself prophesied that it would (Mark 13:10). It is here, however, that

an important difference emerges. On the one hand are those like Karl
Barth and his followers, who insist that the once-for-all sacrifice is applicable to everyone and that all human beings are saved. On the other hand
are those who deny this and say that salvation is given only to those who
believe, while the rest are condemned to suffer the fate that we all deserve
on account of our sins.

There is a further subdivision between those who believe that people
are saved by their own efforts (whether "works" or profession of faith) and
those who insist that they are saved only by the grace of God. In one way,
this latter group is closer to the universalists, because they both believe
that salvation is by grace and not by works, but it is also more faithful to
the teaching of Jesus, who clearly indicated that not all would enter the
kingdom of heaven (Matt. 7:23). It was also Jesus who said that although
everyone would be raised from the dead in order to face the judgment,
only some of those judged would be fit for the kingdom of heaven (25:31–
46). The book of Revelation is equally clear on this point—the dead will
be judged by what is written in the book of life, and those whose names
are not found in it will be cast into the lake of fire and perish (Rev. 20:12,
15). From our point of view this judgment has not yet taken place, since
if it had there would be no point in warning us about it in the way that
Jesus did. He was not telling his hearers what would happen to them but
exhorting them to change their behavior so that they might escape what
would otherwise be inevitable. In this sense, the judgment is future, but it
is also definitive and therefore eschatological. What does that mean, and
what difference does it make in practice?

First, it means that there will be a judgment on time—there is no past
or future in the kingdom of God. The sufferings of the past, whatever
their cause, will be wiped away and forgotten (Rev. 21:4). In this life we
are shaped by where we have come from and what we have gone through,
whether we like it or not. Memories and grudges weigh on us and determine our attitudes and conduct. But when time is removed, these things
will also disappear and we shall be set free to be the people God wants
us to be in his kingdom. This is why salvation cannot be based on works,
because they too will belong to the past that will be swept away in the new
creation. For the same reason, laying up treasure on earth is a waste of
time and energy because such things will have no place and no meaning
in the kingdom of God (Matt. 6:19–21; 1 Cor. 3:11–15).

Second, there will be a judgment on power. The kingdoms of this
world will become the kingdom of our God and of his Christ (Rev. 11:15).

There is no earthly ruler who can compare with him, and therefore all allegiance to the secular state is provisional and relative. We are told to render unto Caesar what belongs to him, but what belongs to him is as nothing compared to what belongs to God (Matt. 22:21). The rulers of this present age have been put in power by God as a means of controlling evil, but they cannot become a way of salvation because they remain ultimately subject to Satan, who is the prince of this world (Rom. 13:1–7; John 12:31; 14:30; 16:11). It is hard for many people to grasp this apparent duality, but in fact it is completely logical. In a world governed by sin the power of the sword is necessary to keep it under control. Although this power is legitimate in the circumstances of a fallen world, it is not good in itself, and to rely on it for salvation is the worst form of idolatry. This is a particularly important message for us today because we are inclined to trust secular authorities (not only governments, but scientific and intellectual establishments of all kinds as well) to bring us the kind of peace and happiness that can only come from God. Law and order are great blessings, but in the final analysis they are a caricature of the kingdom of heaven, where law will be unnecessary and order will be shaped by a common devotion to God.

Lastly, there will be a judgment on what the world calls success. There are no lasting achievements on earth. However beautiful our creations may be and however well they may stand up against the ravages of time, they will not endure forever. We get a sense of what this means every time there is a devastating tornado, earthquake, or tsunami. Thanks to the marvels of modern technology, we can watch in horror as whole cities are destroyed in a matter of minutes and buildings meant to withstand the greatest shocks come tumbling down as if they were made of paper. If natural forces are capable of such destruction, imagine what God will do when he comes in judgment!

It is important to understand this because along with success comes failure, which is usually more common and, depending on one's point of view, may even be the same thing. Was the invention of the automobile, for example, a success? Technologically speaking, we might think that it was, but if we add up the cost in pollution and depletion of natural resources, things might look very different. It is not always easy to know how to evaluate human achievements, not least because their long-term consequences are hidden from our eyes. The Crusaders who captured Jerusalem from the Muslims in 1099 regarded that as a great triumph of the gospel, but centuries later we can see that they achieved nothing and that the Christian communities in the Middle East still suffer from the legacy of that event, for which they are held partly responsible. In the light of that history, can we say that the establishment of the modern state of Israel has been a success? How long will it last? Many Christians believe that it is a sign of the approaching end of time, but what if it disappears in another hundred years or so in the way that the Crusader states (with which the Arabs often compare Israel) did? It is tempting to say that whenever we think we have succeeded at something, we only need to wait long enough and that sense of achievement will disappear as whatever we have done crumbles and is swept into the "dustbin of history" as Marxists like to say. When the kingdom comes, success and failure will be judged together, and both will be swept away by the overwhelming power of God.

At first sight, this may seem discouraging to those who have dedicated their lives to literature and the arts (for example) and who regard great achievements in these fields as monuments of the human spirit that are worthy of God's notice and preservation. There is something in human nature that wants to create and achieve. This is a God-given trait, and he has commanded us to develop the resources that he has put at our disposal (Gen. 1:28). The problem is that the human race has put itself in the place of God and looks to its achievements as a way of salvation. Sooner or later, we are led to believe, mankind's dominion over the earth will solve all problems and people will be able to live indefinitely, if not forever. Man will not only play God, he will be God. It is this, the fruit of the sin of pride, that God will come in judgment to root out and destroy.

The book of Revelation tells us that human potential for achievement will be recognized and honored not by taking our paltry works up to God but by sending the New Jerusalem down from heaven (Rev. 21:10). The city is the symbolic expression of human creativity. God does not despise this or reject it, but he re-creates it according to his will. The New Jerusalem, like the new creation of which it is the centerpiece, will be a gift, an eschatological realization of what God intended for us in the garden of Eden. It will not be a return to the garden but an acknowledgment of all that has happened in human life since Adam and Eve were expelled from it. All that will be left of Eden will be the tree of life, which will stand on its own in the midst of the city (22:2). The one thing that Adam and Eve were prevented from touching will become the distinguishing mark of the kingdom's presence, and its leaves will be used for the healing of the nations.

This is important because it reminds us that the eschatological coming of the kingdom will transform our present reality in a way that will
comfort every sorrow and heal every imperfection. It will put right all that
has gone wrong and bring harmony in place of discord. There will be no
temple in the city because there will be no more need of sacrifice, or even
of worship as we now understand it (Rev. 21:22). The Lord himself will be
its light, and everything we have and are will be caught up in him.

The last thing that needs to be said is that although the judgment will
precede the coming of the kingdom, there is a sense in which it will also
be its end. Once the Son has put all things under his feet, he will give the
kingdom back to the Father so that God may be "all in all" (1 Cor. 15:28).
He will not cease to reign, but the nature of his rule will change. As the
closing chapters of the book of Revelation tell us, the king will become the
bridegroom, elevating his people from the status of subjects to that of co-
heirs and equals with him. The church will be the bride of Christ, becoming one body with him for all eternity. We shall reign with him forever,
but there will be no kingdom other than his body to rule over because
everything will be caught up in him who is the Alpha and the Omega:

> From heaven he came and sought her
> To be his holy bride
> With his own blood he bought her
> And for her life he died.

The words of the hymn say it all.[5] The eternal purpose of God is to unite his
people to himself in a kingdom built out of suffering that is both caused
and transformed by love. Caused, because in love the Son of God came
into the world to become one of us, to take our sins upon himself, and to
die for our salvation on the cross, where he was crowned and acknowledged as king. Transformed, because out of his death has come our life,
and out of his resurrection has come our eternal salvation. Crowned with
him in his suffering, we shall be seated with him on his throne in glory,
and God will be all in all.

In sum, the kingdom of God cannot be understood apart from its
eschatological element because it is that which gives it its meaning and
purpose. From our present point of view it will come in the future, but
when it comes time will end and a new kind of life will be inaugurated.
That life will not be bound by time, nor will its purposes be fulfilled by a

---

[5]From "The Church's One Foundation," written by Samuel John Stone (1839–1900) and published in 1886.

process of cause and effect. In the new creation we shall dwell in a dimension of reality that is beyond change and decay, in which our identity and purpose will be defined by our union with Christ. He will be our king and our bridegroom, the one who reigns over us but who at the same time cherishes us as he cherishes his own body. What we see and know in this life is a foretaste of what is to come, but it cannot compare with the reality itself. For that we must await the coming of the kingdom and the revelation of the king who will come with judgment and with salvation to those who believe.

9

THE KINGDOM TODAY

ANTHONY B. BRADLEY

In recent years there has been a renaissance among evangelicals thinking about the connection between *orthodoxy*, what Christians believe, and *orthopraxis*, how Christians are to live.[1] These two *orthos* are intended to work in harmony with one another. Sadly, however, there often has been tension between some communions that tend to emphasize one side of this equation over the other while pointing fingers and accusing those who emphasize the other side of not being truly Christian. What we have read in this book about the kingdom of God presents unique opportunities to encourage God's people not to pit these two emphases against each other but to bring them into a symbiotic relationship.

The Bible is clear that we are to be a people of faith *and* practice. For example, Jesus teaches that those who love him will obey his commands (John 14:23–24). Paul encourages Timothy to watch his doctrine and life closely (1 Tim. 4:16). James reminds us that faith without works is dead (James 2:14–16). There are simultaneous calls to believe and to do. Herein lies the problem. Even with the best of intentions and commitments we do not always know what is best, and, if we are honest, we must recognize that what is best is not always clear. Our orthopraxis and pursuit of justice means that, in our frailty and imperfections, the best we can do is rely on prudential judgments guided by clear principles. Is there a framework to help us get started? This chapter suggests that God has provided such a framework in his Word and his creation so that the scaffolding of

---

[1] I would like to thank Peter Green, John Halsey Wood Jr., Jake Belder, and Stephen Wesley for their helpful comments and criticisms during the drafting of this chapter.

the kingdom of God presented in the previous chapters can move God's people into mission.

Outlined below are eight principles of orthopraxis and justice that can direct our prudential judgments in good directions in a world complicated by sin, idols, pain, oppression, nation-states, globalization, pluralism, and a host of other issues. We will focus on the question, "What are God's people to do in the kingdom to press the claims of Christ everywhere in creation?"[2] The answer has much to do with how we understand the nature of love, human dignity, our neighbors, and civil society as well as what we believe about what humans deserve, how we are to live in equality, how we reciprocate with others, and what people need.

Love

The primary operating praxis and character of the kingdom of God is love. Love is not characterized by cultural conquest, withdrawal, exclusion, or political agendas. The rule and reign of God the Father, Son, and Holy Spirit compel a praxis-oriented life of love. The person and work of Christ make properly ordered love possible and provide an image of what love looks like in practice. God is the author of love, and his rule over all of life is an extension of his love. To help his followers understand the dynamic reign and rule of the kingdom of God, Jesus sums up what it means to be properly human by teaching that the greatest commandment for us is to "Love the Lord your God with all your heart and with all your soul and with all your strength and with all your mind, and your neighbor as yourself" (Luke 10:27). The Bible gives God's instruction for how to love him well and people made in his image. Scripture teaches us what it means to be faithful stewards over the whole creation. People of the kingdom are people who hunger to practice the art of well-ordered love.

The good news of the gospel is that the hostility of the heart toward God and disordered love toward others are transformed into new affections with a new disposition toward God and all that he desires for his creation.[3] As Christ commands, the primary motive and direction for life in the kingdom of God is love. But to love God is easier said than done. Love for God is the dispositional center of affection, volition, intellect, satisfac-

---

[2]See chapter 2, "Creation," in Albert M. Wolters, *Creation Regained: Biblical Basics for a Reformational Worldview*, 2nd ed. (Grand Rapids, MI: Eerdmans, 2005); and Henry R. Van Til, *The Calvinistic Concept of Culture* (Grand Rapids. MI: Baker Academic, 2001), 205–16.

[3]David Clyde Jones, *Biblical Christian Ethics* (Grand Rapids, MI: Baker, 1994), 38. By gospel I mean "the good news of salvation in Jesus Christ." See John Webster, "Gospel," in *DTIB*, ed. Kevin J. Vanhoozer et al. (Grand Rapids, MI: Baker, 2005), 263–64.

tion, joy, and goodwill in relation to all that God is.[4] Love for God is a life oriented around an uncompromising commitment to love the things God loves. Properly loving one's neighbor predisposes one to a commitment to seeking the good of the other. David Jones explains it this way:

> Love for our neighbor is beneficent affection for persons like ourselves. Love acts for the good of others out of affection for them, which influences the perception of what truly serves their interest and how it may be carried out in the diverse circumstances of human life.[5]

To love in this way requires that we understand what it means to love ourselves within a context of intimacy with God. To "love your neighbor as yourself" demands that we love ourselves well. To love oneself well is to do what is necessary to sustain one's life and to fulfill one's responsibility to preserve one's human dignity, holiness, chastity, property, and reputation and to bring glory to God the Creator.[6] As such, there is nothing sinful about one's desire to pursue one's best interests. Our best interests are to function in concert with God's best interest for his world (Deut. 10:13; Matt. 6:33; 1 Pet. 3:10–12).[7] Sin, however, corrupts what we believe to be our self-interest and leads us to treat others in ways that undermine both their dignity and ours. With love-oriented motives the direction of life in the kingdom becomes more clearly understood as willfully obeying the guidance that God gives about what it means to be truly human. It is an obedient love that submits to God's authority, desires to be guided by his instruction, and determines to carry out his will prudently.[8] Jesus says that those who love him will obey what he commands (John 14:15). This type of love is not an autocratic, coerced love—if there is such a thing— but a love characterized by willful reciprocation out of gratitude because of God's pursuant, liberating, and transformative love first shown to the people of the kingdom (1 John 4:7–21).

The means that God has given his people to properly love him and their neighbors include God's revelation in creation, his Word, the church, and so on, all working through the empowering presence and operation of the Holy Spirit. When Jesus teaches about the connection between love and obedience, he is quick to remind the disciples that the Holy Spirit

---

[4]Jones, *Biblical Christian Ethics*, 44.
[5]Ibid., 50.
[6]Ibid., 56.
[7]Ibid.
[8]Ibid., 59. The way of love is a way of life. Cornel West says, "Love and service are a vocation, not a profession." Cornel West, *Hope on a Tightrope: Words and Wisdom* (Carlsbad, CA: Hay House, 2008), 152.

will be present to help, comfort, and counsel an obedient love in the kingdom (John 14:16; 15:26; 16:7). The praxis of the kingdom of God depends entirely on the activity of God the Father, Son, and Holy Spirit and as such guarantees that the goals and ends of the kingdom will be accomplished.

Praxis as the Pursuit of Holiness

The application of loving God demands a life of hungering and thirsting for righteousness. The whole redemptive story is a story of God using the holiness of his people to accomplish mysteriously his redemptive will for the world. Jesus' teaching on the kingdom of heaven in the Beatitudes explains the normality of desiring holiness for those in the kingdom: "Blessed are those who hunger and thirst for righteousness, for they shall be satisfied" (Matt. 5:6). There is a great satisfaction that comes when one's life is desperate for holiness because by this one fulfills what it means to be made in the image and likeness of God. Righteousness is living out what it means to be truly *human*. Not to be a person desperate for righteousness is to set oneself up for the disordered love of self, neighbor, and creation. Unrighteousness provides a platform for the proliferation of sin and brokenness. As such, the church of Jesus Christ is a community of Jesus-followers committed to doing what is true, honorable, just, pure, lovely, commendable, excellent, and worthy of praise (Phil. 4:8).

Praxis as Loving Others Properly as Image Bearers of God

For followers of Jesus Christ, loving the other has a specific orientation. If we are to love others well we must see people as more than material beings needing material solutions. This materialist assumption is a child of atheism that seeks to sever human beings from their souls. Anthony Hoekema argues that God preserves all of his creation and that every human person is therefore dependent on God daily for his or her existence. Because of the uniqueness of being soul-constrained beings in distinction from the rest of creation, we cannot love others well without sharing the message of the gospel of Jesus Christ. Because of the effects of the fall, every human being sins against the holiness of God the Creator by using God-given capacities in the service of Satan.[9] The only remedy for this soul condition is the liberation, redemption, and rescue of this fallen state by God's sovereign intervention through the work of the Holy Spirit.

---

[9]Anthony Hoekema, *Created in God's Image* (Grand Rapids, MI: Eerdmans, 1986), 7.

The Holy Spirit works through the teaching of the gospel to bring those we love to repentance and faith in the person and work of Christ. The full restoration of human dignity is achieved through the human person's union with Christ. The praxis of the kingdom of God, then, requires the regular practice of evangelism.

By extension, the primary forms of love for people in the kingdom of God are what Jesus called the weightier matters of the law: justice, mercy, and faithfulness (Matt. 23:23).[10] Jesus' identification of these weightier matters is derived from the Old Testament emphasis that justice, mercy, and faithfulness comprise the essence of all that God is calling his people to be and to do.[11] This triad is summarized in Micah 6:8: "He has told you, O man, what is good; and what does the LORD require of you but to do justice, and to love kindness [mercy], and to walk humbly with your God?" It reminds us that believing the good news of salvation in the work and person of Christ is the beginning of living a life of justice, mercy, and faithfulness.

In sum, love is the foundation, orientation, and greatest application of kingdom praxis. Love is the first principle of the kingdom that governs all other principles. Sadly, in a fallen world love alone does not always tell us what the best practices are in every situation. The remaining elements of orthopraxis suggest what is necessary for harmonizing love-driven prudence with good intentions.

Human Dignity

For the second principle of orthopraxis we return to the importance of human dignity. In the kingdom of God, loving others demands viewing them as made in the image and likeness of God. Not only do human beings bear the image of God, they *are* the image of God.[12] As a human being every male and female is a child—the likeness or offspring—of God (Gen. 1:26; 9:6; Luke 3:38; Acts 17:28; 1 Cor. 11:7; James 3:9). Herman Bavinck is quick to point out that this doctrine implies two things: (1) Christ was made human in our likeness (Rom. 8:3; Phil. 2:7–8; Heb. 2:14) and Christians, having been conformed to the image of Christ, are now again becoming like God (Rom. 8:29; 1 Cor. 15:49; 2 Cor. 3:18; Phil. 3:12; Eph. 4:24; Col. 3:10; 1 John 3:2); and (2) that the image extends to the whole person in soul and body, in all faculties and powers, in all conditions and

[10]Jones, *Biblical Christian Ethics*, 77.
[11]Ibid., 78.
[12]Herman Bavinck, *Reformed Dogmatics*, vol. 2, *God and Creation* (Grand Rapids, MI: Baker Academic, 2004), 554.

234   Anthony B. Bradley

relations.[13] To be truly human is to bear the image of God. To love another properly means to want the liberation of the image of God in the other's whole person.

To claim that someone has human dignity is to claim that he is essential because he is the image of God.[14] The vocation of being human has certain attributes that help us to know what it means to love others well. By creating male and female in his image, God gave each person characteristics, capacities, potentials, and functions to live out the freedom, privilege, and responsibility of being coworkers with God in the regal tasks to be carried out in creation.[15] To St. Basil the Great, the mysterious plural used by God in the creation of humans ("Let us make man in our image, after our likeness," Gen. 1:26) is the Trinity deliberating over the creation of the human person. The image of the Trinity is imprinted upon humans in their creation. God loves the human being in his image, and because God is good, his image is good. Nonna Harrison articulates the idea this way: "God shared His own breath with us, which forms a concrete connection between the divine and the human. This shared breath then attracts His love to us as well."[16]

Harrison nicely summarizes the Christian understanding of what it means to be made in the image of God.[17] She notes that:

1) Humans are created to be free to make decisions in cooperation and in harmony with God. We were created to be in union with the triune God for the sake of good.

2) Spiritually, we were created to enter into the lifelong process of being transformed so that we can know and love God and neighbor. The highest aspect of our spiritual psychology is *nous*: reason, mind, or intellect. "The intellect perceives the material world through the senses and organizes and evaluates those perceptions. Yet its highest and more important function is to perceive spiritual realities, including other people in the spiritual aspect, angels, and ultimately God."[18] This transformation rightly orders our passions, impulses, and reason to excel in moral character and so to be freely obedient to the will of God. The other, non-

---

[14]Ibid. See also Dwight N. Hopkins, *Being Human: Race, Culture, and Religion* (Minneapolis: Fortress, 2005), 159–60, and Anthony B. Bradley, *Liberating Black Theology: The Bible and the Black Experience in America* (Wheaton, IL: Crossway, 2010), 183–85.
[15]Gerard Van Groningen, *From Creation to Consummation* (Sioux City, IA: Dordt College Press, 1996), 64.
[16]Nonna Verna Harrison, "The Human Person and the image and likeness of God," in *The Cambridge Companion to Orthodox Christian Theology*, ed. Mary B. Cunningham and Elizabeth Theokritoff (Cambridge: Cambridge University Press, 2008), 79.
[17]Ibid., 78–90.
[18]Ibid., 83.

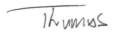

rational faculty is *thumos*, which is the capacity to control our passions. It drives other virtues like perseverance, courage, self-restraint, rejection of evil, and the struggle for justice.[19]

3) As bearers of God's image, all human beings are endowed with a royal dignity. Men and women were created to exercise their royal status by ruling over and simultaneously developing creation.[20] Gregory of Nazianzus says that God created the heavens and the earth, then created the human being as a participant in both to unite them together. As humans we are called with Christ to a cosmic priesthood: to love and care for the earth and all its creatures on behalf of God.[21]

4) Finally, the divine image includes "practical reason" and "practical creativity" that have enabled all human beings to develop and freely use the gifts of creativity through participation in the arts and sciences, economics, politics, business, agriculture, manufacturing, technology, and culture-making.[22] Economic exchange enables humans to share with one another, yet it also produces material things that can tempt us away from God. As humans, we are called to use reason to organize and govern society by implementing wise plans consistent with being made in the image of God the Father, Son, and Holy Spirit. We have been given freedom and creativity to share in the *divine* freedom and creativity.

To treat any human being as if these attributes do not apply is the basis of injustice and the destruction of human dignity. For example, the chattel slavery and racial injustice inflicted upon Native Americans, African Americans, and others in the United States was a grave evil not only because it violated legal principles but also because it refused to see those considered unacceptable to the dominant culture as bearing the image of God and so as having inherent dignity. The history of racism is the repeated narrative of not seeing others as the image of God and committing to treating them accordingly. The catalyst for injustice, oppression, and paternalism is viewing some other person or group of people as having less dignity than those in positions of power. Love in the kingdom of God refuses to see any human being as anything less than the image of God and so desires our neighbors to experience the liberation of being properly human both spiritually and physically. Human dignity, then, is the basis for genuine community.

[19]Ibid., 84.
[20]Van Groningen, *From Creation to Consummation*, 51–70.
[21]Gregory of Nazianzus, *Oration 38, On Theophany II*, as summarized in Harrison, "The Human Person and the Image and Likeness of God," 86.
[22]Harrison, "The Human Person," 87.

Solidarity and Community

If kingdom praxis demands a love for God and love for others, and if the kingdom presses the ontological point that every human person is made in the image and likeness of God, then human beings are, by definition, to live together in community with a sense of solidarity. This is our third principle of orthopraxis: we are interconnected and interdependent. Being human means seeing oneself in connection and relationship to others. One practical dimension of human destiny manifests itself in community. Herman Bavinck helps us to understand that the importance of the image of God in man is beyond any individualistic conception of the human person. That is, it is not simply that each person bears the image of God but that persons *in community* bear his image. It was not good for Adam to be alone; but it was not good for Adam and Eve to be alone together, either, so God inaugurated community through multiplication:

> Not the man alone, not the man and woman together, but the whole of humanity is the fully developed image of God, his children, his off-spring. The image of God is much too rich for it to be fully realized in a single human being, however richly gifted that individual may be. It can only be somewhat unfolded in its depth and riches in a humanity whose members exist both successively, one after the other, and contemporaneously, side by side. . . . Belonging to that humanity is also its development, its history, its ever-expanding dominion over the earth, its progress in science and art, its subjugation of all creatures.[23]

Humanity as a whole, according to Bavinck, is the image and likeness of God.[24] In the kingdom there is no such category as "us" or "them" with respect to understanding our humanity. The interconnectedness of human persons is the image of God, and if kingdom-oriented Christians seek to bring principles of the kingdom to bear in society, then the categories and distinctions that cause us to see ourselves as not in solidarity with certain people groups will be obliterated. We, the people, constitute the image of God. We thus should love people as God intends so that the full expression and implications of the image of God can be realized on earth as God desires.

Because humanity is the image of God, solidarity highlights in a special way the intrinsic social nature of the human person and the equality

---

[23]Bavinck, *God and Creation*, 577.
[24]Ibid.

of all in dignity and rights. This in turn leads individuals to a common commitment to care for each other in community.[25] Thanks to the technological advances and globalizing trend of recent decades, our interdependence and interconnection is emphasized in new and more immediate ways. The inequalities between developed and developing countries, fueled by corruption, exploitation, and oppression, have a negative influence on the internal and international life of many nations.[26] For example, sex trafficking in Eastern Europe, Central and South America, and Asia has direct connections to trafficking cases in the United States as girls, boys, and women are transferred between countries and across oceans for immoral, dehumanizing, and debased purposes. Regardless of one's country of origin, the solidarity of human beings who are made in the image of God makes these global problems *all of our problems* as well. Sex trafficking—just one such issue among many—is a violent breach of human solidarity and defiles the beauty of the image of God.

For the sake of living well together and in acknowledging the twin realities of sin and scarcity, we must order our social institutions so that they manage the web of dependence and the commitments we make to each other.[27] For our interdependent communal relationships to function well, we must develop structures of solidarity through the creation or prudent modification of laws, market regulations, and legal systems.[28] In this context solidarity requires a firm commitment to the common good with a firm and persevering determination to love others well.[29] Loving others properly for the sake of the kingdom orients life toward a readiness to serve the other instead of toward using the other either for personal advantage or to fulfill one's egoism.[30] In valuing the dignity of every human person and the mystery of humanity as the image of God, women and men graciously cultivate a greater awareness that they are debtors of the *vestigia Dei* in the society of which they are a part.[31] The grace of God codified in his covenants with creation makes us thankful for the contributions of all persons, contributions "that make human existence livable," and grateful for "the indivisible and indispensable legacy consti-

[25]Pontifical Council for Justice and Peace, *Compendium of the Social Doctrine of the Church* (Washington, DC: USCCB Publishing, 2005), 84–85.
[26]Ibid.
[27]On scarcity see Victor Claar and Robin Klay, *Economics in Christian Perspective: Theory, Policy, and Life Choices* (Downers Grove, IL: InterVarsity, 2007), 29–34.
[28]*Compendium of the Social Doctrine of the Church*, 85.
[29]Ibid.
[30]Ibid. See also distinctions by ethical and psychological egoism in James Rachels and Stuart Rachels, *The Elements of Moral Philosophy*, 6th ed. (New York: McGraw-Hill, 2010).
[31]*Vestigia Dei* can be translated as "traces of the Creator."

tuted by culture, scientific and technical knowledge, material and imma-
terial goods and . . . all that the human condition has produced."[32]

The liberating mystery of the person and work of Jesus Christ gives
kingdom-oriented followers of Christ freedom not only to see the general
interdependence of humans in the image of God, but also to press the
claims of Christ through the entire creation. Thus, solidarity goes beyond
itself to take on the gospel-centered dimensions of grace, forgiveness, and
reconciliation between God and man and between persons.

> One's neighbor is then not only a human being with his or her own
> rights and a fundamental equality with everyone else, but becomes the
> *living image* of God the Father, redeemed by the blood of Jesus Christ
> and placed under the permanent action of the Holy Spirit. One's neigh-
> bor must therefore be loved, even if an enemy, with the same love with
> which the Lord loves him or her; and for that person's sake one must be
> ready for sacrifice, even the ultimate one: to lay down one's life for the
> brethren.[33]

Loving God, loving others, and recognizing their dignity invites us to
be in solidarity with the poor and the oppressed in new ways. Solidarity
means nothing less for the kingdom-oriented Christian than the impos-
sibility of ignoring the needs of the poor and the oppressed; we are in
solidarity with every human being because everyone together constitutes the image and likeness of God. In the United States, for example,
it should be impossible for Christians to ignore the needs of the communities of so-called white trash. Geographical proximity introduces
particular challenges—or, to put it in more colloquial terms, familiarity breeds contempt—but kingdom priorities do not allow followers of
Christ to ignore the widespread poverty in mobile home communities
in Appalachia. Kingdom priorities introduce new questions about a
Christian's disposition toward Native Americans living in poverty on
reservations, or toward disadvantaged legal immigrants, and so on. As
women and men committed to loving others for the common good, we
are compelled to ask how we are to love those who are truly disadvantaged in accordance with their dignity as human persons, even if they are
what some might call "rednecks" living in rural communities, "ghetto"
men who wear their jeans below their hips, or lower-class residents of

---

[32]*Compendium of the Social Doctrine of the Church*, 86.
[33]Ibid., 87.

New Orleans displaced by Hurricane Katrina. In sum, solidarity, from a kingdom perspective, reminds us that the truly disadvantaged are the disadvantaged for whom we are actually responsible because we long to see them liberated to be the women and men God created all human persons to be.

Subsidiarity and Civil Society

Living together in community requires cooperation and coordination. Within the history of Christian social thought there have been various speculations as to the best context for human flourishing. These have ranged from theocracy to socialist democracy. In both Protestant and Roman Catholic traditions—i.e., Western Christianity—principles such as subsidiarity and sphere sovereignty have proven to be helpful categories for Christians in discerning how to order society in light of human dignity and the reality of sin. These form the fourth principle of kingdom praxis.

The principle of subsidiarity was first introduced by Johannes Althusius, a sixteenth-century Dutch political philosopher, and also has been developed in more specific terms by proponents of Catholic social thought.[34] Althusius theorized that individuals take their part in society as members of a certain social group, such as a family, guild, or commune, but not as independent individuals.[35] Althusius's focus on subsidiarity maintains that "the role of the state is not to regulate a political sphere separate from the social communities but to coordinate and secure their common purposes in symbiosis."[36] This is a social, political, and ecclesiastical principle that finds its classic modern expression in Catholic social teaching, in which it takes the following formulation:

---

[34]Althusius theorized society was composed of different social groups. According to him, sovereignty derives from the social covenant between the society and the sovereign power. See "Johannes Althusius," in *Religion and Liberty* 8 (Sept.–Oct. 1998): 3: "Althusius was born in Diedenshausen in Westphalia in 1557. Beyond a record of his birth, little is known about his early life. Upon receiving his doctorate in both civil and ecclesiastical law at Basle in 1586, he accepted a position on the faculty of law at the Reformed Academy at Herborn. The greatest achievement of his Herborn years was the publication of the *Politica* in 1603. Its success was instrumental in securing for Althusius an offer to become municipal magistrate of Emden in East Friesland, which was among the first cities in Germany to embrace the Reformed articles of faith. Althusius accepted the offer in 1604 and exercised an influence comparable to that of Calvin in Geneva; he guided the city without interruption until his death in 1638." See also Ken Endo, "The Principle of Subsidiarity: From Johannes Althusius to Jacques Delors," *Hokkaido Law Review* 44, no. 6 (1994): 553–652.

[35]For Althusius, man is not self-sufficient, thus he has to form different associations like families, guilds, or communes, and even cities and states. However, even such associations are not self-sufficient, so they must cooperate to sustain themselves and grow. See Bengi Demirci, "The Principle of Subsidiarity in the European Union Context" (master's thesis, Middle East Technical University, 2003), 12.

[36]Aaron Martin, "The Principle of Subsidiarity and Institutional Predispositions: Do the European Parliament, the German Bundestag, and the Bavarian Landtag Define Subsidiarity Differently?" *Working Papers Series* (Munich: Center for Applied Policy Research, 2010), 4–6.

A community of a higher order should not interfere in the internal life of a community of a lower order, depriving the latter of its functions, but rather should support it in case of need and help to coordinate its activity with the activities of the rest of society, always with a view to the common good.[37]

Additionally, Abraham Kuyper developed an idea called "sphere sovereignty," which teaches "that the family, the business, science, art and so forth are all social spheres, which do not owe their existence to the state, and which do not derive the law of their life from the superiority of the state, but obey a high authority within their own bosom; an authority which rules, by the grace of God, just as the sovereignty of the state does."[38] In other words, it is a violation of human dignity and solidarity for higher orders of society to undermine and violate the functions of lower orders, as well as for spheres to extend beyond their expertise, competence, or design into other spheres.[39] If we are to take a kingdom-oriented approach, motivated by love and with the goal of nurturing human dignity for the common good, particular contributions of individuals and institutions to the common good need to be arranged according to the best prudential judgments possible.[40]

The absence of much clear thinking about social differentiation among evangelicals creates a tendency for blind allegiance to political ideologies, which themselves tend toward idolatry, as a way to construct a vision for what provides the best contexts for human flourishing. Political ideologies are based on taking something out of creation's totality, raising it above that creation, and making the latter revolve around and serve it.[41] Every political ideology is based on the assumption that this idol has the capacity to save us from some real or perceived evil in the world.[42]

---

[37]John Paul II, Encyclical Letter *Centesimus Annus* (1991), paragraph 48.

[38]Abraham Kuyper, *Lectures on Calvinism* (Grand Rapids, MI: Eerdmans, 1931), 90.

[39]Anthony B. Bradley, "The Elements of Social Justice," WORLDMag.com, http://online.worldmag.com/2010/04/28/the-elements-of-social-justice/ (accessed January 29, 2011).

[40]The social, political, and economic arrangements either encourage human flourishing or delimit it. It will require a differentiated approach to the roles of church, state, education, the arts, business, and other spheres to provide proper contexts for individuals to renew the dignity of people in society. See Samuel Gregg, *On Ordered Liberty: A Treatise on the Free Society, Religion, Politics, and Society in the New Millennium* (Lanham, MD: Lexington, 2003), 89–104.

[41]David T. Koyzis, *Political Visions and Illusions: A Survey and Christian Critique of Contemporary Ideologies* (Downers Grove, IL: IVP Academic, 2003), 15.

[42]Ibid. Here Koyzis highlights several ideologies with which many Christians align themselves in attempts to do what is right and just. For example, Christian classical liberals (libertarians) usually treat individual liberty as an idol and identify government as the great evil in the world instead of the Devil, the real enemy of God and humanity. Christian conservatives tend to idolize tradition and history while resisting the "evils" of change. Christians who embrace collectivist ideologies will mostly idolize the potential of wealth-redistribution as a legitimate avenue of justice—as we find in nationalist and socialist ideologies—and tend to distrust the

Followers of ideologies often wish to impose their own simplistic conception of a monolithic social order on the complexities of real society.[43]
Christians tend simply to align themselves with secular and idolatrous
ideologies, and they do this without integrating fully into their thinking
the ways in which kingdom priorities ought to arrange a Christian's perspective on the society by holding love, human dignity, and solidarity in
healthy tension. This blind alignment with ideology is a tendency toward
syncretism.

A kingdom-oriented approach, however, transcends political ideologies. In such an approach, different institutions serve different functions
to contribute to human flourishing. We must be diligent in protecting
the integrity of these institutions by giving them freedom to do what they
do well while at the same time limiting their propensity to affect spheres
outside of their competence and expertise.[44] Civil society requires coordination and cooperation that cannot be driven by the fleeting promises of
political ideologies. Because of the doctrine of sin, the Christian tradition
has consistently resisted the state's tendency to overreach its authority by
extending into areas such as the family, education, caring for the poor, and
so on. The point is that the state is not to undermine or usurp the healthy
growth of other institutions because those spheres are also created by God
and derive their authority and structure from God's design for human
flourishing. We see these tensions more acutely when Christians wrestle
with deciding who is responsible for meeting the needs of the poor. For
some, the primary responsibility lies with government while for others
government is the last resort.

For example, let's look at the matter of caring for orphans. The Bible
is clear that caring for the fatherless is a demonstration of true religion
(James 1:26–27).[45] Orphan care is not a church program but a normal way
in which God's people live in the kingdom. Nowhere does the Bible suggest

potential evils of individual freedom and markets by preferring centralized approaches. Lastly, the Christian
egalitarian vision of democracy idolizes equal voices of the people and tends to locate the evils of society with
the existence of the have-nots.
[43]Ibid., 16. See also James Davison Hunter, *To Change the World: The Irony, Tragedy, and Possibility of Christianity in the Late Modern World* (New York: Oxford University Press, 2010), 93–175.
[44]Using Christianity to justify democratic and collectivist ideologies, as one finds in writers such as Jim Wal-
lis and Shayne Claiborne, to name two, tends to alignment with the Democratic Party's political platform in
general or, on the other extreme, to the libertarianism of someone like Gary North.
[45]By "orphans" I mean "true orphans." True orphans have no parents at all or are children for whom parental
rights have been completely terminated. See U.S. Department of Health and Human Services, "Children in
Public Foster Care On September 30th of Each Year Who Are Waiting to Be Adopted, FY 2002–FY 2009," US
Department of Health and Human Services; Administration for Children and Families; Administration on
Children, Youth and Families; Children's Bureau, http://www.acf.hhs.gov/programs/cb/stats_research/afcars/
waiting2009.pdf (accessed January 29, 2011).

that caring for the fatherless is the responsibility of governments. As such, in America, if we were to ask the church whose responsibility it is to care for orphans, we would have to look to ourselves. As a matter of fact, we could say boldly that the only reason the United States has true orphans in the foster care system is that Christians are not loving their neighbors in ways outlined in the Bible. As a result, orphans, then, are subjected to the oversight of the state, which cares about their material well-being but is not designed, nor competent, to ensure that orphaned children are cared for spiritually and holistically. Because the people of the kingdom recognize that every orphan is made in the image of God, Christians would seek the best for children even beyond their material provisions and would want to see them flourish in order to become the kinds of people that God created human persons to be. In this sense, it is the people of Christ's church who are best at caring for orphans. But the Christian community's role in providing this holistic care can be undermined by institutions such as government even when those institutions have the best intentions. Taking subsidiarity and sphere sovereignty seriously in the kingdom forces us to stop and ask ourselves, "What institutions has God established to best meet the needs of society, and what can be done to see those spheres flourish by fulfilling their respective roles well in light of human dignity?"

The Question of What People Deserve

Who or what determines what the truly disadvantaged deserve—or what any of us deserve for that matter? This brings us to our fifth principle of kingdom praxis. What people *deserve* depends on how we care about ourselves and those who are suffering; it depends on what we think about others as humans and what we expect from people relationally. If we love people and seek their good, what people deserve are opportunities to live out their vocations as human beings—the freedom to do the things that humans were created to do.[46] If the kingdom is the context for understanding what people deserve, then the context of God's grace, manifested in providence and provision, matters. David Schmidtz helps us to understand desert by framing the argument with this thesis:

> There is more than one way to be deserving, and in particular, more than one way to deserve an opportunity. We sometimes deserve X on the basis of what we do after receiving X rather by what we do before.[47]

---

[46]Bradley, "The Elements of Social Justice."
[47]David Schmidtz, *Elements of Justice* (Cambridge: Cambridge University Press, 2006), 40.

Framing the discussion in terms of what happens *after* receiving something opens the possibility that desert is more connected to what we do with what we have been given materially than it is with whether there is something intrinsic to human persons that warrants deserving certain things over others. For example, rereading the parable of the talents (Matt. 25:14–30) in this light would imply that the two servants who cultivated the talents they had been given to produce more were deserving. On the other hand, the servant who did nothing but hide his talent could be said to be undeserving because of his inaction after receiving provision. In this sense, we demonstrate that we are deserving of our opportunities by not wasting them and by giving them their due.[48] Again, in this framework, desert is not evaluated on what was present beforehand but concerns how one takes advantage of given opportunities.[49]

If we apply Schmidtz's formulation to praxis, we will see that we must make better distinctions between what people *deserve* and what people should *earn*. What a person deserves has more to do with his opportunities and freedom; what a person earns has more to do with a person's work, i.e., his or her job. In ethics this tension arises most often in discussing wages. Does human dignity demand that society determine what wage must be paid? Or does human dignity demand that people deserve opportunities to be good stewards of what they have been given to meet their needs and the needs of those for whom they are responsible? In other words, do people deserve a high wage arbitrarily, or do people deserve a wage appropriate to their services rendered?

A good example of the confusion about desert emerges in the context of seeking a just wage for those working on coffee plantations. This good concern has given rise to the fair trade coffee movement that is popular among many evangelicals. Fair trade coffee is coffee that is purchased directly from the growers for a higher price than standard coffee. The idea is that with the higher prices workers will be paid what they deserve. Using Schmidtz's analysis, the critical question should not be, "What coffee wage do workers receive?" but rather, "What should workers earn given the nature of their work in a global economy?" Victor Claar does a superb job of highlighting the problem of confusing earning and deserving in the coffee industry.[50]

---

[48]Ibid., 41.

[49]I am making no connection to discussions of soteriology in this section. A more useful analogy would be an employment situation in which an employee demonstrates that he or she is deserving of the job by flourishing in the position and making the most of the situation.

[50]Victor Claar, *Fair Trade? Its Prospects as a Poverty Solution*, Studies in Christian Social Ethics and Economics 2, ed. Anthony Bradley (Grand Rapids, MI: Acton Institute, 2010).

Sadly, fair trade coffee does not help the poor in the developing nations for several reasons. First, the primary reason that coffee prices remain low is that "there is too much coffee being grown by vast segments of the world's global poor who will work for low wages and who have no better option available to them."[51] Second, technological advances and better fertilizers yield better crops and increase the overall coffee supply.[52] Third, people around the world drink less coffee than is produced; therefore, the prices are lower than they would be if production could not keep up with demand.[53] Fourth, growing coffee therefore pays poorly because many countries around the world heavily subsidize coffee production in ways that deflate the price.[54] Finally, fair trade coffee networks miss the majority of the world's coffee growers—large and small—because of restrictions imposed by the fair trade Labeling Organization International (FLO).[55] The great irony of the Fair Trade movement is that it perpetuates the low prices and market saturation that keep wages low.[56] As such, what low-wage coffee workers deserve are new freedoms and opportunities that provide them with what they need to make it in a world of scarcity. Keeping poor coffee workers stuck in an industry structured for low wages, even through well-intentioned approaches like fair trade products, is not giving them what they deserve because they are unable to earn a sufficient living by making use of their God-given creativity to produce something better.

What human persons deserve are opportunities to live out what it means to be human in light of the providential reality that "we are not born having done anything to deserve advantages as rewards."[57] Because of differentiation in society, the focus of justice is not income disparities but a pluriform principle of distribution to provide every human being

---

[51]Ibid., 14. See also Tim Hartford, *The Undercover Economist* (Oxford: Oxford University Press, 2006).

[52]Claar, *Fair Trade?*, 14.

[53]Ibid., 13. Claar states, "In 1962, Americans over the age of ten drank about 3.1 cups per day. Owing largely to the expanding market share of soft drinks in the beverage market, by the 1900s a typical American drank just 1.6–1.9 cups of coffee daily." See also *The Economist*, "Voting with Your Trolley," December 7, 2006.

[54]Claar, *Fair Trade?*, 17–19.

[55]Ibid., 22. Claar continues, "FLO limits entry into the Fair Trade network to cooperatives of small coffee growers. This restriction means that farmers operating on larger scale farms are locked out of the Fair Trade network." Further, according to Claar, "Poor growers face two additional restrictions on gaining access to the fair trade network. First, FLO restricts the overall number of entrants into the fair trade network. That is, there is a *de facto* quota on fair trade coffee. Second, a cooperative of poor coffee farmers that aspire to enter the network must pay a hefty entry fee. In 2004, it cost each organization $3,200 to gain FLO certification." Ibid.

[56]Ibid., 44. Claar explains, "If the fundamental problem with the coffee market is that prices are low because there is too much coffee, then it would appear the Fair Trade movement may be making matters worse rather than better because it increases the incentives to grow more coffee. As early as 2001 the FLO stated that it was reluctant to register any additional coffee cooperatives. And in 2002 the FLO temporarily closed its registry, thereby shutting out most of the world's poorest coffee growers."

[57]Schmidtz, *Elements of Justice*, 53.

opportunities to advance, by his or her own efforts and in solidarity with others, toward the common good.[58] This requires the direct work of the church in evangelism and moral formation as well as Christians pressing the claims of Christ in every sector of culture. Schmidtz adds:

> One reason to give people what they deserve is that it renders people willing and able to act in ways that help them (and the people around them) to get what they need. Welfare considerations are not desert bases, but they can still provide reasons for taking a given desert maker seriously (for example, for respective people who work hard).[59]

In the kingdom those born with certain advantages are not honored more than others. What matters is the extent to which solidarity and differentiation provide human persons opportunities to do what they can to deserve what they have been given, regardless of the quantity—whether it be five talents or two.[60] Desert claims become confused when driven by principles of entitlement that acknowledge our status as separate agents not in solidarity. Principles of desert acknowledge our status as active and dignified agents interdependent in a culture of life that honors human dignity, solidarity, and the legal protections that enable us to do justice by embedding opportunities in our differentiated civil society.[61] What would make fair trade coffee fair is not the wage but rather new opportunities for workers to take advantage of what they have been given to meet their needs and the needs of others—including incentives to grow something other than coffee that will bring a higher wage. If we love people made in the image of God and seek to give them what they deserve, we want to put them in a position to be fully human co-creators with God. This can be done through reciprocity.

Reciprocity

No human person was born having earned anything given by God's providence. The air we breathe, the food we eat, the shelter in which we live were not given in response to anything we did prior to receiving them. We have no prior claim on the goodness that has been lavished on us.

---

[58]This may or may not lead to homogeneity of income across cultures, but it does enliven human dignity. In light of the *imago Dei*, what people deserve is a chance to be free from the personal and social manifestations of sin and brokenness that prevent people from bearing God's image properly. See also ibid., 59.
[59]Schmidtz, *Elements of Justice*, 60.
[60]Ibid., 67. See also Aristotle, *Nicomachean Ethics*, trans. 2nd ed., Terence Irwin (Indianapolis: Hackett, 2000), 67–77.
[61]Schmidtz, *Elements of Justice*, 70.

246   Anthony B. Bradley

Every good thing that we have is a consequence of God's grace. But how
should we respond? We cannot reciprocate in kind, but we can be men
and women who are agents of grace by passing that grace on to others.[62]
In the kingdom, reciprocity is understood in terms of giving praise to God
and loving our neighbors by passing grace on to them—that is, showing
grace to others because it was first shown to us (1 John 4:7–12). If we
really do love people, if we recognize their inherent dignity, if we are in
true solidarity with them, if we desire their good socially and economi-
cally, and if we want to give them what is due, the best we can do for them
is to honor the grace given to us by sharing that grace with them. This is
the nature of reciprocity in the kingdom. David Schmidtz argues, "When
people reciprocate, they teach people around them to cooperate. In the
process, they not only respect justice, but also foster it. Specifically, they
foster a form of justice that enables people to live together in mutually
respectful peace." Understanding reciprocity in this way harmonizes love
with concerns about human dignity, solidarity, and civil society. Those in
the kingdom are to be models of reciprocity because of the positive effect
it has in neighborhoods, communities, schools, and places of employment to invite people to "taste and see that the LORD is good" (Ps. 34:8).
Reciprocity requires the types of relationships that do not exhaust the
demands of human dignity but provide an essential thread to the fabric of
a virtuous community.[63]

The clearest expression of the principle is articulated as "transitive
reciprocity."[64] The only fitting response to the grace of God in the kingdom is not to attempt to "pay God back," because that is impossible, but
rather to pass grace on to others. This is the essence of loving one's neighbor as a citizen in the kingdom of God—i.e., an emphasis on being an
agent of grace to the other. Schmidtz describes it this way:

> When a teacher helps us, we are grateful. However, it is both odd and
> ordinary that we acknowledge debts to teachers mainly by passing on
> benefits to those whom we can help as our teachers helped us. I call
> this transitive reciprocity. Having received unearned windfall, we are in
> debt. The moral scales are out of balance. The canonical way to restore
> a measure of balance is to return the favor to our benefactor, as per
> symmetrical reciprocity. However, the canonical way is not the only

---

[62]Ibid., 76. We simply cannot return the goodness of God in proportion to the good we have received from him.
[63]Ibid., 81.
[64]Ibid., 82. See also David Schmidtz, *The Limits of Government: An Essay on the Public Goods Argument*, illus.
ed. (Boulder, CO: Westview Press, 1990), 138–60.

way. Another way is to pass the favor on, as per transitive reciprocity. Transitive reciprocity is less about returning a favor and more about honoring it—doing justice to it. Passing the favor on may not repay an original benefactor, but it can be a way of giving thanks.[65]

In response to grace, every human person is expected to acknowledge the Creator and respond accordingly in loving obedience (Rom. 1:18–25).[66] The only way to rightly respond to the grace of God is to worship God and pass the grace of God on to others (Lev. 19:18; Matt. 28:18–20). Christians honor God and do justice to grace by loving God and loving their neighbors who are made in God's image, share creational space, live in communities, and are due an encounter with the people of God. Believers thank God by living a life of worship and praise, being obedient to virtue, and by being committed to loving the other. The other-centered approach is a distinctive characteristic of life in the kingdom. There is a desire to love others in the same way that God loves his people.

Passing grace on is at the core of what motivates the work of the International Justice Mission (IJM) under the leadership of Gary Haugen. In his book *Just Courage*, Haugen explains that Christians in the kingdom are the men and women who have transitioned from "rescued to rescuer."[67] Haugen reminds us that "we who have been rescued by Christ come to understand that our rescue has not been simply for ourselves but for an even more exalted purpose . . . our rescue is God's plan for rescuing the world that he loves."[68] This is a variation on the theme of Isaiah 61. The people of God have been redeemed, healed, and liberated to do the work of the kingdom: to be agents of healing and liberation for others, to "build up the ancient ruins" (v. 4), to "repair the ruined cities" (v. 4), to be called "ministers of our God" (v. 6), and to pass on the grace that has been given so that it reaches as far as the curse is found.[69] God's people have been rescued by grace out of darkness so that they can be the light of the world.[70] As the women and men of IJM rescue others from injustice, it is an act

---

[65]Schmidtz, *Elements of Justice*, 83.
[66]For followers of Jesus, those having received the unmerited and unearned graces of salvation and sanctification, the moral scales are out of balance.
[67]Gary A. Haugen, *Just Courage: God's Great Expedition for the Restless Christian* (Downers Grove, IL: InterVarsity, 2008), 25–35. International Justice Mission is a Washington DC–based human rights agency that secures justice for victims of slavery, sexual exploitation, and other forms of violent oppression. IJM lawyers, investigators, and aftercare professionals work with local officials to ensure immediate victim rescue and aftercare, to prosecute perpetrators, and to promote functioning public justice systems. Learn more at http://www.ijm.org.
[68]Ibid., 29.
[69]See Michael D. Williams, *Far as the Curse Is Found: The Covenant Story of Redemption* (Phillipsburg, NJ: P&R, 2005), 63–82.
[70]Haugen, *Just Courage*, 31.

of praise and thanksgiving to God for his redemptive work in their lives. Being agents of justice is nothing other than transitive reciprocation.

Equality

What the kingdom puts on display is a vision of a community where transitive reciprocity is normative. Passing the grace of God on to others enables people to live as reciprocators so that virtuous citizens may accept some individual responsibility for fostering their community, each one enabling reciprocity in solidarity with others. The challenge in the kingdom is to think critically about how reciprocity creates the conditions for true equality—that is, treating every human being in ways that are consistent with God-given dignity. In many ways we reciprocate with others by restoring the other person's dignity. This is a foundational principle of justice as explained by David Jones: "Justice means that every human being should be treated according to what it means to be one who bears the image of God and who has a divine calling to fulfill."[71] The demands of love, solidarity, and justice call for treating people equally as human beings. Defining equality, however, remains difficult because we all have different visions of what equality is as seen from God's perspective. For some, equality is determined materialistically in terms of distribution of resources; for others, equality is defined by a society that does not show favoritism but treats all people according to the same rules. In the Bible, it seems that equality obliterates the divisive cultural distinctions that sinful men and women assign to others and prefers to speak about humans in terms of their standing before God. All persons stand in need of a savior because all have sinned and fallen short of the glory of the God (Rom. 3:23). What is *not* emphasized or promised in the Scriptures is a definition of equality determined by whether or not human persons have equal proportions of material goods and social power on earth. The zero-sum approach to justice, one that obsesses with material inequality, is a hindrance to a just distribution of need.

The reality of the kingdom requires thinking differently about justice with regard to the question, "Does equal treatment imply equal shares?"[72] The short answer to this is no, but this may require some explanation. Discussions of equality demand a much larger treatment than we have space for here, but we are mindful that at times the definition of equality

---

[71]Jones, *Biblical Christian Ethics*, 83.
[72]Schmidtz, *Elements of Justice*, 109.

is subjectively constrained by what constitutes evidence of equality and the means required to achieve those definitions. For example, if equality is determined by evidence of the equal distribution of wealth, then committing other forms of injustice in pursuit of the articulated evidence of justice becomes permissible. The ends will justify the means. In this sense, embracing one kind of unequal treatment is simply the price of securing equality of a more subjectively important kind.[73] However, if equality is determined by evidence of equal treatment by rules that apply to all, no matter what, we focus not on the ends but on the justice of means.

There is no biblical evidence demonstrating that equality of proportion of shares is promised in this life (Matt. 26:11). We only care about disparities because of the fall, which breeds a culture of envy in which equality is reduced to material manifestations. What matters in the kingdom is that every man and woman is treated according to what it means to be made in the image of God and that every person is given an opportunity to live out a human vocation in peaceful solidarity with others. Society is not a race but "needs to be a place where people do not face arbitrary bias or exclusion, where all people have a real chance to live well, as free, virtuous, and responsible members of a community."[74] Moreover, the imperfections of life mean that equal treatment according to one's dignity may result in disparities that may not be immoral but merely a consequence of the laws of creation.[75]

If we love the other we will be compelled to put people in positions where they have real opportunities to live out the implications of human dignity. In a civil society, dignity is coordinated by the multiple institutions that are kept in check by the social virtue. These institutions commit acts of injustice when they prevent human beings from living the human vocation of bearing God's image. Equality is given opportunity to flourish first within the family through the love and service of relatives and extends out into the larger society with a focus on loving neighbors in light of the common good. Preventing people through injustice or neglect from participating in the institutions that form and cultivate virtues is the very essence of what it means to be inhumane.

---

[73]Ibid., 111.

[74]Ibid., 117. See also John Locke, *Two Treatises of Government*, 3rd ed. (Cambridge: Cambridge University Press, 1988), 269–72.

[75]Even economic communitarians such as Stassen and Gushee do not agree that equality of proportion represents justice. Equality of outcome is "superficially attractive" and "ultimately founders because it fails to take the mandate of work with adequate seriousness." Glen H. Stassen and David P. Gushee, *Kingdom Ethics: Following Jesus in Contemporary Context* (Downers Grove, IL: InterVarsity, 2003), 422.

Confusion about equality often arises when comparing incomes between racial groups, for example. A prevailing assumption is that income gaps are evidence of injustice and that what is needed are redistributive measures that bring more income equality. For example, when looking at the disparities in income, child poverty, home ownership, and unemployment, communitarians Stassen and Gushee conclude that the cause is "systemic injustice in the distribution of income and economic benefit in American society."[76] However, when some do better than others, for various reasons, this is not necessarily proof of structural injustice, nor is it proof that someone is winning at the expense of someone else's losing.[77] Moreover, while giving a nod to the long-term economic consequences of single parenthood, Stassen and Gushee fail to see that income alone is not an accurate indicator of quality of life and that family income is affected by myriad issues that have much to do with the moral virtues of those lagging behind and so on. Therefore, income is not a good basis for defining systemic injustice. Systemic injustice does not account for, nor can it be blamed for, the fact that nearly 70 percent of black children are born outside of marriage, that 94 percent of all murdered black people are murdered by other black people, or the fact that in many major cities black males have a high school dropout rate of more than 50 percent—all of which factors impede one's ability to succeed financially.[78] Many, if not all, of these issues are, at their root, moral in nature and cannot be solved through material means. What black people need is not redistributed wealth but unhindered opportunities to participate in the institutions of society that form virtue and make contributions to the common good so that they can meet their needs as people of freedom and dignity. Equality in the kingdom stresses giving indiscriminate opportunities for people to live lives of dignity, and though this may lead to material inequalities it does not constitute the basis of injustice.

Need

If we take human dignity seriously, how does the rule and reign of Christ over all things help us better articulate what human persons *need* in order to become fully human? First, as Christians, we recognize that every human person has a need for communion with the triune God—Father,

---

[76]Ibid., 394.
[77]Schmidtz, *Elements of Justice*, 178.
[78]Anthony Bradley, "Stop Blaming White People," WORLDMag.com, http://online.worldmag.com/2007/11/07/stop-blaming-white-people/ (accessed January 29, 2011).

Son, and Holy Spirit. As created beings this is our deepest need, which renders us distinct from the rest of God's creation. It is only with human beings that the triune God has chosen to have eternal intimacy, even despite the infidelity of his people. As an aspect of his kingdom's communication of his grace, God refuses to abandon the people he calls to himself through the work of the Son and the Spirit.

Outside of our spiritual needs, humans have other differentiated needs that demonstrate the reign and rule of Christ over all things and that properly order human activity toward God's intention for his creation. As we think about justice, we are challenged, in light of the principles discussed thus far, to ask better questions. If this is true about love, human dignity, solidarity, civil society, desert, reciprocity, and equality, it seems that kingdom-oriented praxis demands that what people really need are opportunities to explore the beautiful potential of what it means to be image bearers of God with dignity. When it comes to the needs of the least advantaged, we want to avoid a materialistic framework that tends to have little interest in human dignity or the right ordering of human passions. Such an approach often reduces the meeting of such needs to the redistribution of resources, sometimes called distributive justice. Rather, from a kingdom-oriented perspective, we must ask better questions, being careful that any initiatives we propose are designed to meet the *real* needs of people on the margins. Again, David Schmidtz is very helpful:

> In many contexts, distributing according to need does not result in people getting what they need. It induces people to do what *manifests* need rather than what *merits* need . . . if we care about need—if we really care then we want social structures to allow and encourage people to do what works. Societies that effectively meet needs, historically speaking, have always been those that empower and reward exercise or productive capacities by virtue of which people meet needs.[79]

In other words, if we truly love our fellow human beings and want to meet their real needs, we will strive to place them in contexts where their human potential can be unlocked and empowered in ways that make real contributions to the common good and bring glory to God. Life in the kingdom demands cultural moral formation that occurs through the preaching of the gospel and the right ordering of God's creation toward

---

[79]Schmidtz, *Elements of Justice*, 167.

good ends by his people in their culture-making activities.[80] What we
have seen historically is that large-scale, one-size-fits-all, undifferenti-
ated, need-based distribution approaches have never been effective at
making people less needy.[81]

In light of human dignity all human persons need contexts that foster
moral virtue and excellence. We need a culture in which virtuous people committed to the good aid in unlocking the potential of creation in
their culture-making through their contributions to all aspects of society.
These contributions in turn meet the needs of other people and enable
them to flourish so that they, too, may make other-oriented contributions
to the building up of society and the ongoing development of the kingdom story. As we consider the long-term sustainability of such a virtuous society, our emphasis shifts from materialistic reductions about how
much people have toward a consideration of what is necessary for people
to live well together.[82] The mystery of Christ's concern that we focus on
the needs in front of us compels us to pursue not a results-oriented utopia on this side of Christ's return, but rather to pursue endeavors that
support human dignity by establishing frameworks of trustworthiness
so that people can plan to deal with one another in mutually beneficial
ways.[83] What people need is to live in a society that recognizes fundamental human rights, "thereby enabling us to have a system of expectation and
trust, which allows us together to transform our world into a world with
greater potential. When we cannot count on others to treat us as rights-
bearers with separate lives, we are living in a world of lesser potential,"
says Schmidtz.[84]

If we truly seek a virtuous society that desires to meet the needs of the
disadvantaged and to bring glory to God, then the church must recognize
its call to serve vibrantly and robustly as the key institution that forms
and shapes the moral virtues of society. Without the faithful preaching
and teaching of the whole counsel of God to people in every sector of
society we cannot expect to foster virtuous cultures that render to human
persons the dignity and opportunities that they are due as image bearers
of God. In this sense the moral dispositions of societies matter:

---

[80]Andy Crouch, *Culture Making: Recovering Our Creative Calling* (Downers Grove, IL: InterVarsity, 2008), 63–67, 256.
[81]Schmidtz, *Elements of Justice*, 167.
[82]Ibid., 171. See also John R. Ehrenfeld, *Sustainability by Design: A Subversive Strategy for Transforming Our Consumer Culture* (New Haven, CT: Yale University Press, 2008), 58–77.
[83]Schmidtz, *Elements of Justice*, 171.
[84]Ibid. See also John Witte Jr., *God's Joust, God's Justice: Law and Religion in Western Tradition*, Emory University Studies in Law and Religion (Grand Rapids, MI: Eerdmans, 2006), 148–63.

Moral institutions constrain the good's pursuit because the good is pursued by individuals. If the good is to be realized, then institutions—legal, political, economic, and cultural institutions—must get the constraints right, so as to put individuals in a position to pursue the good in a manner conducive to the good's production in general.[85]

The church's role in the kingdom is vital because the church nurtures and grows God's faithful people, who press the claims of Christ's lordship in every sphere of society so that they may be well ordered toward the Creator. One dimension of loving our neighbors is for God's people to influence the social good by making moral contributions through the arts, business, economics, literature, the sciences, technology, entertainment, and every other field of endeavor. We love our neighbors by helping to give them the type of society they need to bring glory to God. We move along in our lives in ways that complement and bless others rather than hinder their efforts to make contributions to the common good as well.[86] Again, life is not about "keeping up with the Joneses" or making sure people have what they need to live better than someone else. Our goal is to ask what is necessary for the least advantaged to flourish. What human persons need is agency and self-efficacy. If people are made in the image and likeness of God, and if we love them accordingly, then we will do all that we can to make sure people know that their moral virtue matters for the rest of us and that they can be real agents for change as we all seek together to make the world a better place.

As a case in point, if we want to address the problems with inner-city public education from a kingdom-minded perspective, we will have to ask better questions than society in general has been asking in this regard. Public schools are failing minorities in America, but they are failing no group more miserably than black males. The numbers are shocking. The Schott Foundation recently reported that only 47 percent of black males graduate from high school on time, compared to 78 percent of white male students.[87] This revelation is beyond disturbing because it exposes the fact that many public schools serve as major catalysts for the desolation of unemployment and incarceration that many black youths face. In many places the disparity between whites

---

[85]Schmidtz, *Elements of Justice*, 174.
[86]Ibid.
[87]See Anthony Bradley, "Teachers Unions, Civil Rights Groups Protect Failed Schools," *Detroit News*, August 27, 2010, and The Schott Foundation for Public Education, "Yes We Can: The Schott 50 State Report On Public Education and Black Males," Black Boys Report, http://blackboysreport.org/ (accessed January 29, 2011).

and blacks is nearly unbelievable. In Nebraska, for example, the white/
black graduation gap is 83 percent for whites compared with 40 percent
for blacks; in New York the ratio is 68 percent to 25 percent. Urban
districts are among the worst at graduating black males: Atlanta, 34 percent; Baltimore, 35 percent; Philadelphia, 28 percent; New York, 28 percent; Detroit, 27 percent; and St. Louis, 38 percent.[88] This is such a great
tragedy because these blacks are foregoing what they need to live with
dignity as men contributing to the good and are missing opportunities
to learn to meet their own needs.

What, then, do at-risk black males need? Specialized approaches
that affirm their dignity as black men and set them up for success. This
may mean rethinking how we educate inner-city black males from broken homes. Even with mounting evidence demonstrating that single-
sex education for black males from low-income households represents
one of the best opportunities for graduation, the National Education
Association (NEA) petitioned the Department of Education in 2004 to
prevent single-sex options from becoming nationally normative. The
NEA balked because "the creation of an artificial single-sex environment [will] ill prepare students for life in the real world."[89] This statement ignores the proven success of such institutions as the Eagle
Academy for Young Men, a charter school in the Bronx comprised of
primarily black and Latino students and the first all-male public school
in New York City in thirty years. The academy boasts a high school
graduation rate of 82 percent. In the summer of 2010, Chicago's Urban
Prep Charter Academy, with a 100 percent graduation rate, graduated a
class of 107 black male students, all of whom attended college in the fall
of 2010. These schools are success stories because they are specialized
to meet the actual needs of at-risk black males in inner cities. Funding
for such institutions is neither the problem nor the solution. At-risk
males need a different educational environment. In the end, thinking
about need in terms of human dignity focuses less on short-term solutions and more on doing what is necessary so that humans can live in
harmony with God's design. In sum, what people need are structures
and contexts that allow them to flourish morally and socially as image
bearers of God.

---

[88]Bradley, "Teachers Unions."
[89]Diane Shust and Randall Moody, National Education Association, to Kenneth L. Marcus, Assistant Secretary for
Civil Rights U.S. Department of Education, Washington DC, 23 April 2004. http://www.ncwge.org/documents/
comments_NEA.pdf.

Conclusion

The glory of God and the image of God matter in the praxis of the kingdom of God. As ambassadors of this kingdom, we are actively working to make this rule of God known in all of life and to all of creation. In this chapter eight elements of praxis are offered as ways to help the church ask better questions about what should be done here and now in ways that are in harmony with the priorities of the mission of God. Love, human dignity, solidarity, subsidiarity, desert, reciprocity, equality, and need are all elements that must be considered with prudential judgment before deciding on a course of action. If we do not take these elements seriously as a starting point and fail to ask better questions about what God expects of us and what people truly need, we run the risk of doing more harm than good. Good intentions are simply not enough without principled, biblically informed prudence. For example, if we recognize the spiritual and social roles of the family, these eight elements can keep us from supporting programs or policies that create perverse incentives that work against encouraging people to get married, be committed to their children, participate in their children's moral formation and education, and so on. As such, these elements do not answer all justice-oriented questions in every situation. But they can serve as a guide to deliberations about what God has revealed as his will for his creation and his redemptive mission. Our goal in the kingdom is to respond to God's grace by putting his glory on display so that we may invite others to taste and see how good it is to be in covenant with the triune God.

SELECTED BIBLIOGRAPHY

Arnold, Clinton E. *Powers of Darkness: Principalities & Powers in Paul's Letters*. Downers Grove, IL: InterVarsity, 1992.

Augustine of Hippo. *The City of God*. Translated by Marcus Dods. Peabody, MA: Hendrickson, 2009.

Bartholomew, Craig G., and Michael W. Goheen. *The Drama of Scripture: Finding Our Place in the Biblical Story*. Grand Rapids, MI: Baker, 2004.

Beasley-Murray, George R. *Jesus and the Kingdom of God*. Grand Rapids, MI: Eerdmans, 1986.

Blaising, Craig A., and Darrell L. Bock. *Progressive Dispensationalism*. Wheaton, IL: Victor, 1993.

Bright, John. *The Kingdom of God: The Biblical Concept and Its Meaning for the Church*. Nashville: Abingdon, 1953.

Caragounis, Chrys. "Kingdom of God/Kingdom of Heaven." In *Dictionary of Jesus and the Gospels*. Edited by Joel B. Green and Scot McKnight, 417–430. Downers Grove, IL: InterVarsity, 1992.

_____. "Kingdom of God, Son of Man and Jesus' Self-Understanding (Part II)." *Tyndale Bulletin* 40 (November 1989): 223–238.

Childs, Brevard S. *Biblical Theology of the Old and New Testaments: Theological Reflection on the Christian Bible*. Minneapolis: Augsburg Fortress, 1993.

Chilton, Bruce. "Kingdom of God, Kingdom of Heaven." In *New Interpreter's Dictionary of the Bible*. Edited by Katharine Sakenfeld, 3:512–523. Nashville: Abingdon, 2008.

Cho, Youngmo. *Spirit and Kingdom in the Writings of Luke and Paul: An Attempt to Reconcile These Concepts*. Milton Keynes, Buckinghamshire, UK: Paternoster, 2005.

Chrupcała, Lesław Daniel. *The Kingdom of God: A Bibliography of 20th Century Research*. Jerusalem: Franciscan Printing Press, 2007.

Clifford, Paul Rowntree. *The Reality of the Kingdom: Making Sense of God's Reign in a World Like Ours*. Grand Rapids, MI: Eerdmans, 1996.

Du Toit, Andreas B. "The Kingdom of God in the Gospel of Matthew." *Skrif en Kerk* 21, no. 3 (2000): 545–563.

Eichrodt, Walther. *Theology of the Old Testament*. Translated by John A. Baker. London: SCM Press, 1961.

Ekström, Bertil. "The Kingdom of God and the Church Today." *Evangelical Review of Theology* 27 (October 2003): 292–305.

Evans, Craig A. "Inaugurating the Kingdom of God and Defeating the Kingdom of Satan." *BBR* 15, no. 1 (2005): 49–75.

France, R. T. "Kingdom of God." In *Dictionary for Theological Interpretation of the Bible*. Edited by Kevin J. Vanhoozer, 420–422. Grand Rapids, MI: Baker, 2005.

Glasser, Arthur F. *Announcing the Kingdom: The Story of God's Mission in the Bible*. Grand Rapids, MI: Baker, 2003.

Goldsworthy, Graeme. *According to Plan: The Unfolding Revelation of God in the Bible*. Downers Grove, IL: InterVarsity, 1991.

_____. *Gospel and Kingdom: A Christian Interpretation of the Old Testament*. Carlisle, Cumbria, UK: Paternoster, 1981.

_____. "Kingdom of God." In *New Dictionary of Biblical Theology*. Edited by T. Desmond Alexander and Brian S. Rosner, 615–620. Downers Grove, IL: InterVarsity, 2000.

Hahn, Scott W. "Kingdom and Church in Luke-Acts." In *Reading Luke: Interpretation, Reflection, Formation.* Edited by Craig G. Bartholomew, Joel B. Green, and Anthony C. Thiselton. Vol. 6 of Scripture and Hermeneutics Series, 294–326. Grand Rapids, MI: Zondervan, 2005.

Henry, Carl F. H. *God, Revelation and Authority.* Vol. 4. Wheaton, IL: Crossway Books, 1999.

_____. "Reflections on the Kingdom of God." *Journal of the Evangelical Theological Society* 35 (March 1992): 39–49.

Hill, Charles E. "Paul's Understanding of Christ's Kingdom in 1 Corinthians 15:20–28." *Novum Testamentum,* 30 (October 1988): 297–320.

_____. *Regnum Caelorum: Patterns of Millennial Thought in Early Christianity.* 2nd ed. Grand Rapids, MI: Eerdmans, 2001.

Howard, David M. "The Case for Kingship in Deuteronomy and the Former Prophets." *Westminster Theological Journal* 52 (Spring 1990): 101–115.

Kelber, Werner H. *The Kingdom of God in Mark: A New Place and a New Time.* Philadelphia: Fortress, 1974.

Klappert, Bertold. "King, Kingdom." In *New International Dictionary of New Testament Theology.* Edited by Colin Brown, 2:372–389. Grand Rapids, MI: Zondervan, 1986.

Kraybill, Donald B. *The Upside-Down Kingdom.* 3rd ed. Scottsdale, PA: Herald, 2003.

Ladd, George Eldon. *Crucial Questions about the Kingdom of God.* Grand Rapids, MI: Eerdmans, 1952.

_____. *The Gospel of the Kingdom: Scriptural Studies in the Kingdom of God.* Grand Rapids, MI: Eerdmans, 1959.

_____. *Jesus and the Kingdom: The Eschatology of Biblical Realism.* New York: Harper & Row, 1964.

_____. "The Kingdom of God and the Church." *Foundations* 4 (April 1961): 164–171.

_____. *A Theology of the New Testament.* Grand Rapids, MI: Eerdmans, 1974.

Leithart, Peter J. *The Kingdom and the Power: Rediscovering the Centrality of the Church.* Phillipsburg, NJ: P&R, 1993.

Malina, Bruce J. *The Social Gospel of Jesus: The Kingdom of God in Mediterranean Perspective.* Minneapolis: Augsburg Fortress, 2001.

Maloney, Elliott C. *Jesus' Urgent Message for Today: The Kingdom of God in Mark's Gospel.* New York: Continuum, 2004.

Marshall, I. Howard. "The Hope of a New Age: The Kingdom of God in the New Testament." *Themelios* 11 (Spring 1985): 5–15.

Moltmann, Jürgen. "Jesus and the Kingdom of God." *Asbury Theological Journal* 48, no. 1 (Spring 1993): 5–17.

Moore, Russell D. *The Kingdom of Christ: The New Evangelical Perspective.* Wheaton, IL: Crossway, 2004.

Neusner, Jacob. "The Kingdom of Heaven in Kindred Systems, Judaic and Christian." *BBR* 15, no. 2 (2005): 279–305.

Pannenberg, Wolfhart. *Theology and the Kingdom of God.* Philadelphia: Westminster, 1969.

Patrick, Dale. "The Kingdom of God in the Old Testament." In *The Kingdom of God in 20th-Century Interpretation.* Edited by Wendell Willis, 67–79. Peabody, MA: Hendrickson, 1987.

Pennington, Jonathan T. *Heaven and Earth in the Gospel of Matthew.* Grand Rapids, MI: Baker Academic, 2009.

Perrin, Norman. *Rediscovering the Teaching of Jesus.* New York: Harper & Row, 1967.

Reynolds, J. L. "Church Polity or The Kingdom of Christ in its Internal and External Development." In *Polity: Biblical Arguments on How to Conduct Church Life (A Collection of Historic*

Baptist Documents). Edited by Mark Dever, 295–404. Washington, DC: Center for Church Reform, 2001.

Ridderbos, Herman N. *The Coming of the Kingdom*. Philadelphia: P&R, 1962.

Rowe, Robert D. *God's Kingdom and God's Son: The Background to Mark's Christology from Concepts of Kingship in the Psalms*. Boston: Brill, 2002.

Saucy, Mark. *The Kingdom of God in the Teaching of Jesus: In 20th Century Theology*. Dallas: Word, 1997.

Saucy, Robert L. "The Presence of the Kingdom and the Life of the Church." *Bibliotheca Sacra* 145, no. 577 (Jan.–Mar. 1988): 30–46.

Scobie, Charles H. H. *The Ways of Our God: An Approach to Biblical Theology*. Grand Rapids, MI: Eerdmans, 2003.

Shogren, Gary. "Is the Kingdom of God about Eating and Drinking or Isn't It? (Romans 14:17)." *Novum Testamentum* 42, no. 3 (2000): 238–256.

Stassen, Glen H., and David P. Gushee. *Kingdom Ethics: Following Jesus in Contemporary Context*. Downers Grove, IL: InterVarsity, 2003.

Twelftree, Graham H. *Jesus the Miracle Worker: A Historical and Theological Study*. Downers Grove, IL: InterVarsity, 1999.

Van Til, Henry R. *The Calvinistic Concept of Culture*. Grand Rapids, MI: Baker, 2001.

Vickers, Brian J. "The Kingdom of God in Paul's Gospel." *Southern Baptist Journal of Theology* 12 (Spring 2008): 52–67.

_____. "Mark's Good News of the Kingdom of God." *Southern Baptist Journal of Theology* 8 (Fall 2004): 12–35.

Viviano, Benedict T. *The Kingdom of God in History*. Wilmington, DE: Michael Glazier, 1988.

Vorster, Nicolaas. "Transformation in South Africa and the Kingdom of God." *Hervormde teologiese studies* 62, no. 2 (2006): 731–753.

Vos, Geerhardus J. *The Teaching of Jesus Concerning the Kingdom of God and the Church*. New York: American Tract Society, 1903.

Wadell, Paul J. "The Subversive Ethics of the Kingdom of God." *Bible Today* 41, no. 1 (2003): 11–16.

Waltke, Bruce K., with Charles Yu. *An Old Testament Theology: An Exegetical, Canonical, and Theological Approach*. Grand Rapids, MI: Zondervan, 2007.

Weiss, Johannes. *Jesus' Proclamation of the Kingdom of God*. Translated and edited by Richard H. Hiers and David L. Holland. Lives of Jesus Series. Philadelphia: Fortress, 1971.

Wenham, David. *Paul: Follower of Jesus or Founder of Christianity?* Grand Rapids, MI: Eerdmans, 1995.

Williams, Michael D. *Far As The Curse Is Found: The Covenant Story Of Redemption*. Phillipsburg, NJ: P&R, 2005.

Willis, Wendell, ed. *The Kingdom of God in 20th-Century Interpretation*. Peabody, MA: Hendrickson, 1987.

Witherington, Ben, III. *The Indelible Image: The Theological and Ethical Thought World of the New Testament, Volume 1: The Individual Witnesses*. Downers Grove, IL: InterVarsity, 2009.

Wolters, Albert M. *Creation Regained: Biblical Basics for a Reformational Worldview*. 2nd ed. Grand Rapids, MI: Eerdmans, 2005.

Wright, Christopher J. H. *The Mission of God: Unlocking the Bible's Grand Narrative*. Downers Grove, IL: InterVarsity, 2006.

Wright, N. T. *Jesus and the Victory of God*. Minneapolis: Fortress, 1996.

AUTHOR INDEX

SUBJECT INDEX

SCRIPTURE INDEX